Preaching and Professing

PREACHING AND PROFESSING

Sermons by a Teacher Seeking to Proclaim the Gospel

Ralph C. Wood

WILLIAM B. EERDMANS PUBLISHING COMPANY
GRAND RAPIDS, MICHIGAN / CAMBRIDGE, U.K.

© 2009 Ralph C. Wood

Published 2009 by
Wm. B. Eerdmans Publishing Co.
2140 Oak Industrial Drive N.E., Grand Rapids, Michigan 49505 /
P.O. Box 163, Cambridge CB3 9PU U.K.

Printed in the United States of America

14 13 12 11 10 09   7 6 5 4 3 2 1

Library of Congress Cataloging-in-Publication Data

ISBN 978-0-8028-6446-8

www.eerdmans.com

Contents

Part VII: Death and Eternal Life

Preface

Recently, when I was giving lectures at a major state university here in the American Southwest, my visit was sponsored by a consortium of campus ministry groups. As a gesture of good will, and to show local academics that not all Christians are intellectual cowards, my host asked the local English Department faculty whether they would like me to give a lecture in their behalf. No honorarium would be requested; my lecture would be a "freebie." Sending along my CV to demonstrate that I have at least minimal intellectual bona fides, my sponsor explained that I would be willing to talk on any of the several writers whose work has figured large in my research and publication: Flannery O'Connor, Walker Percy, William Faulkner, John Updike, Peter De Vries, G. K. Chesterton, J. R. R. Tolkien, C. S. Lewis, P. D. James, even John Bunyan or George Herbert. When I called my host to ask which of these writers the English faculty wanted me to address, he began to back and fill and hem and haw. It was clear that he didn't want to give me a straightforward reply. Finally, I compelled him to speak plainly about why the local English Department had no use for me. At last he came out with it: "They say you're more of a preacher than a scholar."

With a splendid shock of recognition, I knew instantly that the local literati who had meant to dismiss if not damn me had, instead, got me exactly right: I am indeed more preacher than scholar. Thus am I a professor only in a qualified sense, that is, as a Christian who professes the faith as well as one who teaches in the classroom. Perhaps my sense of gospel urgency, even in the classroom, stems from my having benefited from the ministry of outstanding preachers of the gospel. First, there was Joseph L. Gilmore who, together with his lovely wife, Shirley, was a model of Christian ministry at the First Baptist Church of Linden, Texas. Not only did Gilmore prepare his sermons with considerable care and deliver them with both eloquence and passion; he was also a serious student of Scripture, with a large library on the shelves of his office. It was under Gilmore's excellent ministry that I experienced my own call to ministry as a high school senior in 1958. My college minister, Julius ("Slats") Stagner of the First Baptist Church of Commerce, Texas, was not a scholarly preacher at all, but he announced the gospel with prophetic passion and insight. On the race issue, for example, Stagner was uncompromisingly courageous, enabling our Baptist Student Union to invite William Lawson, a distinguished black Baptist pastor from Houston, to give the first public address by an African-American on our all-white campus. And then, from 1971 through 1985, it was my enormous privilege to have heard, Sunday in and Sunday out, the sterling preaching of Warren Carr at the Wake Forest Baptist Church in Winston-Salem, North Carolina. I make no apologies for my frequent references to Warren Carr in this book, since nearly everything good in my life is due to his ministry — a ministry not only of faithful pulpit proclamation but also of profound personal care and friendship.

In all three of these ministers, I was confronted with something of St. Paul's own urgency: "Woe be unto me if I preach not the gospel." I acquired from them the burning conviction that the gospel is not one spiritual choice among others, that Christianity is not (as Walker Percy wittily declares) "a member in good standing of 'the world's great religions,'" least of all that Christian faith is merely my personal quirk or hobby. The Reverend Thomas Marshfield, John Updike's protagonist in *A Month of Sundays,* may be terribly unfaithful in his moral life, and far from orthodox in his theology, but about one thing he is unmistakably correct. Marshfield declares, ever so faithfully, that the ministry is "not only my life; it's my afterlife." Though I've never found any Christian community willing to lay hands on me, and while I thus remain a layman called primarily to the classroom rather than the pulpit, I gladly confess that my academic work has been, whether for good or ill, a form of proclamation: a *profession* of the things that matter both temporally and eternally.

These sermons are my *overt* pulpit proclamations made during the last two decades, the years during which I could compose and preserve them electronically. I am sure that there were earlier messages, but they seem to have disappeared, perhaps blessedly so. When Bill Reimer at Regent College first suggested that I collect these more recent homilies, I was surprised at the idea of making them into a book. When I discovered that there were more than sixty of them, I was surprised again at having been asked to preach so often. Even more surprising, as well as grateful-making, was the willingness of my brother-in-law and dear friend, John Myrick, to sift through the whole lot, seeking to garner at least a little gold amidst all the dross. Then, when Bill Eerdmans agreed to publish this collection, even though my editor, Reinder Van Til, pruned them by a third, I remained gratefully surprised. These confessions of amazement are not signs of false modesty. Some of my so-called friends sometimes say about me what we often said about our real friend, the late president of Wake Forest University, James Ralph Scales, namely, that I am the only person who gets greater applause when he stands up than when he sits down. My wife Suzanne has also been known to declare, not altogether encouragingly, that she has never heard me give a sermon or speech that was too short. But she has more than atoned for her caustic truthfulness by having pored over the text with her sharp eye for errors.

Willing to concede as much as forty-nine percent accuracy to my critics, I concede to being an essayist who has never learned to write for the ear but only for the eye. Yet this may not be altogether a vice, given Luther's sharp directive: "When you hear the Word of God proclaimed, stick your ears in your eyes." I remain a manuscript preacher, yet always seeking to announce the Glad Tidings imaginatively, enabling my hearers to *image* the Word. Thanks to a challenge from Cindy Caldwell, my friend and former student, I have gradually weaned myself from my written text. "Since you don't read your lectures in the classroom," she once asked, "why should read your sermons in church?" Instantly, I knew that she had probed to the quick: she had seen that, as something of an aesthete, I was unwilling to trust that the Spirit would give me utterance. I valued safe precision over risky proclamation. Rather than reading my manuscript, thanks to her, I have come gradually to preach from an outline, even while sometimes stumbling and blundering.

It is not completely accidental that these sermons were preached in a variety of settings and at many different churches. Perhaps the obvious explanation for this diversity is that I haven't often been invited back for encores! Even so, I can honestly report that I've preached whenever I've been asked. And so I have held forth in places both great and small, mainly small. Thanks to friends and former students, I have preached at the Cathedral of the Immaculate Conception in Atlanta and at the First Baptist Church of the City of Washington, D.C. Yet I've omitted a sermon preached in Rockefeller Chapel at my alma mater, the University of Chicago. Despite the kind offices of my dear friend Bernie Brown, who was then the dean of Rockefeller Chapel, I laid a homiletical egg so huge that they are still making omelettes from it in Hyde Park. The more happily memorable occasions, I confess, came in country churches in North Carolina, often on Baptist College Sunday, when there were only a few score of folks present. On every occasion, both grand and humble, I have sought to address the people before me, seeking always to envision their situation — even if from the safe aerie of my upper-story office. These are not sermons spoken "to whom it may concern," therefore, but rather my personal words seeking to become God's own Word, announced to particular people on specific occasions and at definite places.

Looking back over them, I notice that, with the exception of the cathedral in Atlanta and the chapel at Regent College in Vancouver, all of these sermons were preached in Baptist, Methodist, Presbyterian, and Episcopal churches. This happily ecumenical fact attests to the ecumenical character of the universities where I've taught: for twenty-six years at Wake Forest in Winston-Salem, North Carolina, for an interim year at Samford in Birmingham, and for the last decade at Baylor University in Waco, Texas. During my nine years of membership at the First Baptist Church of Winston-Salem, North Carolina, my pastors Paul Craven and David Hughes were especially generous about inviting me to occupy the pulpit. It was also my extraordinary privilege to serve as the supply preacher for the Paddington Chapel United Reformed Church in London during a sabbatical semester in 1988. This remnant — often numbering only a dozen or so — of a once-grand congregation patiently listened to this visiting American academic. There at Paddington I served alongside one of the lesser-known but truly eminent preacher-theologians of the twentieth century church, the late Daniel Jenkins. Then in the twilight of his career, Daniel taught me the true character of ministry when he once declared, without any prompting from me, "I've spent my life trying to get out of God's way, teaching and preaching so as to wedge a small opening for the Spirit to enter and do its huge work." That God so magnificently used Daniel Jenkins' subdued and self-effacing kind of ministry, in both the written and the preached word, prompts me to dedicate the publication of these sermons to his blessed memory.

There is one ecclesial omission here that attests also to the one notable repetition that readers will encounter. I did not preach a single one of these sermons in the church where I first learned the gritty and angular and comic quality of the gospel, namely, the Wake Forest Baptist Church. The reason is not hard to discern. The excellence of Warren Carr's preaching during those sixteen years (1971-1987) meant that the congregation was not eager to hear other ministers, except (by necessity) during Carr's brief summer vacations. Why go beyond Winston-Salem when one of the best preachers in the country was already in the pulpit? When someone once complained about my over-frequent quotations and references to Carr, I found myself suddenly confessing what I have come ever more surely to believe: Warren Carr is the only great man I have ever had the privilege of knowing. I've known others more intelligent, more academically accomplished, far more culturally refined. But none has approached the depth of his gospel wisdom, his prophetic insight, his holy courage. It is altogether fitting that this collection should end with my eulogy at his memorial service.

This miscellany opens with sermons devoted to the nature and character of Christian proclamation. It gives me special delight, as a layman, to pay tribute to preachers and preaching. And so I here include the sermon that opened the Warren Carr Preaching Series in 1998, another that accounts for the minister's multiple roles, and finally a tribute to three people who have announced the Word of God in both word and deed. Part II contains a set of sermons on the church. I have become increasingly convinced that a low regard for ecclesial life is the chief bane of many, perhaps even of most, evangelical Christians. I attempt, therefore, to make a Protestant reclamation of the ancient doctrine called *extra ecclesiam nulla salus:* "Outside the church there is no salvation." That some of these sermons are alarmist is altogether to the point, for they express my worry over the perilous state of Christ's body.

It may come as a surprise to the reader to find that Part III is devoted to suffering no less than service. I trust that there is nothing morbid or self-pitying here, though I do confess to being haunted by death. My father dropped dead of a cerebral hemorrhage when I was eighteen and he was fifty-five; my splendid college minister, Richard Norton, died of nephritis at age thirty-three; a groomsman in our wedding who was also a brilliant first-year medical student, Jim Mayfield, committed suicide at age twenty-two; and some of my finest Wake Forest and Baylor colleagues have been struck down in their prime. My long devotion to Flannery O'Connor, a writer who spent the last dozen years of her life dying from disseminated lupus erythmatosus at age thirty-nine, has helped me thus to understand why all Christians should embrace one of her most drastic claims. "Death," she said, "has always been a brother to my imagination, and I can't imagine a good story that doesn't end in death."

The supreme image of death, Christ's cross, does not lead to dolefulness and melancholy because it is a joyful summons to service. That is, it is a summons to the death that brings life, to the slavery that is liberty, as the Book of Common Prayer attests: "In thy service is perfect freedom." It was a special delight to find in Tolkien's hobbits a fine paradigm of what we Christians are meant to be as well: the little people of the world. It was also a privilege to preach a farewell sermon — in the conviction that God honors our service without regard to our success, much less our numbers — to the small congregation in London as they struggle to remain faithful while their little flock dwindles.

The seven sermons on doctrine and the moral life in Part IV are concerned not only with the obvious evils of terrorism and war, of abortion and the death penalty, but also with the lesser noticed expressions of what Pope John Paul II called "the culture of death," especially our abominable neglect of the elderly and our false counsel about what it means to be human. Convinced with the late Baptist theologian James Wm. McClendon that Christianity remains a vigorous set of doctrines and morals precisely as our preaching and ethics give shape to our worship and living, I have sought to show that justification and sanctification — faith and works — must be held in their properly contrapuntal relationship.

I was reared in a small-town Baptist church whose Christian year offered but slight modifications of the American year. It began with Youth Sunday on the last Sunday evening following Christmas (the "dead" Sunday when the pastor was given a small break), then the Sweetheart Banquet in February, followed by Easter Sunday (when we sang "Up from the Grave He Arose" without much acknowledgement that Christ had been crucified and buried), then the celebration of Mother's Day, and sometimes Father's Day (but the Fourth of July for sure), with everything culminating in Christmas itself (preceded, of course, by the annual "cantata"). Yet there were also fall and spring revivals, plus two weeks of Vacation Bible School in the summer, just to make sure that we Baptists could not be accused of Christian indolence. Not for a minute would I cast scorn on these faithful folks who spawned me. They gave me the most important gift in the world, and I owe them an unpayable debt of gratitude. Even so, I discovered in my mid-twenties, as a graduate student at the University of Chicago, that there is another calendar that helps Christians live by, another clock than the world's chronometer — namely, God's holy time ensconced in the church's grand rhythm of feasts and fasts. This liturgical life has been one of the chief blessings of my Christian life. Part V thus includes assorted sermons on Advent, Lent, Palm Sunday, Maundy Thursday, and Ascension Day.

My oft-repeated mantra that "many of my closest friends are my former students" attests to my unbounded gratitude for the high privilege of spending more than three and a half decades of my life in the classroom. Scores of these students have invited me to share their lives by offering counsel in times of trouble, being present amidst sickness and sorrow, as well as celebrating their joys and achievements whether close at hand or from afar. Part VI includes sermons on two of the most joyful occasions, marriage and ordination. How to say what needs saying about the enormous delights and difficulties of Christian ministry and marriage? That I treat them as vocations indicates that they are indeed holy callings that require God's sacramental grace for their sustenance.

The sermons in Part VII were at once the most rewarding and the most demanding, both to write and to preach. To announce the gospel at funerals is an even greater honor than to give homilies at weddings. Many nuptials are only minimally Christian events, as the paraphernalia — the flowers and the wedding dresses, the music and the pomp, the reception and the photographs — seem to shove lonely Jesus into the shadows. By contrast, funerals are often maximally Christian occasions: the time when we are privileged to proclaim the one Word that the world cannot declare to itself, that divine life and transworldly hope are the final realities, not earthly death and hellish despair. And so this assemblage of my sermons concludes with a selection of eulogies that I have been honored to deliver at the final homegoing of several family members and friends, even one of whom was a suicide. Here, as in all of these other homilies, I have been preaching to myself and not only to the congregations who have so patiently listened.

PART I

PREACHING AND HEARING

The Primacy of Preaching in Protestant Worship

THE WARREN CARR PREACHING SERIES

First Baptist Church
Elkin, North Carolina
June 7, 1998

We live in a time of homiletical famine, a drought of the preaching and the hearing of God's Word. Hence my conviction that we must be less busy doing and less noisy talking in order to become better hearers of the Word. Yet we will not become gospel listeners unless we have preachers who believe that their first and last call is to proclaim what eye has not seen nor ear heard, what has not entered the human heart: the unparalleled Good News prepared by God for those who love him (1 Cor. 2:9). Everything else derives from this fundamental fact that we cannot hear and know Jesus Christ without the proclamation of his Word by authentic preachers: "How shall they hear without a preacher?" (Rom. 10:14). Perhaps because I am not an ordained minister myself, but one who has benefited from excellent proclaimers of the Word, I have come to believe that the pastor's many other responsibilities and privileges spring from and center on this pulpit-act of preaching.

My aim here is to show that worship is the proper context for the hearing of God's Word, and that the sermon lies at the center of Protestant worship. This is especially true of Baptists, even if it is not true for other traditions. Episcopalians and Lutherans have a fixed liturgy as the heart of their worship. Methodists and Presbyterians also have the creeds to carry the weight of worship. Baptists have no formally prescribed liturgy, and we do not often (if at all) recite the creeds. Yet this is not merely a Baptist worry; much of evangelical worship suffers from the same liturgical lack. Our services of worship frequently have a homemade air and a rather crude quality about them. We need to do better by way of our pastoral prayers and congregational responses, so that they are not mere off-the-cuff effusions. The words "just" and "share" have been used so mindlessly that we should banish them from the lexicon of our supplications.

Neither does evangelical worship often transport us into the presence of the transcendent and holy God by way of our anthems and the congregational singing. In all of our noncreedal traditions, hymns become the real bearers of our beliefs. When I find myself in moments of extraordinary glory or terrible crisis, it is the hymns of Watts and Wesley, of Fanny Crosby and B. B. McKinney, that come pouring forth: "O God, Our Help in Ages Past," "I Know Whom I Have Believed," "O Jesus, I Have Promised," "Come Thou Fount of Every Blessing," "Love Divine, All Loves Excelling," "On Christ the Solid Rock I Stand." This explains why the displacement of gospel songs and traditional hymns by so-called praise music has such deadly theological consequence. Our people will eventually come to have a faith, I fear, that is as trite as our entertainment-driven music. True preaching, by contrast, should always find its appropriate echo and reinforcement in music that glorifies rather than trivializes God.

The black preacher from Jackson, Mississippi, who is also president of the Foundation for Reconciliation and Development, John Perkins, was once asked how many points a good sermon should have. "At least one," he wisely replied. At the risk of not having even a single worthy point, I offer these three theses concerning the centrality of the sermon for Protestant worship: the primacy of hearing, the primacy of preaching, and the primacy of the preacher.

The Primacy of Hearing

Isn't it interesting that Scripture puts such great emphasis on hearing rather than seeing God? Notice well the biblical claim that no man shall see God and live. From Adam and Abraham to Noah and Malachi, nearly every major Old Testament character *hears* God, though few ever see him — except Moses, who sees only God's hind end as he passes by, while Moses remains hidden in the cleft of the rock! So it is in the New Testament: there we who are the new Jews called Christians are instructed to walk by faith rather than by sight, to listen to God rather than to behold him face to face. "Blessed are those who have not seen and yet believe" (John 20:29). Only in the life to come will sight of the holy God bless rather than destroy us. It is in "this hope [that] we were saved. Now hope that is seen is not hope. For who hopes for what he sees? But if we hope for what we do not see, we wait for it in patience" (Rom. 8:24-25).

Why is God invisible? Wouldn't it be an immense help if God were palpable, so that we could see and touch him and thus know that he is real and not merely imagined? Most pagan religions indeed do make their gods visible by creating statues and images of them. Such visibility is what the God of Israel and Jesus Christ expressly forbid: "Thou shalt not make a graven image of me." Nowhere is the strangeness of the unpictured God made more remarkable than in the Roman destruction of Jerusalem in AD 70. As they razed the Temple, the Roman soldiers eagerly entered the Holy of Holies, the sanctuary of sanctuaries, the place where the pagans hoped at last to find the image of the Hebrew God, there to smash it in triumphant glee. To their huge disappointment, they found no such statue or figure, but only the Ark of the Covenant: a box containing mere scrolls. This bizarre religion with an unimaged god was unlike anything they had ever encountered! To the good pagan, a god who cannot be cast into bronze or carved from marble or wood is not worthy to be called a god. The early Christians encountered similar complaints. Their refusal to worship any other deity than the God of Jesus Christ caused them to be branded as atheists. In Paul's sermon on Mars Hill, recorded in Acts 17, we learn that the Athenians had erected an idol even to an unknown god. And though Paul sought to appeal to this pagan love of likeness in their gods by showing that Jesus is God in the flesh, he notably failed to make many converts.

God wants to be heard even before he can be seen. An obviously visible God would be a tyrant. There would be no room for faith or trust, no place for doubt or struggle, if God were open to view. Therefore, the young Samuel does not request that God show himself: such a sighting would make Samuel's obedience compulsory rather than voluntary. "Speak, Lord," we hear Samuel pleading, "for thy servant heareth" (1 Sam. 3:10). A palpably undeniable God would be a dictatorial deity. And we would hate him for being such a silent bully.

I wonder whether there may be a link between the decline of audibility and the rise of unbelief. Ours is a supremely pagan and thus a supremely visual culture. Almost everything important comes to us through the eye, almost nothing through the ear. It is not by chance that rock music issued in MTV: it is not sufficient to hear but also to see the hypersexualized music enacted. That the lyrics are mangled and indecipherable does not matter. Gyrations and other visual stimuli take their place. The literary critic Irving Howe once said that we Americans have become virtual mushrooms: we grow only in the dark, by the light of a flickering screen. George Will doubts whether we really grow very much at all. Will has observed, for example, that there is more imaginative work in reading any cheap Harlequin romance or detective thriller than in watching the most sophisticated movie. Film is a lazy and passive medium insofar as it requires no image-making labor but depicts everything for us. Such sensory bombardments enervate the imagination. Because we are the passive recipients of such relentless stimuli, we come to believe that the rest of the world operates in similar fashion. We are rapidly losing the capacity for both moral discernment and analytical thinking — indeed, for much thinking of any kind at all — and thus all the more prone to violence.

In *The Screwtape Letters,* C. S. Lewis speaks of the dread modern triumph of the eye over the ear. The cosmetic and fashion and advertising industries celebrate this mighty victory of seeing over hearing, as we come to have increasingly superficial notions of beauty and attractiveness. It is not the human face alone that reveals our souls; it is also the human voice. Thus do I encourage my students to fall in love not only (or even chiefly) with another's image but also with his or her voice, for lasting friendship and commitment and true love are found in the voice, the promise-making and promise-keeping faculty. We are what we declare, what we speak, what we pronounce and announce. Bunyan and Wesley, for example, still used the word "conversation" to mean outward behavior. Our ancient Christian forebears understood the primacy of hearing over seeing. Thus did the saints of the early church practice what they called "the discipline of the eyes," being even more careful about what they saw than what they heard.

Why is the spoken and heard word so much more important than its written and read versions? It is interesting to note that neither Jesus nor Socrates, the two most famous teachers in world history, left anything in writing. They both failed to publish, wags have said, and therefore they perished. Both men were killed, in fact, for their action-inciting words. Speech is our unique gift, the very image of God in us.

Animals can do everything that we humans can do, except the most important thing of all: they cannot speak. This explains why, given the awful choice between sight and hearing, the wise and courageous person would choose sound, giving up the enormous ease and pleasures of the visible world for the irreplaceable world of the human voice. Winston Churchill was not the first to note that deafness is infinitely more isolating than blindness: it squeezes us out of the human circle, cutting us off from true communion.

Therefore, we ought to reverse the trite aphorism about sticks and stones: they merely break our bones, while words can truly help or hurt us. A word of care and kindness can heal the deepest of wounds. A word of spite and deceit can rankle and fester forever. Once words are out of our mouth, we cannot retract them, any more than we can unscramble an egg or put toothpaste back into the tube. Their effects are permanent, for good or ill. Words are so powerful that the Epistle of James calls the tiny tongue the most dangerous of all bodily organs, far more hazardous than the genitals. A single word, therefore — most especially when it is the Word of God — is worth more than a thousand pictures.

The Primacy of the Sermon

When Luther and Calvin and the Anabaptists revolted against the medieval church, they did so in protest that the proclaimed Word had been eclipsed by the works-centered religion that Paul opposes in his Epistle to the Romans. The Reformation was thus a preaching movement intended not to create a special branch of Christendom so much as to renew the whole church in the doctrines of grace. The sermon thus became the Protestant sacrament, our equivalent of the Roman mass, the very center of the worship and praise of God. In fact, the Old Testament scholar Walter Brueggemann argues that Israel understands God in fundamentally verbal terms. It is not God's miraculous acts in history nor his divine being in himself that matters so much as it is the unique Word that issues from God's revelation to Israel.

Scripture refers far more often, in fact, to God's speaking than to his doing. God is indeed a doer — the Maker and Redeemer of the universe — but he acts chiefly by his speaking. In the first chapter of Genesis, God speaks the cosmos into being. God doesn't take things into his own hands and fashion the world out of something prior to it. Instead, he says, "Let there be." We know, of course, that Genesis 1 is a theological story and not a scientific report. God is not a material being but the divine Spirit. He has no mouth or tongue, and he doesn't speak Hebrew or Greek, English or Ebonics. God speaks through his people Israel and finally through his son, Jesus Christ, the one man in whom he has fashioned his own image.

The sermon is the center of most Protestant worship, our veritable sacrament, because there we encounter Christ himself in the heard Word. The Swiss Calvinists of the sixteenth century went so far as to declare (in the Second Helvetic Confession of 1566) that "the preaching of the Word of God is the Word of God." Thus the gospel is not only something to be preached: *the gospel is preaching itself.* This is a radical claim, but I think it is exactly Paul's point. *Fides ex auditu.* "Faith cometh by hearing," we remember from the King James translation, "and hearing by the word of God." Note exceedingly well what St. Paul does not say: He does not say that faith comes by seeing, and that what is seen comes by writing, and that what is believed comes through reading. G. K. Chesterton noted that a book cannot be put on the witness stand; it cannot be interrogated so as to confess its meaning and truthfulness. In his second letter to Corinth, Paul explicitly warns against an overemphasis on the merely written word. There he says that the word that is written down often serves to kill, while the Spirit, acting through the proclaimed Word, gives life (2 Cor. 3:6).

We can close our eyes to what is seen. We can put down a book and either daydream or go change a light bulb. We cannot so easily dismiss the spoken and the heard Word. We have eyelids for shutting out pictures and scenes that we don't want to see, but the ear has no flap for fending off either human words or the Word of God. Our earlobes are meant to increase our hearing, not to close it off. Jesus does not say, "Let those who have eyes, see," but rather "Let those who have ears, hear." "Stick your eyes in your ears," said Luther, "when you hear the Word of God preached." Luther calls us to see in a new way: through the verbal imaging of the proclaimed Word. We thus learn to look rightly at the world when we have first truly heard the Word. It follows, said Luther, that "the church is a mouth-house, not a pen-house." At church we don't write essays or take notes, lest our scribbling become a clever and pseudo-academic means of stopping our ears to the God who engages us as we listen rather than write.

It needs to be said that evangelicals run a great risk in focusing on the sermon. Christian worship that is centered on the proclamation of the gospel is not the safest but the most perilous activity of the week. The worship hour is the hour of great risk. Something splendid occurs when we come to hear the Word proclaimed, or else something terrible. When the Word is not preached, everything else fails; indeed, an awful sacrilege has occurred. Nothing can salvage a service that is void of true proclamation. Someone has described hell as a perpetual church service minus the presence of God. I would add that hell is an interminable sermon without the proclamation of the gospel.

Faithful preaching is even more dangerous than its unfaithful counterpart. Calvin confessed, for example, that the truly proclaimed Word makes the world at once better and worse off. "For while there was no preached Gospel," he declared, "all the world was without care and at rest. There was little to argue or dispute about." The world remained at ease in its self-serving slumbers, even when the somnolence was of a highly ethical sort. But with the true preaching of the gospel, Calvin added, "the world is plunged into conflict." Faithful preaching, Calvin is saying, permits no neutral response, as if we were attending a civic club luncheon or parents-and-teachers meeting. It makes us either hugely glad or unbearably sad. It either saves or else it damns. To hear God's Word is gladly to acknowledge his grip on our lives. It makes us eagerly seize the brass ring of grace for all we are worth. It prompts us joyfully to practice the faith every day and every night until our last day and last night. Or else it forces us to turn away in wrath and scorn, spitting and scoffing at this call to devote our lives to Jesus Christ and to none other. There is no convenient middle path between these drastic extremes: whether we know it or not, we are either hearers of the Word or else we are haters of the Word.

The early British Baptists were so convinced of what is dangerous and drastic about the proclaimed Word that they became suspicious of the merely written Word. Lest the Bible become a substitute for hearing the living Word, our foreparents in the faith prohibited their people even from bringing their Bibles to church. You may recall that Warren Carr never asks the congregation to follow along in their Bibles when he reads the sermon text. As he wittily puts it, such a request must mean that we don't really trust him to read it right. And so he begins with a sharp one-word command: *Listen!* He wants us to hear the Word of God, not read it. The sermon is where such hearing reveals God's Word to be sharper than a two-edged sword, piercing even to the joint of bone and marrow. We are called to let it rend our hearts and cleave our souls. We are summoned to let it wound us to the quick, lancing the suppurating sores of sin, that it might heal us forever.

How many of us could truly confess Jesus Christ if the sermon had not been the focus of our worship? And without treading too fearlessly and foolishly on angelic ground, how many here would contest that Warren Carr literally preached this congregation back into unity and reconciliation after it had been so bitterly divided? You were brought back to health not by an intentional interim — as if all other interims were accidental! — but by a providential interim. He was not a consultant trained in conflict management, as if the church were another business or governmental agency. This church was revitalized as God's faithful people by a faithful preacher who rightly regards the sermon as the center of Protestant worship.

The Primacy of the Preacher

"How are men to call upon [the Christ] in whom they have not believed?" asks St. Paul. "And how are they to believe in him of whom they have never heard? And how are they to hear without a preacher?" This brings us to a final claim as simple and drastic as it is startling and dangerous: the voice of Jesus Christ is none other than the voice of the one who proclaims his Word. The faithful preacher, I again repeat, is the voice of the living Lord. The first and still the greatest Protestant, Martin Luther, said it outrageously: "When the Holy Spirit enables me to preach the Word of God, it is no longer Martin Luther but Jesus Christ who speaks." John Calvin, our other chief founder, made a similar case. "The Word of God," said Calvin, "is not distinguished from the words of the Prophet." The God of the Gospel, Calvin added, "is not separated from the minister." The preacher of the Word actually does God's own work.

These are perilous sayings indeed. We all know preachers who think that they not only proclaim Jesus but that they have become Christ himself. Thus do they lord it over their people according to this terrible self-perception, which is, of course, self-delusion. They swagger and bully and dominate their flock as though they were not only the audible but also the visible God. They do a lot of shouting as well as a lot of eating. Notice that they are often as gross as they are loud, having been made obese with their own egotism rather than lithe with the Word of God. (Yet let me speak a word in defense of the innocently fat: a fleshy lady from my wife's East Texas hometown says that she would rather shake than rattle!)

We who are not fundamentalists have become so afraid of preacherly authoritarianism that we have sadly diminished the role of the preacher. We are reluctant to speak of the pastor as having primary authority within our Baptist churches. Instead, we call him our "servant-leader" or (God forbid!) our "congregational facilitator." These are weasel phrases that serve to dodge the true primacy of the preacher. Warren Carr has often noted the result: there are very few jokes about preachers. We make fun only of those things that we take seriously. Notice, therefore, that most of our jokes are sexual — sex being the last thing that our culture takes with utmost seriousness.

To diminish the primacy of the preacher is to ignore the fact that — in a tradition such as ours, which makes preaching the central act of worship — the preacher is bound to be the center of the church's witness and its religious life. Willy-nilly, he or she is the shepherd of the flock, the preacher of the Word, and thus the primary figure in the congregation. My friend, the British theologian Daniel Jenkins, sums up the matter well. The Protestant pastor, he says, serves as the exemplary Christian. He or she is set apart by the local congregation to do directly and full-time what the other church members are able, because of other exigencies, to do only indirectly and part-time: to proclaim and enact the Word of God. And as J. Don Reeves reminds me, the preacher is not the political but the spiritual head of the congregation. Therefore, when the church is in conference, the preacher is indeed one among equals: one person, one vote. Even so, I confess that I always eagerly await the pastor's word about any important matter that we are voting on.

Richard John Neuhaus makes a similar claim about the primacy of the preacher in his splendid book entitled *Freedom for Ministry*. Neuhaus argues that ministers are called to serve as a virtual lightning rod: to receive fire from both God and man. Precisely because of the authoritative Word that they proclaim, preachers are the singular individuals through whom the divine presence is brought to earth, even as they are the people through whom the hard human questions are clarified and rendered creative rather than destructive. One of my former students, now a Methodist minister, illustrates the point powerfully. He tells about the death of two members of his congregation, a mother and father who were run down by a drunk driver as they innocently walked along the roadside. Four children under the age of thirteen were instantly orphaned. Great was the grief and distress of the family and friends who quickly assembled.

God was by no means absent from that terrible scene. Prayers had already been made, and assurances had already been given, by the time my friend arrived. God was already at work. Yet everything changed when the preacher entered that house. Those prayers now had a single voice, and those assurances came from one who spoke not only for himself but also for the God of the gospel. Now the great grief and the furious anger had both a focus and a target: the preacher himself. There he acted as no mere servant-leader or pastoral counselor or congregational facilitator. There he became God's own surrogate, the one through whom Christ himself was made manifest.

It is not only during times of great crisis that the preacher's primacy should be observed. It should also happen during ordinary times. Preachers who are not afraid of their own authority and primacy will have such startlingly original things to say on Sunday that we who are their parishioners will seek their counsel during the week. Knowing that we have heard what can be heard nowhere else, we will not confine our conversations to polite palaver. We will not be content with mere congeniality. We will engage our preachers in the deep and hard and joyful things of the gospel — precisely because they have first engaged us in these very things. Such vital exchanges between preacher and flock will symbiotically feed our preachers' own proclamation of the Word. No longer will they take their illustrations from television shows or sermon books but from felt and lived experience. No longer will they preach what I call "messages to the cosmos": *Time-Life* discourses addressed virtually to anyone and thus truly to no one in particular. Or, as the comic novelist Peter De Vries suggests, they will avoid prayers that might be entitled "In Case Anyone Is Listening." Instead, our preachers will speak, as the Quakers used to say, to our fallen and redeemed condition.

"How shall they hear without a preacher?" The answer for most of us Protestants lies in making the sermon serve as the center of our worship. There we will help restore the priority of hearing over seeing in a culture that will soon blind as well as deafen itself. There we will give unabashed preeminence to the preaching and hearing of the Word. And there we will acknowledge the true pastoral primacy of the preacher in the faithful life of God's flock. Amen.

Be Hearers of the Word and Not Doers Only

Romans 10:14-17

THE WARREN CARR PREACHING SERIES

First Baptist Church
Elkin, North Carolina
June 7, 1998

We are a famished people because there is so very little preaching and hearing of the gospel today. This may seem to be a strange claim. Our churches, as well as our television stations and our radio networks, seem quite well nourished with preachers. Indeed, we are bloated with them. Yet, for all our religious fatness, we remain a scrawny, even an emaciated people. We are anorexics and bulimics of the Word. We stuff ourselves with preaching, but then we put our finger down our throat in sickness at these thousands of words that constitute no real Word.

This famine of the Word marks our great divide from Jesus himself. He was physically famished after his forty days of temptation in the wilderness. Satan promised him power to turn the desert stones into nourishing bread, if only he would bow down and worship the prince of this world. Jesus replied that there is a starvation far worse than having nothing to eat. He tells the devil that men will die if they try to survive on the foodstuffs of the world. Only the Word that proceeds from God will nourish our souls. Eight centuries earlier, the Hebrew prophet Amos made a similar prediction of our late-twentieth-century condition. Amos prophesied that God would send a time of dearth and drought on sinful Israel. It would be a famine that would make mere hunger and thirst seem nourishing. God would unleash, instead, a famine that would devastate his people at their very core: a famine of "hearing the words of the Lord" (8:11).

I believe that something similar has happened in our time. I believe that God has sent a terrible famine of the Word. Why would the good God do so horrible a thing? Why would he prevent the hearing of his Word? God is no capricious and arbitrary deity who acts without reason, much less a monster-god who delights in our misery, tearing the wings off flies to see them squirm. As always, God acts for our good, even when his actions seem hurtful. He sometimes takes good things away from us to awaken us to their real value and thus to prompt our eager return to them. We often learn the privilege of health only when we've fallen sick, the value of money when we've gone broke, the sweetness of victory when we have suffered the bitterness of defeat, the blessedness of hearing when we've become deaf. The nineteenth-century Danish poet and prophet Søren Kierkegaard explained the matter well. He declared that God would eventually take the gospel away from Europe — and America, I would add — as the final way to convince us of its truth. I believe that Kierkegaard has proved to be right: God is deliberately starving his churches and his people so that we might learn to feast on his true food. My purpose is to identify the reasons for this awful famine that God has sent upon us, this awful dearth of the Word. For if we can discern why we have grown deaf to the voice of God, we might yet again become hearers of his holy Word. In religion as in medicine, diagnosis is two-thirds of the cure.

We Are Too Busy Doing

In Romans 10, the apostle Paul wrestles with the problem of his own people's deafness to the Word: Why do his fellow Jews refuse to receive Jesus as the Anointed of God, as the Messiah of Israel and thus of the whole world. Paul poignantly confesses, in the very first verse, that "my heart's desire and prayer is that [Israel] may be saved." Earlier Paul has admitted, in one of the darkest lines in all Scripture, that he would be willing to be damned if Israel could be brought to redemption (9:3). His people have rejected Christ, Paul says, not because they are so wicked but because they are so good. This is usually the case: we are undone by our solitary and unbalanced virtues far more than by our manifold yet singular vices. We sin against God and man more often through our strengths than our weaknesses. The intelligent person looks with scorn on the stupid, the courageous man despises the cowardly, the beautiful woman has contempt for the ugly. Our blessings become our curses.

So it was with ancient Israel: she became deaf to God's Word precisely because of her obedience to the Law. God had given his elect nation the precious gift of the Law to be the means of her salvation. Unlike all other races, Israel was set apart as the one people whom he would graciously enable to live in faithful obedience to the Law. Thus would Israel become ever more reliant on God, since the Law could be fulfilled only through the covenant of forgiveness that God had made with her. Israel could not keep the Law of her own accord, but only by means of God's own goodness and power. This explains, by the way, why an Alabama judge is wrong to think that posting the Ten Commandments on his courtroom wall will make the people there more righteous. It may have the opposite and terrible effect of making them self-righteous. For if we think we can make the state do the work of the church, as if we could obey God's Law by our own might — that is, apart from the worship and service of Jesus Christ — then we are indeed damnably mistaken.

We Americans are nothing if not doers. This can-do spirit is our great national talent. Living in Europe will quickly make you wish you had someone who could do something and not just stand there. After we had spent a year in Italy, my family and students joked that the Italian national gesture is a quizzical shrug of the shoulders, and the national motto is *Forse domain* ("perhaps tomorrow"). Yet as I have suggested, our virtues become our vices. We Americans make long lists of things we have to do, as if the world would cease to turn if we stopped our desperate doing. Even middle-schoolers now carry calendars to keep up with their busy schedules. Parents wear themselves out running the taxi service that takes their kids from one activity to the next.

Our busy-ness comes in two kinds, the unworthy and the worthy. Our frenetic activity often constitutes a secret attempt to fill our emptiness: we hurry and scurry lest we might have to stop and reflect on the bundle of furious activity that we have become. Early in my years at Wake Forest, I learned that people always find time to do the things they really want to do. I confess to being one who cannot sit still and do nothing. I must be up and about, bustling to and fro, wanting to get something done. Our busy-ness is thus a hidden excuse for not accomplishing our true work, the difficult and time-consuming tasks to which we are called. Hence Pascal's harsh truth: "Most of the world's mischief is due to the inability of men to sit still in their room."

There is a second kind of busy-ness that is even more dangerous because its activities are constructive rather than self-interested and escapist. Surely you will ask what is wrong with constructive activity, especially when it occurs in the church? What is wrong with the father who gives up his entire weekend to work on a Habitat for Humanity house? What about the mother who surrenders her vacation week to accompany the young people of the church to summer camp? What about high school and college students who devote their spring break to helping storm victims clean up property devastated by tornado or hurricane? What about the family who is here every time the church doors open? Surely these are all worthy activities, and surely they are to be commended. Yet such noble doings are strangely dangerous. They threaten to become substitutes for what must always come prior to them: the hearing of God's Word. We should be active only and precisely because Christ acts, not in secret fear that God will do nothing unless we ourselves get busy.

My first call, therefore, is for us to slow down and to listen, to hear God's word before we too eagerly do it. Jesus Christ is the steady center of our lives, the stable stackpole around whom the harvested grain of our lives is to be gathered. He is not a helpless bystander to our furious activity, a mere hanger-on to our godless striving. We cannot work our way into the Kingdom, though we most certainly can work our way out of it. We are saved not by our works — not even by the noblest of activities — but by grace through faith, as hearers of the Word and not doers only.

We Are Too Noisy Talking

If busy-ness and activity are the first reason that God has sent a famine of the Word upon us, then our noisyness is surely the second. Ours is an age frightened of silence. We can't even shop in the stores, or be put on hold as we use the telephone, without the ever-present racket of Muzak in our ears. When I complained about the high-decibel background music in a local grocery store, the manager told me that it was required by company policy, as that was specified in far-off Cincinnati, Ohio! We fear the prospect of being silent and alone with our thoughts, much less with our prayers. And so we fill our lives with constant noise. We leave the television on even when we are not watching or listening to it. Young people turn up their supercharged car radios so loud that the whole machine shakes — as do all other cars in the vicinity — with the deafening sexual throb of the music. Yet we adults are no better able to withstand silence. Many of us now use sleep machines to make the soothing noises that help us drop off at night. How ironic that the silence that was once the precondition of sleep has now become its dread enemy!

Yet it is not only mechanical noises that make us very poor hearers of the Word. It is also our own noisy voices that silence the voice of God. We gab and rattle on about everything and nothing. Again, it was Søren Kierkegaard who gave the right name to our time: the "Talkative Age." He meant that, in our age, everyone has an opinion about nearly everything, but few of us have convictions about much of anything. We are eager to attitudinize about this and that, but we are reluctant to take a stand — to live and to die — for the sake of the gospel. We can all give our opinion about Al Gore or George Bush, about Tiger Woods or Deion Sanders, about rock stars and movie stars. But when it comes to our convictions about Jesus Christ as God's saving Word incarnate, we hem and haw and stew and stumble. Or if we are professors or preachers, we are likely to chatter endlessly about those awful fundamentalists or those terrible liberals. Thus do we become noisy gongs and clanging cymbals, not only because we lack the love of God but also because we have not listened to the God of love.

To hear God speak, we must first fall silent. The Bible puts considerable emphasis on silence. Elijah hears the voice of God, not in the tornado winds, not in the thunderous earthquake, not in the crackling and consuming fire. God speaks to Elijah out of the silence that enables him to hear "a still small voice" (1 Kings 19:12). Because God does not shout, we must first be quiet if we are to hear his own quiet Word. "Be still, and know that I am God," declares the Psalmist (46:10). Hebrew scholars tell me that this is a polite rendering of a rather harsh declaration that would better be translated, "Shut up, and listen to me." To know that God is truly God — our Father, not our Daddy — we must first stop our mouths, sit still, and listen. St. Thomas Aquinas wisely declared that "silence honors God." When we are noisy, God refuses to speak; instead, he sends a terrible silence of the Word. But when we stop prattling and rattling, God will indeed speak. And when he speaks, he will enable us both to hear and to do his Word.

There Are Not Many Preachers of the Word

We fail to become hearers of the Word not only because we are too busy and too noisy, but also because there are not many preachers. Here, I believe, the fault lies less with us laypeople than with our ministers. To say that there are not many preachers may seem an odd claim. In the Baptist southland, there often seem to be more preachers than believers. It is obvious that I am using the word in St. Paul's special sense when he says that "faith comes from what is heard, and what is heard comes from the preaching of Christ" (Rom. 10:17). There are not many pastors who preach nothing but Jesus Christ and him nailed. Yes, there are many storytellers who string together interesting narratives and call it preaching. Yes, there are many expositors who make verse-by-verse commentary on Scripture while the congregation faithfully takes notes, as if the church were a lecture hall. Yes, there are many counselors who offer psychological help to the hurting by "feeling our pain" and telling us how to accept our brokenness. Yes, there are many social reformers who lead their churches to engage in worthy projects for the poor and the needy. Yet it is not necessary to be a proclaimer of the Word in order to accomplish these worthy things.

I receive occasional requests from churches to recommend preachers to fill their empty pulpits. It's always an embarrassing moment when I have to confess that I know only a handful of preachers. I quickly add that I know several ministers who would make fine denominational servants and excellent administrators, who would visit those in hospitals and counsel the troubled, who would become well-regarded citizens of the community, who would join all the right civic clubs and be seen in all of the right public places, who would smile a lot, shake a lot of hands, slap a lot of backs, and offend absolutely nobody. Again, one doesn't need to be a proclaimer of the gospel to do these things. On the contrary, I contend that one had better not be a preacher if one believes that this is what it means to be a minister of the Word. "How shall they hear without a preacher?" asks Paul. The answer is that God will send a famine of the Word against those who preach without having anything truly redemptive and revelatory to say — against those who preach without preaching the gospel.

Who, then, is a true preacher of the Word? It is a man or a woman who has been encountered by the crucified and risen Christ, who has been saved by God's grace from all busy and noisy activity (albeit of the worthiest kind), who has been called and commissioned to announce the only news that can redeem the world from sin, death, and the devil. True preachers of the Word are those men and women who wrestle daily with the dangerous God of the gospel. Thus do they have a Word to declare that we can hear from no one else. They refuse to repeat the tired and boring (or even the fresh and interesting) truths that we can learn from television or from the public schools and the universities. They confront us with the Good News that, while we were yet sinners, Christ has died for us, that he has risen from death's bonds to set us free from our busy and noisy lives, and that he reigns at the right hand of God to put real life in us — new life, abundant life, eternal life. These preachers declare to us the one Word that remains the same yesterday, today, and forever: Jesus Christ. Therefore, God will lift our present famine of the Word when we cease from our busyness and noisyness, when we sit still and listen to this one voice, and thus when we all become hearers and thus doers of the Word.

With uncommon self-restraint, I have refrained from quoting the man whom this preaching series honors. Since nearly everything I know about the gospel I have learned from him, this amounts to an almost miraculous silence. Yet I cannot end without this single personal reference. This emboldened minister of the gospel told me recently that many people, especially those strange folks who calls themselves moderates, want to salute him for having been the first Southern Baptist pastor to ordain a woman to the gospel ministry. They also want to honor him for having been one of the first Southern white preachers to insist that we must not deny black people their rightful place in society. Already in the 1950s, this courageous witness to the truth was preaching that blacks are our fellow human beings created in the image of God, and also that most of them are our brothers and sisters in Jesus Christ. So it is with women: in Jesus Christ there is neither Greek nor Jew, neither bond nor free, neither male nor female. In him alone are we all one. It is a gross sin against God, this man preached, to exclude blacks and women from their rightful place in our churches and in our society.

The liberation of women and blacks is hugely important, as is the struggle against the other sundry and sorry forms of oppression and self-absorption. But these are not the things that Warren Carr regards as his chief accomplishment. He was a doer of the Word because he was first and last a hearer and preacher of the Word. He explained the matter recently by telling me about a phone call he received from a pastor in Charleston, South Carolina. This man had attended the Watts Street Baptist Church in Durham, North Carolina, during the 1950s. Under Warren's ministry, this pastor had been called to become a minister of the gospel, to proclaim and to enact the saving Word of God. "That," said Warren Carr, "is the witness I hope to be remembered for." Amen.

The Minister as Parson, Preacher, and Pastor

Acts 20:17-24

Poplar Springs Baptist Church
Elkin, North Carolina
October 16, 1988

Paul has come to bid farewell to his congregation at Ephesus. He knows that his own end is near. He has been warned that the trip to Jerusalem will probably mean his death. At the very least, he will face affliction and imprisonment. And so it is a time for summing up his life and ministry, for encouraging and strengthening his people, for putting his case in the simplest terms possible. Paul does it in a single pithy sentence: "I do not count my life of any value nor as precious to myself, so that I may accomplish my course and the ministry which I received from the Lord Jesus, to testify to the gospel of the grace of God."

It would be hard to find a more compact and straightforward declaration of what it means to be a witness to Jesus Christ, and thus of what it means to be a minister of the gospel. I've come here today to address this question. You are a church without a pastor, and I am layman who has not been ordained. Perhaps this makes us a good match, and perhaps I can be of service to you by describing what I envision a true minister of the gospel to be.

I can say to you, in both honesty and gratitude, that I would not be a Christian and a professor of religion today were it not for my ministers. It is a noteworthy fact that I can remember every one of my pastors — from the time as a mere child I was first able to understand that the man in the pulpit was someone immensely important, to this very day some forty years later, when my pastor is also my closest companion in the faith. Like Dilsey in Faulkner's *The Sound and the Fury,* I've seen 'em come and I've seen 'em go. And I've seen some I wish might have gone sooner than they did, just as I've beheld others whom I wish we could have kept much, much longer. Taking my cue from St. Paul, I maintain that a true minister of the gospel has three essential characteristics: the minister is first of all a parson and thus a man or woman of God; the minister is also a preacher of the Word in all of its incomparable gladness; finally, the minister is a pastor who not only feeds the sheep but who also knows who the True Shepherd is.

The Minister as Parson

Our word "parson" has an old-fashioned ring to it. Yet it ought not seem so quaint, for it means simply "person." The parson is thus our true person, the man or woman who represents what it means to be a human being — namely, a man or a woman living before God as our Father, alongside Jesus Christ as his incarnate Son, and filled with the inner testimony of the Holy Spirit. We are — all of us — nothing less than witnesses to the glorious thing that God has done as Father, Son, and Spirit. In our words and our deeds, in our living and our dying, we give testimony to him who spoke and acted in our behalf, who died and rose again that we might live now and forever in God's presence. This is what really counts for every one of us as Christians. But it is the parson whom we ordain to declare and to act out in a public way this great fact.

The Greek word for "person" comes from the giant masks that actors wore in performing the great public dramas of Athens and other Greek cities. The masks enabled actors both to project their voices and to clarify the tragic or comic nature of their character. *Persona* thus means *character:* we are what we declare, what we speak, what comes sounding through us. Our word "parson" has the same root: a parson thus wears a mask, dramatizes a character, plays a part, perhaps even pretending to be what he or she knows we all ought to be but often are not — men and women living in the presence of God.

Our masks are our necessary restraints on our worst behavior, as well as necessary projections of our best behavior. A world where everybody told the total truth would be brutal indeed. In fact, the little Epistle of James warns against the tongue that tells the unbridled truth.

This little flap of flesh can become what James calls "an unruly evil, full of deadly poison." The tongue kindles a fatal fire when it tells the truth in order to wound and destroy. Such false truthfulness is set alight by hell because it takes pleasure in another's misery. The poet William Blake put the matter ever so sharply:

A truth that's told with bad intent
Beats all the lies you can invent.

None of us could survive if we did not wear a mask and play a role. My own chief persona is that of a teacher. My role as a professor enables me to be something larger and truer than my miserable little self! The old saying that "a man is as good as his word" thus needs drastic alteration. We are not as good as our word. We are all contradictions of what we profess to be. We are hypocrites. We are whited sepulchers. We are miserable sinners who lack integrity. Yet we would do well to remember the claim of the poet W. H. Auden that there is no real distinction between the sincere and the insincere, but only between the sane, who know that they are acting, and the insane, who do not.

That your parson is an actor performing a role means that he or she may not be a better person (in the ordinary sense) than you are. Indeed, his or her failings may be very great. We will have to judge and forgive their sins if they are truly our parsons, even as they must indict and pardon our own offenses if we are truly their people. They remain our parsons because God has summoned them to do what no one else can accomplish: to ascend the hill of the Lord like Moses, to stand in the holy place, and thus to know the horror of our sin and the glory of our salvation in Christ Jesus.

This means, above all, that our parsons should have deep personal faith: they must first of all be men and women of God and not merely of the world. We don't want our parson to be known primarily for his hobbies or athletic ability, nor for her singing voice or hairdo. And God forbid that they should be merely a nice folks with pleasing personalities who are good at going along and getting along. Least of all should the parson be a "hale fellow well met," a backslapping good ol' gal or boy, a Gleaming Gums with a blinding smile. True parsons are no such fakes and frauds.

They are real persons because they are real people of prayer. Prayer is the one place where there can be no pretense: there we are made totally transparent. There we wear no masks, because there God sees right through us, and yet loves us still. There we are enabled to be the real and natural selves that God intends us to be. *Ora et labora* was the ancient motto of the monks: pray and work. Prayer comes first, else all the work of your parsons will be in vain. In prayer they turn away from their own efforts. In prayer they leave themselves and their work behind. In prayer they stand before God without one plea, but that Christ's blood was shed for thee and them. Many parsons are burning out these days without any visible signs that they were on fire. If your parsons have been set alight by prayer, they will not burn out. Instead, their light will shine like a beacon in the darkness; for thus will they act out our true personhood in Jesus Christ.

The Minister as Preacher

Over and again Paul calls himself a preacher of the gospel. "I preach nothing else," he says, "but Jesus Christ and him crucified." "Woe be unto me if I preach not the gospel." "I am eager to preach the gospel to you also who are in Rome," Paul also declares in the opening chapter of his Epistle to the Romans. Preaching is thus an activity like none other: it is the continuing miracle that occurs right here in our midst, the annunciation of God's kingdom so as to make it actually happen. "Faith comes by hearing," declares the apostle again in Romans, "and hearing comes by the preaching of Jesus Christ." Words speak to the heart and conscience, as even the most powerful pictures and music do not. This, among many other reasons, is why I am troubled by the fact that our children are growing up in a world of images and sounds but not of words. It also explains why the electronic church will never be a true church. The preached Word, when it announces the call of Jesus Christ — not to a faceless audience but to you and me — is the most stunning of all human things. There God enables the preacher's mere mortal words to become nothing less than God's own redeeming Word.

In other Christian traditions, liturgy and sacrament largely take the place of preaching. But not in our own Baptist tradition and other evangelical traditions, where preaching is the heart of the matter. A minister who cannot preach — no matter how fine a parson and pastor he may be — will sooner or later fail. In Texas we are fond of the saying "That dog won't hunt." It is just as silly to say, "That preacher can't preach," for it means that he or she is no preacher at all. Yet good preaching is not fundamentally a matter of eloquent oratory. One of the most powerful sermons I ever heard was by a man whom I could hardly understand because he had a cleft palate. And I often hear primitively clear proclamations of the gospel from uneducated fundamentalist preachers on the country radio station out of Mt. Airy, North Carolina. Their realism is often admirable. One of them, in describing the scene in Gethsemane where Peter takes a sword to Malchus, declared recently: "It wasn't old Peter's fault that Malchus ducked. For he sure wasn't going after no ear. He wanted his head!"

To be a good preacher is to have something utterly original and radically important to say, for the gospel is nothing less than radical and original. Bad preaching comes from the attempt to give human advice as if it were the Word of God. This doesn't mean your preacher needs to have a doctorate; indeed, that might be the worst of hindrances! But she or he must surely be a student of Scripture and of other books. Don't saddle them with a thousand trivial tasks when they should be hard at study. And make sure that they are not at the shopping mall or on the golf course when they should be at their desk. Further, be careful to engage your preachers in conversation about their preaching. Tell them when it speaks to you and when it doesn't. An authentic preacher would much rather be told that he is dead wrong than to be given a polite "I enjoyed your sermon." (Of course, I may be setting myself up for some deadly responses!) But such is the risk and the wonder of preaching. It is not meant to make us comfortable but to make us godly and gracious.

What I'm trying to make clear is simply this: if your ministers are preachers worthy of their hire, they will certainly cause offense. Paul says that he did not shrink from declaring anything that was profitable. His proclamation of the gospel made him real and terrible enemies. This is, alas, as it must be. The Catholic wit G. K. Chesterton said that Christ commands us to love our enemies, not that we should have none. I would add the corollary that those preachers who make no enemies for the sake of the gospel are no friends of God.

It is evident that Paul is not at all concerned with his own reputation. He says that he does not account his life as precious and valuable to himself — as something that must be protected like fragile glass. And Paul wants no one else to protect him from the truth. He simply and straightforwardly preaches the gospel without worrying what people will think. He counts all such worldly repute as mere garbage, all such so-called gain as real loss. And he does it for the surpassing joy of knowing and preaching Jesus Christ. Thus do I urge you to make sure that your minister is first and last a preacher of the gospel.

The Minister as Pastor

The word "pastor" appears only once in the New Testament — in Ephesians 4. Even there it really means "shepherd," which is of course what a pastor truly is: one who tends sheep amidst the pasture. True pastors lead and guide their lambs; they guard and protect their flock from the wolves of this world. This means that ministers must constantly be among their people if they are to be their shepherd. Pastors who are distant and aloof from their flock are no pastors at all. Yet I fear that this is the deadly failing of many modern pastors. They are secretly suspicious of their calling, deeply embarrassed at having the church as their career, thus often wishing they could be elsewhere than among the people of God. May God deliver us from such false shepherds!

Authentic pastors who abide with their flock draw sustenance from their sheep. Not only do they feed the flock when they are hungry but, what is equally important, the flock feeds them when they need nourishment. My own former minister says that, when he was troubled and downcast, he always turned to his own people for strength and hope. He went to visit the sick and the elderly, the heartbroken and the dying, not only in order to fulfill his pastoral duty, but also to hear an encouraging word. As you have surely learned from your own experience, a visit to the needy and the helpless almost always ends with your receiving ever so much more than you have given. And the most important thing that pastors receive from dwelling among their people is learning their real joys and griefs. And only as you, in turn, open yourselves to your pastors will they be able to address the gospel to your own condition rather than preaching to the walls and windows.

Notice, finally, that Paul says he has shed many tears with his people. This the greatest of the apostles is no proud sophisticate who is too cultivated to weep when the occasion demands it. Yet Paul is not the advocate of a blubbering emotionalism. The church's ancient desert fathers and mothers spoke of "the gift of tears": they were not referring to any kind of sentimental emotionalism but rather to true sorrow over their sin and true joy over their salvation. The pastor whose eyes moisten even as ours do can never be our master but always and only our minister. The word *minister* literally means "the little one." This is who our pastor truly is because that's who we truly are — the little ones. God alone is Master, the great one; Jesus Christ is the true shepherd, while the pastor is but his helper, and we are all his sheep. May God thus grant us good parsons and good preachers and good pastors who lead us to do but one thing: to follow the Good Shepherd, Jesus Christ. Amen.

Hearing the Voice of God

A CONVOCATION SERMON

Samford University
Birmingham, Alabama
September 23, 1997

Paul declares in Romans 10:17 that "faith comes from what is heard, and what is heard comes through the preaching of Christ." This is my text and my theme for today because it has proved profoundly true in my own life. I have never seen or heard God himself. He has not revealed himself to me through sky-writing or loudspeakers. The God of the Bible doesn't often engage in such stupendous visible and hearable acts. Such world-shattering displays would make God obvious, and an obvious God would not be the self-hidden and self-identifying God of Scripture. Such a plain and indisputable God would be coercive. He would be a bully, and he would force our obedience. This is not the God of Abraham, Isaac, and Jacob, not the God of Jesus Christ. The true God is always the God of invitation and persuasion, the God who commands only because he also enables us to do his will. And he enables us to do his will in life-giving trust through others who announce his gospel to us. Therefore, I want briefly to describe three people who have enabled me to hear the voice of God summoning me to faith and obedience.

I

I must have been four or five years old the first time I heard God speak through the agency of another human being. To say that God spoke to me through Zuma Allen is not quite right, since this woman did not speak a single word to me. It was the deadly look she gave me that enabled me to hear the voice of God as I had never heard it before. Zuma Allen was our black maid. My family was far from wealthy, but, like nearly all other white families, we had a black maid. Perhaps because African-American maids were paid so poorly, even schoolteacher parents like mine could afford one. I can still see this woman's long black fingers — not really black underneath but nearly pink like mine — smoothing down the collars and cuffs of my father's starched white shirts as she ironed them.

But one summer day — it must have been the summer of 1946 or 1947 — I spoke a word in Zuma Allen's presence that had a devastating effect on me. No sooner had I uttered that word and seen Zuma's wounded look than I knew I had done something absolutely dreadful. I crawled under the bed and hid myself there, it seemed, for hours. I did not want to come out from that dark hole. I did not want her ever to see me again, so horribly ashamed was I for the thing I had said. I knew, in my childlike way, that I had crossed a barrier that should never have been crossed: I had demeaned and diminished another human being — unforgivably.

Yet the word I had let slip was not an unusual word. It was a word that I had heard my parents use, that my friends and I frequently used, that all white people and even some black people used. It was the word that formed the entire basis for our segregated society. It was the word that helped "keep Negroes in their place," their supposedly deserved place of subjection and inferiority. This single word made clear that black people could not stay in the same hotels or drink from the same water fountains or use the same bathrooms or attend the same schools that I did. Everyone knows the word I'm talking about. I don't need to repeat it.

Why, then, did my use of these two syllables in the presence of an illiterate black maid have such a horrifying effect on me? I assure you that it was not because I was a good little boy with an innocent soul. There is no such thing. Like everybody else, I was already an accomplished sinner at age four or five. I was devastated that summer day in 1946 or 1947 because I had first heard another word spoken to me in Sunday school and proclaimed to me in church. Perhaps, alas, I must explain what this other two-syllable word was. It was the word "Jesus." I had read this word in the Bible, and I had sung it in a Baptist group that only the bald and the gray will recognize. We were called the Sunbeams, and we were taught to sing: "Jesus loves the little children, all the children of the world. Red and yellow, black and white, they are precious in his sight. Jesus loves the little children of the world."

The people who had taught me this other word did not intend for it to have such a life-reversing impact. It was supposed to be a safe word, a nice word, a sweet word. It was a word meant to keep things rather much as they were. It was a word intended to get me into heaven but not to get too much of heaven into me. Yet this was the one word that my well-intentioned preachers and teachers and parents could not control. This word could not be tamed and housebroken because it is no ordinary word: it is the Word of God made flesh. Already as a first-grader, therefore, I had been shaped without knowing it by this word "Jesus." It had set me upon a path that would lead to a place where I did not intend to go. It was the word that would not let me speak as I was naturally inclined to speak. It would not let me violate another human being who had been made in God's image and redeemed by God's Son without feeling the horror of God's wrath. Thus did I hear the voice of God in the injured eyes of a black maid named Zuma Allen.

II

If faith comes by what is heard, and what is heard comes by the preaching of Christ, I heard the voice of the gospel in a fresh and startling way when I was a seventeen-year-old freshman attending a small state college in Commerce, Texas. This time the voice was that of an English professor named Paul Barrus. He was the most learned man I had ever met. He spoke both French and German; he read both Latin and Spanish; and he commanded our English tongue like no other speaker I had ever heard. His voice was cultivated, eloquent, humane. It was also a Christian voice in a quiet and understated way. This professor did not raise his voice in boasting about his Christianity; much less did he feel any need to be loud and defensive about his faith. Yet this strong and sure voice of my professor was not without its doubts and fears. I can still recall the day he told our class that the lines of his face were his battle scars.

This Christian teacher left his deep mark on me because he was not afraid to face the toughest opponents of the gospel. Precisely in order to test the strength of his own Christianity, Paul Barrus had written his doctoral dissertation at the University of Iowa on Ralph Waldo Emerson, the great unbelieving saint of American literature. Only if the gospel could meet and match Emerson's pantheistic paganism, Barrus believed, was it worthy of intelligent assent. This teacher wanted to make sure, therefore, that we naïve Christians did not live by what Dietrich Bonhoeffer would call "cheap grace," namely, an easy and convenient faith that costs us nothing in the way of thought or word or deed. And so Paul Barrus taught us to have great reverence for the honest doubters of traditional Christianity. He totally immersed his mainly Baptist students in Emerson and Thoreau and Whitman, in Melville and Hawthorne and Twain. This deeply Christian teacher thus enabled me to hear the gospel in a startlingly new way by insisting that a willfully unintelligent faith is a contradiction in terms. A deliberately unthinking Christian, he showed us, is an affront to the God whose Son is the truth incarnate. This God doesn't require us to have brains in order to be saved, but he surely requires us to use all the brains we've got, precisely because they're the brains he's given us.

Yet there was a rattle in this splendid teacher's voice that I had been taught not to like. For it turns out that Paul Barrus was not a Baptist nor a Methodist, not a member of the Church of Christ nor the Assembly of God — the only four churches in my provincial little East Texas town. He wasn't even a Presbyterian or a Lutheran or an Episcopalian — whoever they were. He wasn't even a Protestant. God forbid, he was a Roman Catholic. Just as I had been taught that blacks are natively inferior, so had I learned that Catholics are not even Christians. Before I went to college, I had met only one group of Catholics, a family who had already proved strange if not subhuman because their daughter was a nun. Yet here as a freshman I was confronted with the deepest and most Christian voice I had ever heard, and it was a Roman Catholic voice. It broke open the cocoon of my narrow faith. Against my will and utterly to my surprise, this Catholic teacher released my little Baptist butterfly from its confining cage. He turned me into an ecumenical Christian. Thanks to Paul Barrus, I would spend the rest of my works and days studying and teaching, not the Baptist faith as it was narrowly construed, but the Christian faith in its widest and deepest expressions — Catholic and Orthodox and Protestant.

III

"Faith comes by what is heard, and what is heard comes by the preaching of Christ." This ringing Pauline claim from Romans 10:28 became literally true to me in the third and final instance. I was twenty-nine years old, a recent product of the University of Chicago, and a first-year university teacher. Rarely has anyone presumed to know any more or been any more confident about what he supposedly knew than this new instructor. I was a hot academic property. I was sophisticated. I was cultured. I had read great books, and I had been taught by great teachers. I had seen great museums and heard great orchestras. Above all, I had left behind, once and forever, the narrow and provincial stuff of my Texas Baptist past. Like the Peter De Vries character who calls himself a pilgrim in reverse, I was trying to escape my Baptist Jerusalem for the worldly wonders of Athens and Babylon. And I hoped to turn my naïve Christian students into fellow sophisticates like me. (No one had yet told me that a sophisticate is a person who has been educated beyond his intellectual abilities.)

I was rescued from such a silly sophistication by yet another voice. This time it was not the voice of God speaking through the injured eyes of a black maid, nor through the Christian eloquence of a Catholic teacher, but through the prophetic witness of a Baptist preacher named Warren Carr. I tried to ignore and avoid him in every way I could. He represented the constricting past whose shackles I had already slipped. But like Jacob wrestling with the angel at the River Jabbok, this preacher would not let me go until I had blessed him. It turned out that he, too, had read a lot of books, indeed that he had written a couple of his own. He could stand up intellectually to any academic on the campus. And he was the funniest human being I had ever met, a man whose glinting humor remains wonderfully alive in this, his eightieth year.

Yet it was not Warren Carr's sharp mind and wild wit that drew me to him. It was his voice. He spoke with an authority that I had never heard at the University of Chicago. It was a deliberate and careful voice, neither quick-paced nor especially eloquent. It was a voice that reverberated with enormous moral and spiritual strength, a voice that had known deep personal suffering. It was the voice of a courageous Christian witness who had faced death threats when his white Baptist church in Durham, North Carolina, had welcomed blacks in the same year that the 16th Street Baptist Church was bombed here in Birmingham. Yet this preacher did not announce to me the tired tidings of moral effort. He did not tell me to become socially and politically righteous. He declared the unsurpassably Good News that all the sophistication and morality in the world would not save me or anyone else. My only hope, he declared, was the world's only hope: salvation by God's grace alone through the gift of faith alone in Jesus Christ.

Warren Carr called me to hitch my tiny cart of conscience and learning, if it was going to go anywhere good, to the great gospel train. If I did not locate my life and work in the God of grace and glory, I would end in a self-created hell of presumption and false righteousness. And so my life took another drastic turn that I could not have predicted. The voice of this Baptist preacher converted me to a true understanding of my vocation: he showed me that I had not been called to sophisticate the naïve but to educate both myself and my students in the way, the truth, and the life of the incarnate God. There is no greater calling because there is no greater gospel. Faith comes through hearing it, even as I have heard it spoken to me through a black maid, a Catholic teacher, and a Baptist preacher.

IV

It's obvious that God has not used glamorous acts to get my attention. Many doors have been slammed in order that others might be opened. My search for a worthy mission in life thus illustrates the strangely nonvoluntary quality of the gospel. God often corners us into the place where we are supposed to be. Already as a freshman in high school, I knew that I was not meant for the athletic life — even if in Texas you were not likely to get a date if you didn't play football. I was the proverbial ninety-eight-pound weakling who had no capacity to bang other bodies around and who didn't want my own puny little carcass banged around. A first door thus was closed. I found that I could play a trumpet instead. I had such a hot horn, in fact, that I aspired to be a professional trumpeter, the next Harry James. But at the regional band contest in my senior year, an eighth-grader from Jefferson, Texas, made me sound like a beginning bugler. Another door was slammed shut. Because I had done well in high school math, I thought that perhaps I might become a collegiate math major. I did make an A in freshman algebra, but only with the help of a friend — often late at night, after he had come in from bowling or movie-going — who enabled me to solve the problems I couldn't solve on my own. A third door now plainly read: "Do Not Enter."

The first hint that perhaps I was being compelled into my proper mission came during my senior year, when my math-whiz friend knocked on my door around midnight. We were both taking a course on the history of the English language under Paul Barrus, who had assigned us the task of reciting the Lord's Prayer in Anglo-Saxon. My friend had brought his tape-recorder with him, and he asked me to repeat that blankety-blank prayer into his machine so that he could go back to his room and listen to my recitation over and over, into the small hours of the night — until at long last, perhaps, he could pronounce those alien Old English words. Thus did God begin to corner me into the profession I thought I was meant to avoid. Since my parents were both high school teachers, I had naively rejected teaching as my calling. I thought, for a while, that God might have called me to pulpit ministry instead. It was foolish, I can see in retrospect, for me to become a boy-pastor at age nineteen, shepherding a rural Baptist flock outside Commerce in Fairlie, Texas. Those country Christians were amazingly patient with my greenhorn efforts. My outsized ego found a natural outlet in preaching; but my irascible temper was ill-suited (at least then) for the pastoral care that needs to be given to fellow sinners. And the thought of raising an annual budget while keeping everybody happy put the well-known willies into me. Door four now seemed fastened from the outside.

Vacillating between seminary and doctoral study, I was driven to seek a master's degree in English because Paul Barrus had brought Flannery O'Connor to our campus in 1962. She had set fire to my theological imagination. My wife, Suzanne, agreed, in turn, to work on her own master's degree in biology — patient as always in providing this interim period for Providence to suborn me into his service. The English department assigned me two sections of remedial composition, teaching yahoos who were barely literate (they had rightly renamed the course "retarded composition"). Yet the classroom proved delightful. There was a deep juncture, I discovered, between words and the Word. I was meant to make sure that subjects and verbs agree, that pronouns have proper referents, that participles do not dangle, that gerunds still survive. Forty-five years later, I'm still feasting at the table to which I have been so happily compelled — chiefly, of course, at the Lamb's Supper, but also at the lectern and the chalkboard and the endless papers yet to be graded. Amen and amen.

PART II

THE CHURCH

"Compel Them to Come In": The Gospel as Divine Command, Not Consumer Choice

Luke 14:15-24

Regent College
Vancouver, British Columbia
July 25, 2006

Second Baptist Church
Lubbock, Texas
September 17, 2006

Compelle intrare: compel them to come in. These, said C. S. Lewis, are perhaps the most frightening words in the New Testament. We do not like to think of Jesus as the Lord who compels but rather as the Christ who invites, who allures, who welcomes, who persuades. Certainly, these latter metaphors of divine grace and action are right and good and true. Yet, as Lewis himself urges, we must also engage with the most difficult of the biblical sayings, wrestling hard with the hard words of our Lord. We must beware all things obvious. If it will fit on a bumper sticker, we can be virtually assured that it is false. There is, of course, a fundamental simplicity about the gospel, but it always remains a simplicity lying on the far side of complexity. I maintain, therefore, that this complex parable of the Great Banquet requires our careful attention, not because it offers an odd departure from the gospel, but because it drills to the very core of it. "Compel them to come in" is a phrase that illumines the whole nature of the Christian life as obedience to the Savior, and thus of the church as the community of such obedience.

I

There is not much talk about election and predestination in evangelical circles these days. Poor John Calvin — the theologian with the worst press in the history of the church — is very much out of favor among us Baptists, even though we were birthed from English Calvinism in the seventeenth century. In fact, Calvin and his theology have become embarrassments in many Christian circles. Yet we ought to have sympathy for dear dour Calvin, if only because he was afflicted with hemorrhoids in an age when horseback was the only means of travel! At the minimum, we should join Calvin in hymning Romans 8:28: "We know that in everything God works for good with those who love him, who are called according to his purpose." Yet we shouldn't be made edgy and nervous by the two following verses that Calvin insisted also on heeding: "For those whom he *foreknew* he also *predestined* to become *conformed* to the image of his Son. . . . And those whom he *predestined* he also *called;* and those whom he *called* he also *justified;* and those whom he *justified* he also *glorified.*" So it is with the celebrated "watchword of the Reformation" found in Ephesians 2:8: "For by grace you have been saved through faith; and this is not your own doing, it is the gift of God — not because of works, lest any man should boast." It is not legitimate to acclaim these words without also joining my friend Gregory Pritchard in quoting the verse that follows, with its radical moral implications: "For we are his workmanship, created in Christ Jesus for good works, which God prepared beforehand, that we should walk in them."

The words I have emphasized make us tense, I suspect, because we resent the idea that our freedom is found in the foreknowledge and predestination and preparation of God, in the election of Israel and Christ, in the calling and command that we are given in and through the church. These good theological terms threaten our virtual idolatry of choice, our American notion that to be free is to face utterly untrammeled options between one thing or another, in sheer undetermined choices between this and that: between Avis and Hertz, between Democrat and Republican, between good and evil, even between God and the devil. I once heard a well-intentioned radio evangelist offer the following appeal: "God has cast a vote for you, the devil has cast a vote against you, and now it's up to you to break the tie." This claim is actually a remarkable accomplishment, for it harbors at least half a dozen heresies in single sentence! The problem is not chiefly that it commits the fatal error of dualism, making God and Satan equal and opposing powers over whom we have final control; more important, it envisions salvation as a choice that we make like any other consumer choice. This ancient heresy, called Pelagianism, has become virtually unrecognizable to most evangelical Christians because it constitutes such a perfect mirror of the American individualist gospel of autonomous self-determination.

The most difficult lesson we choice-enthralled Americans need to learn is that true freedom lies always and only in the doing of the good. To reject the right and to reach for the wrong is, as St. Augustine taught, not to act freely but slavishly. We surrender rather than exercise our freedom when we thus act. We exhibit not the liberty but, as Luther also taught, the bondage of our wills. And with every bad choice, we gradually close the window of our freedom, until finally it is slammed shut, in utter and wretched entrapment — as any crack addict can testify. The poor and the maimed, the blind and the deaf and the halt are the souls who act freely. In their destitute state, they know that they are not masters of their own destiny, captains of their own souls. They are not deluded, therefore, by the false gospel of "I am whatever I choose to be." These marginalized characters come to the master banquet eagerly because they have been welcomed peremptorily. They give their glad assent to the great invitation because they do not regard the kingdom feast merely as one delight among others — to be accepted or rejected as they see fit, by means of their own solitary and autonomous decision.

To decline this, the one feast that must not be missed — the only gift too good to be turned down — is not to make a free decision so much as a terribly bad choice. This dark truth is what the three ingrates will learn to their own sorrow. The man who must first visit the piece of property he's recently bought (an expensive new house), the one who must first inspect the five yoke of oxen he's purchased (a fancy new automobile from a windfall on the stock market), the husband who must first go home to his newly married bride (perhaps a trophy wife whom he has taken on a Caribbean honeymoon) — these men have not acted freely but unfreely. They have thrown away the only key that unlocks the door to liberty. And so they are judged with a dread finality: "I tell you," says the master to his servant, "none of those men who were invited shall taste of my banquet."

This disturbing parable finds its natural resonance in those discomfiting words we heard earlier about election and foreknowledge, about predestination and calling. Such complex concepts do not make the mistake of giving God's time-bound knowledge of the future, as if he were mapping out and maneuvering our lives like pawns on a chessboard. Rather do the thorny old terms get at this radically paradoxical matter, namely, that nothing other than the incarnate and crucified and risen Jesus has both the right and the power to make absolute demands on us. Thus did our forebears, both Catholic and Protestant, speak of "prevenient grace." The original Latin *praevenire* ("to come before") makes it clear that this gift goes ahead of us and thus makes possible our very acceptance of and obedience to it. It's not as if God makes an offer — meeting us halfway — that we must then accept and enact if the offer is to have validity. On the contrary, divine grace and human freedom are bound inextricably together, as T. S. Eliot reveals in the witty puns of "East Coker." Though we are sick Adamic souls who have turned God's good world into a gigantic infirmary, the fatherly physician relentlessly attends us, curing us by killing us:

> The whole earth is our hospital
> Endowed by the ruined millionaire,
> Wherein, if we do well, we shall
> Die of the absolute paternal care
> That will not leave us, but prevents us everywhere.

God, in his terribly and wonderfully prevenient grace, not only forestalls us from falling into sin; he also enables us to do the good things that, as Paul confesses in Romans 7, we would not and could not do on our own. In sum, this is the one gift that prompts our very reception and enactment of it.

II

Our failure to understand this paradox lying at the core of Christian faith takes its most pernicious form, I believe, in the notion of punctiliar salvation: the idea that our eternal destiny and worth are determined by a single, autonomous, often highly emotional decision that we are required to make at a particular *punctum*, at a singular and unrepeatable point in time. I'm aware, of course, that such decisionistic revivalism has lain at the modern center of my own Baptist tradition, and that many of us would not be Christians at all if our forebears had not been "saved" at such revival meetings — often "protracted" for several weeks, as long as the Spirit lingered. That a fresh crop of illicit babies, perhaps sown by the evangelist and his assistants, was harvested nine months later is only partially to the point. As the late Timothy Smith and many others have reminded us, these revivals also issued in radical social reforms, not only in Wesley's England but also in the great American heartland. Thus did the decisionistic revivalism of the nineteenth century often have the enormous good effect of helping to end slavery and other evils. One of my Methodist friends, Steve Blakemore, puts this real accomplishment of such revivalism exactly right: "The purpose of salvation is not to get us into Heaven so much as to get Heaven into us." And when the kingdom of God comes to dwell in our midst, it means that we had better get the hell out!

The notion of punctiliar salvation has a largely deleterious effect on contemporary evangelical life because it leads many Christians to believe that, because once upon a time we made a solitary "decision to accept Jesus Christ as our personal Lord and Savior," then nothing much else is required. I myself once made such a decision and thus "got saved" as a raw youth who dwelt behind the Pine Curtain in eastern Texas. No one bothered to explain that my baptism was the most important event of my life — not because I could now "go to Heaven," but because all of my earthly allegiances had been transferred to a new Lord. I had been initiated into the body of Christ, into the church as a public and radically communal way of life. Moreover, this transformed and alternative community was intended to be drastically unlike the world around me. All such notions went right past me. Instead, I kept doing my daily Bible readings and attending both Sunday school and Baptist Training Union, not to mention periodically "rededicating my life" at our biennial revivals. It hardly needs to be said that I also continued not to drink or smoke, or to dance or fornicate. Far from denigrating these small virtues, I am merely pointing out that they did not require a commanding and redeeming Lord to perform them. If I had been brought truly into his discipleship, my friends and I would have ceased tormenting a poor retarded classmate named Wayne Burrow. We would have sought, instead, to make him our companion. I would also have seen what was fundamentally wrong about being paid exactly the same wage (sixty cents an hour) as Hive Stevens, the black man with a large family who worked beside me on our family farm. Instead, I was content to believe that I had been "saved" and thus that, since all was well with me, all was well with my community and society.

We must find a way to counteract this fundamentally false idea of the Christian faith as essentially a private matter of an inward and hidden relationship between Jesus and ourselves. To make it an individual affair decided utterly by and for ourselves is to make the gospel another consumer choice at the great American emporium of religious goods and services. We need a fresh set of metaphors for describing both God's action in the world and our participation in it. Stanley Hauerwas offers the staggering suggestion that we should think of Christian faith as fundamentally nonvoluntary. Offensive and counterintuitive though it may be, there is an undeniable nonvoluntarism at work in the Gospels. St. Paul's unflinching insistence on God's prevenient grace finds its perfect counterpart in the imperative verbs of Jesus. Only the Christ who is able to atone for the sins of the world can make demands whose fulfillment he alone can produce. Nowhere does the Lord provide his audiences with mere choices. He doesn't urge them to consider the benefits of his service, its potential penalties, much less its retirement package. Rather than offering mere options, he issues imperious commands: Come and follow me. Take up your cross. Seek first the kingdom of God. Lay down your life for my sake. Abide in me. Love your neighbors. Forgive your enemies. Bless those who curse you. Go into all the world and preach the gospel. Teach, baptize, heal, bind up — on goes the list of divine directives. Therefore, "compel them to come in" thus belongs in a long line of our Lord's peremptory orders.

The church is a nonvoluntary community precisely because Jesus Christ does not offer invitations to solitary choices but gives commands to communal obedience. So long as we think of it as a mere voluntary society, the church does not differ essentially from the Lions, the PTA, the Democratic and Republican parties, even the university — worthy organizations all. Yet the gates of hell shall finally prevail against these institutions, for they are prompted and sustained chiefly by human effort. Hence my astonishment at a college dean who, though a Christian, said he didn't attend or support the church because he belonged to too many clubs already! If this man ever asks his congregation to take him off its rolls, the church should indeed do so, but only on one condition: that he come forward at the end of the next service and publicly renounce his baptism. For then he might be shown what most of us so miserably fail to understand: that the church is not a club or fraternity from which we can go inactive.

There is no such thing as "going inactive" from the kingdom. This would be possible only if Christ were a "lord" whom we could choose for ourselves; for then we could just as easily "unchoose" him, whenever discipleship becomes costly or merely inconvenient. We would do better, I believe, to describe the triune God as drafting us into his cause, commandeering us into his kingdom, sweeping us up in the great movement of his work in the world, ordering us into his compulsory and gladsome service that constitutes the kingdom. Jesus must have had such a drastically nonvoluntary discipleship in mind when he declared, in John's Gospel, "You did not choose me, but I chose you and appointed you that you should go and bear fruit and that your fruit should abide" (John 10:15).

My preacher-exemplar Warren Carr attests to the compulsory character of the gospel in explaining how he was given the huge honor and privilege of Christian ministry. Having heard the gospel, he struck out after God, figuratively chasing him down, grabbing him by the nape of the neck, pleading that he, too, might become a proclaimer of such Good News. None of this silly stuff about "surrendering to preach," as if he had made a burdensome decision to become the "servant-leader" of another "voluntary" society. Carr knew that he had not himself bravely and autonomously chosen to live in the conviction that "God was in Christ reconciling the world unto himself" (2 Cor. 5:19). The matter was exactly the other way around: this one true conviction and this one commanding Lord had chosen him. So it is with us: we have been compelled to the great involuntary banquet of the Lamb. Let us keep the feast. Amen.

The World's Heroes and the Church's Saints

1 Samuel 17:41-49; 1 Corinthians 1:23-31

First Presbyterian Church
Brookings, South Dakota
October 2, 2005
World Communion Sunday

Not long ago my friend Stanley Hauerwas mentioned, in one of his typically pungent throwaway lines, that heroism is not a Christian category. This seemed to me a cockamamie claim, especially in view of the many heroic acts we have recently witnessed, as people from far and near have risen to the aid of those blasted and inundated by Hurricanes Katrina and Rita. Hurrying to my concordance, I discovered, alas, that the words "hero" and "heroism" do not appear anywhere in Scripture. How surpassingly strange! What seem to be obviously biblical turn out not to be biblical at all. And so I set myself the task of reflecting and preaching on this anomaly, asking why we Christians do not make heroism central to our faith and practice, while also seeking to determine why the church puts a far more radical notion in its place.

I

The world's heroes are those who exceed the human norm by human means in the realization of human ends. They are heroically superior to the rest of us because of their moral excellence. Heroes are those extraordinary souls who, seemingly by means of their own strength and courage, outpace us ordinary mortals in seeking the common good.

They perform such splendid deeds of ethical sacrifice that they either inspire or scandalize us: we are either inspired to follow the noble path that they have blazed, or we are scandalized by our own cowardice and complacency. The Greeks and the Romans were verily obsessed with heroes and heroism. It suffices merely to cite some of their names: Odysseus, Ajax, Hector, Achilles, Aeneas. By contrast, we moderns have been far more skeptical about our heroes, perhaps because our so-called great men often turn out to be evil men. After they have done deeds of immense daring, they often want to be exalted for their heroism. Beethoven learned this lesson after dedicating his *Eroica* symphony to Napoleon Bonaparte. To his horror, he then discovered that Napoleon had declared himself emperor of France (as he would later make himself king of Italy). Beethoven ripped out the dedicatory lines.

In fact, the modern world has become so suspicious of heroes that our major writers have turned away from heroism as the chief subject of their work. They know that we have been led horribly astray by allegedly great men, by men eager for power and thus also for war and domination, by such moral monsters as Hitler and Stalin, Mao Tse-tung and Pol Pot. Lest we Americans prematurely congratulate ourselves, let us not forget that our own Woodrow Wilson promised us a war that would end all wars, when in fact it marked our arrogant entry into a century-long marathon of killing. Nor can we forget Hiroshima and Nagasaki, Dresden and My Lai. Ours is, alas, an epoch whose annals are written in blood: roughly 180 million people slaughtered during the past ninety-five years, most of them by their own governments, and more than in all the previous centuries of history combined. In such a time incarnadine, in such an age of ashes and blood, who can still believe in heroism? There is little mystery behind the decision of our chief authors to turn away from the depiction of heroism and to concentrate, instead, on stories of the inward journey, quests for personal wholeness, explorations of the individual psyche.

Yet plenty of heroes still remain, even if they remain largely unhonored in our literature. These latter-day heroes are often not prominent men or women at all. Instead, they are obscure and unsung souls who have performed extraordinary deeds of moral excellence, sometimes in the face of massive evil. Tom Brokaw has recounted American instances of such heroism in *The Greatest Generation,* while Gilbert Martin, in *The Righteous,* has reported hundreds of stories of gentiles who heroically rescued European Jews from the Holocaust.

Even in these last several weeks after the tsunami that struck Southeast Asia, we have again witnessed countless heroic acts in response to storm-caused calamities. It should be obvious, then, that I am not disparaging heroism but praising it. The world would not long endure without its heroes, including its secular heroes, who do not acknowledge God. Yet God surely acknowledges them, since they often do his will unawares. We Christians ought to be staggered with gratitude, therefore, when the world's heroes accomplish such great good. Praise and thanks indeed for their heroism!

II

Even so, the scandalous claim remains: heroism is not a Christian category. We put a far more radical word in its place, for ours is a far more radical calling. We are called not to become heroes but saints. We would do well, therefore, to heed the reminder of the eminent French Catholic writer Georges Bernanos: "Christians aren't supermen, [and] saints [are] still less [superhuman] since they are the most human of human beings. Saints are not sublime, they have no need of the sublime; it is rather the sublime that needs them. Saints are not heroes in the manner of Plutarch's heroes. A hero gives the illusion of surpassing humanity. The saint doesn't surpass it, he assumes it, he strives to realize [his] humanity in the best possible way. . . . He strives to approach as nearly as possible his model, Jesus Christ, that is, to come as close as possible to him who was the perfect man, with a simplicity so perfect that in reassuring others he disconcerts the hero; for Christ did not die only for heroes — he died for cowards too."*

Far from comprehending that the saints are those who have been made fully human by Jesus Christ, we have come to be embarrassed by the word. "Sainthood" implies either a smarmy piety or else an oily morality. No one wants to be Mr. or Miss Goody-Good. Yet sainthood has little to do with being conventionally pious or even conventionally moral. When Paul addresses the church at Corinth, he clearly does not refer to their moral and spiritual excellence, since drunkenness, fornication, gossip, and heresy were constant problems in the Corinthian church, just as they continue to infect our own contemporary churches.

* "Our Friends the Saints," in *The Last Essays of Georges Bernanos* (Henry Regnery, 1955).

Yet the apostle persists in calling them saints, even as he also addresses his letters to the squabbling and sinning churches at Rome, Ephesus, and Galatia with the following greeting: "to the saints. . . ." Is he flattering them? Is he merely careless about his use of words? Far from it: he is making the scandalous claim that Christians are called to become not heroes but saints.

Unlike heroes, who stand apart from the average run of humans, saints are utterly ordinary believers. Far from excelling others, saints are often undistinguished in their natural gifts. When I once complained about the mediocrity of the religion majors at Wake Forest — and thus about the undistinguished future they would have as pastors and professors — my philosopher friend Gregory Pritchard pulled me up short. Like Paul, he reminded me that God doesn't summon MENSA members or other heroes of either mind or body to be the bearers of his kingdom. The apostle tells the church at Corinth that God does calls not the noble, nor the powerful, nor the wise — not at least as the world marks wisdom. Instead, God calls the foolish to shame the worldly-wise, the weak to shame the pseudo-strong, the lowly and the despised to bring all human vanity to naught. Three chapters later, Paul declares that the Roman world has such contempt for Christians that it regards them as "refuse and off-scouring" — rather polite terms, I suspect, that could perhaps have been spelled more succinctly with four letters rather than the five the King James Version uses when it says that ancient Corinth dismissed Christians as "filth." Yet the strange point still holds: Christians are called to become not heroes but saints.

Saints are ordinary Christians struggling to live faithful lives, often in the midst of their own moral failures. They are seeking to live by faith rather than their own strength. They are seeking to die to their own self-will so that God's will might be done in their lives. Above all else, they are seeking to honor God rather than themselves. The celebrated "roll call" of saints found in Hebrews 11 contains a surprising catalogue, a list of biblical stalwarts that is far from impressive. Noah built the ark and thus preserved the world from extinction, but then in his knee-walking drunkenness he shamefully exposed himself. Abraham answered God's call to be the father of God's people and a blessing to all the nations, but then he sought to save his own skin by passing his wife Sarah off as his sister. When Sarah, in turn, learned that she was wondrously enabled by God to bear a child in her old age, she laughed in God's face. And when that son, named Laugher (Ishmael), was born, Abraham banished his concubine, Hagar, and the son she had borne him to the wilderness. Isaac, the late-born son of Abraham and Sarah, is another of these suspect saints. He survives the terrible threat of Abraham to sacrifice him on Mount Moriah, when God miraculously provides a ram for the slaughter; yet Isaac becomes such a passive and lackluster figure that he lets his scheming wife Rebekah and their clever son Jacob cheat the twin brother Esau out of his birthright. Finally, the trickster Jacob, though much to be commended for wrestling with the angel of God at the Jabbok, is himself tricked. He is fooled into first marrying the dull Leah when he had desired the lovely Rachel.

Consider also David, perhaps the unlikeliest saint of all, especially in view of his adultery with Bathsheba and his scheming to have her husband, Uriah, killed. Even so, David is numbered in the roll call of saints. Perhaps it is because of the faith he displayed as a mere youth in his defeat of the swaggering Philistine warrior named Goliath. King Saul first seeks to arm young David with a mighty array of his own weaponry: breastplate, sword, and shield. David discovers, alas, that he is utterly shackled by such heavy armory. It swallows him in size, and perhaps it makes him look like an idiot as well! Perhaps David senses, spiritually no less than militarily, that small arms would best avail against the heathen bravado of mighty Goliath. And so he asks for nothing more than string and sticks. When the boy approaches the behemoth armed only with a slingshot, Goliath is hugely insulted. "Am I a dog," he growls, "that you come to me with sticks?" Yet the real wonder of this story is not that the youthful shepherd slays the hulking giant with a single stone flung at his forehead. Nor should we focus on the grisly beheading that follows. Instead, we should be stunned by David's warning to the giant before the battle is even begun. It's an admonition containing the key that may unlock the mystery of sainthood: "I will strike you down," says David to Goliath, "that all the earth may know that there is a God in Israel, and that all this assembly may know that the Lord saves not with sword and spear; for the battle is the Lord's and he will give you into my hand."

III

"That all the earth may know that there is a God in Israel" — there, I believe, lies the essential distinction between heroes and saints. Saints are not those who exceed the Christian norm, not those who go beyond the limits of their calling. On the contrary, saints are Christians who fulfill their calling: Christians who struggle, like David, to live and to die faithfully. God is not a brute deity, and his people are not swaggering warriors. The battle belongs to the Lord because he conquers with plowshares and pruning hooks. Left to our own human devices, we would surely brandish the sword and spear of our own heroic effort. Saints, by contrast, are called to wield the slingshot of the gospel. It would seem to be so negligible a weapon, so small and ineffective, as to deserve the world's contempt. Yet this little stick and string called the Good News is the world's true and lasting hope. It alone can cast down the giants of slaughter and mayhem no less than the gremlins of hatred and contempt. Therefore, we do not hear the apostle Paul preaching heroism, not even Christian heroism. He could hardly be more contrarian: "We preach Christ crucified," the one "whom God has made our wisdom, our righteousness and sanctification and redemption" (I Cor. 1:23, 30).

In the way of the Cross alone is there hope greater than heroism, the hope that the vicious cycle of our wounding and being wounded can be broken, in fact, that it has already been broken in the man who hangs from a Roman gibbet. Without the gospel, the world turns ever in upon itself, repeating its dreary round, however much its heroes may and must temporarily relieve the suffering. Saints must also relieve suffering, but only by proclaiming the Good News that the right kind of suffering — the sacrifice of our self-will to the good will of God — is the way to joy. It's a joy that can be found right in the midst of our misery. The Westminster Shorter Catechism gets this Pauline point exactly right. "What is the chief end of man?" it asks in the very first question. "Man's chief end," it answers with splendid succinctness, "is to glorify God and enjoy him forever." Saints live first and last for the glory of God.

About this we must be ever so clear: we Christians cannot glorify God — by loving him with all our hearts and minds and souls — unless we also love our neighbors as ourselves. Yet the two commands are not the same. The love of God always comes first, for it is only by his love that we can rightly order our own loves, as St. Augustine profoundly taught. In loving and giving glory to God, saints do not live and act by human means nor always for human ends. As we have seen, they are often disagreeable characters, at least as the world agrees on things. Augustine himself was no moral exemplar, even after his conversion; but he was a saint because he lived and taught and died for the gospel. In our own time, Martin Luther King Jr. was also a man plagued by moral failure, especially in his marital vows. But he was a saint for having lived and died so that all the world might know that there is the God of Israel and the church, and that this God does not judge and save people by the color of their skin but by the content of their character.

This, then, is the heart of the matter: the glory of God alone is the motive force and the measuring rod for the life of sainthood. When saints have completed and fulfilled their task, usually in death, the church canonizes them. Thus, alongside St. Paul and St. Augustine, St. Thomas and St. Francis, St. Perpetua and St. Catherine, we will soon witness the beatification of the late Mother Teresa and Pope John Paul II. In the meantime, the rest of us who call ourselves Christians are saints in the making, struggling to follow the high calling of God in Christ Jesus, to run the race all the way to the end, finishing the course and keeping the faith.

IV

Some of these saints are much further down the road than the rest of us. Millard and Linda Fuller, seeing that their marriage was falling apart and that their lives were becoming morally ever emptier as they became materially ever richer, stopped off in Americus, Georgia, to ask for help. They looked up a Baptist named Clarence Jordan, the founder of an interracial effort in sainthood called Koinonia Farms. Jordan told the Fullers that they ought to give up their financial heroics and set out for ordinary sainthood by selling everything they owned and giving it to the poor. We should not be astonished, because Jordan's counsel happened to be Jesus' own admonition to the wealthy young nobleman. But we are astonished, of course, that the Fullers literally followed it. We all know "the rest of the story," as Paul Harvey would say. The far from ethically exemplary Fullers created Habitat for Humanity in 1976. Thirty years later, that organization has built more than

175,000 homes for the poor; they are located in every state of this nation as well as in eighty other countries.

Lest we idealize Millard and Linda Fuller, let us not forget the saints in our midst. They, too, are seeking to take up their cross and to die to self-will, to follow the hard road that passes through the narrow gate, to maintain a radical integrity before the God who saves by his mercy and grace alone. There are saints in this very sanctuary who are struggling with their own personal demons — with alcoholism and depression perhaps, with addiction to hard drugs and internet pornography, with adultery and all the other vices that make up Satan's arsenal against the saints. Yet saints are formed not chiefly by the evils they struggle against, but by the goods they seek to embody. Flannery O'Connor put well the paradox that joy is to be found in discipline and suffering when she confessed that she never thought less about herself than when she was writing, and yet that she was never more fully herself than when she was writing.

Allow me to enumerate some of these saints-in-the-making. There are care-giver saints who glorify God by visiting the elderly in the nursing homes, refusing to kill them by the neglect that has become so common that the average retirement home resident has, on average, not even a single visitor per year. There are banker and business saints who glorify God by earning only a reasonable and not an exorbitant profit. There are lawyer saints who glorify God by seeking a just verdict rather than the exoneration of their guilty clients. There are artist saints who glorify God by plumbing the deep things of life in their poetry and music and drama, rather than merely titillating their audiences. There are physician saints who glorify God by seeking the true health of their patients, even giving them permission to die, rather than deluding them with the demonic notion that the purpose of life is to stay alive as long as possible. There are counselor and social worker saints who glorify God by dealing patiently and graciously with the troubled and the down-and-out, refusing to treat them as mere victims, insisting instead that they are people of dignity and responsibility because they bear the image and likeness of God.

There are teacher saints who glorify God by teaching their subjects ever so well and by upholding high academic standards, rather than pandering to students with easy grades and faddish ideas. There are homemaker saints who glorify God by making their homes into welcoming and hospitable places, even for strangers and aliens, not luxuriant displays of plush furnishings. There are farmer and gardener saints who glorify God by working as faithful stewards rather than ruthless exploiters of the earth. There are scientist and engineer saints who glorify God by employing their skills for the betterment of humankind, not for our mere comfort and convenience. There are journalist saints who glorify God by giving us discomfiting truth rather than sensationalist entertainment. There are soldier saints who glorify God by discharging their duties within the strict limits of the Christian just-war tradition, refusing to take revenge even on enemies, killing them only as a last resort. And there are politician saints who glorify God by enacting public policy that will redound to the common good, especially of the poor and needy, rather than their own personal advantage.

Surely someone will ask whether such lives cannot be just as readily lived in ordinary human terms rather than by means of such an inflated honorific as "sainthood." The answer is, of course, that human life can indeed be so lived. That's what our humanist friends are seeking to do: to live heroically moral lives by human means and for human ends. Paul is candid in saying that Christians are not thus called and not thus equipped. In fact, the apostle is worried about Christians who want to make themselves into heroes by proclaiming their own righteousness. Saints are called, he says, to give up all such moral and spiritual heroism, lest it lead to the awful business of boasting, lest it make us think that God owes us payment for our righteousness. As Reinhold Niebuhr declared with prophetic wisdom, "Christians are never in a more dangerous position than when they have done good deeds." One of the most generous men I know, for instance, turns livid whenever those who benefit from his largesse don't offer him proper gratitude.

Paul gets at this matter of not seeking rewards — but living only for the glory of God — by declaring that Christians "have died" and by insisting that our lives are "hid with Christ in God" (Col. 3:3). What he means, I think, is that to be saints-in-the-making is to do nothing for our own glory or worldly recognition. We are called like ancient Abraham to live *coram Deo,* to walk before God with integrity. The merciful Lord alone can keep our eye off the bottom line of praise and profit. He alone can preserve us from self-congratulation. He alone guarantees the harvest of our efforts long after we are dead. He alone enables us to play without panic our own small role in his great cosmic drama of redemption. He alone calls us to live by the singular criterion of having "Christ in [us]" as the only true "hope of glory" (Col. 1:27).

Thus do we come to this table remembering Luther's saying that we come as nothing other than beggars. At this feast there is no meat and there is no drink meant only for heroes. They usually insist on providing their own meals, paying their own bills, and thus going debt-free. We are gathered to confess that we are utter debtors and sinners, and that God judges us Christians far more stringently than he assesses pagans and secularists. Alas, they have no such table. Rather than boasting, we pray for the candor and the humility to approach this holy meal as we should — not as the world's renowned heroes but as the church's struggling saints. Amen.

A Call for a Latter-Day Reformation of the Church

First Baptist Church
Hendersonville, North Carolina
January 5, 1997

> *For by grace you have been saved through faith; and this is not your*
> *own doing, it is the gift of God — not because of works, lest any man*
> *should boast. For we are his workmanship, created in Christ Jesus for*
> *good works, which God prepared beforehand, that we should walk in*
> *them. (Eph. 2:8-10)*

You and I, if we are Christians at all, probably owe our lives in Christ to these two verses from the Epistle to the Ephesians. This sterling claim was, in fact, the watchword of the Protestant Reformation. It was never far from the minds and the lips of Martin Luther and John Calvin. Nor did our Baptist ancestors in England and early America ever forget it. For them also, this was the gospel in its purest essence: everything else stood or fell in relationship to this fundamental declaration. This was the *sine qua non,* that without which everything else is nothing at all. Luther was referring to his unrelenting defense of precisely this definition of gospel — as divine redemption through grace alone by faith alone — when he stood before his accusers and stubbornly declared: *Hier stehe ich; ich kann nicht anders.* "Here I stand; I can do no other."

I have come, as a pathetically lesser Luther, to call for a new Reformation of the church. This means that I must first report the alarming news that we are again in danger of losing the gospel. As in the early sixteenth century, so in the late twentieth, the problem lies not chiefly with the world but with the church. The most sinister sins are often committed by Christians rather than pagans, if only because we ought to know better, indeed, because we have been shown and forgiven our own evils as they have not. Surely if we are faithful we will know that this awareness is what distinguishes us from our pagan counterparts. We need only to look into the mirror of Jesus Christ to see ourselves as we truly are. Our secular friends have no such mirror: they stare back only at themselves. This is why the cosmetic and physical fitness industries flourish. Pagan America is desperate to find a prettier face, a better body, a finer physique. Like Abraham Lincoln, who said that there comes a time when every man becomes responsible for his own face, we Christians know that, apart from the new face we have been given in Jesus Christ, we are sinfully ugly.

When I call for a Reformation of the church, please do not hear me as saying that there is nothing much wrong with the world. I am deeply alarmed about the state of our society. Christians have cause to be concerned, as Charles Colson has recently been reminding us, about the dread state of our pagan culture. Colson has made the stunning claim that the day may soon come when we Christians will have to withdraw our support from the United States government. For it is a government that seems ever more perversely bent on making demands that many Christians regard not only as unacceptable but as outright damnable, especially concerning such matters as partial-birth abortion and euthanasia.

I share Mr. Colson's concern but not his solution. I believe that we need a Reformation of the church even more drastically than we need a reordering of the state. Important as these latter matters are, we know that even the best governments come and go; in contrast, the kingdom of God will stand forever. Not even the gates of hell shall be able shut out its coming in. And it is in God's kingdom that we have our true home, not only in the world to come but also in the here and now. Yet we will not find our true place there until we recognize that we are strangers and aliens from the kingdom. Though we are meant to be strangers and sojourners in the world, we have become falsely at home in the world and aliens to the kingdom. I believe that the reason is not hard to find: it is because our churches have largely abandoned the doctrine of salvation by grace alone through faith alone. On both the left and the right, among both liberals and conservatives, this is the doctrine that many Christians no longer believe. Hence my call for a latter-day Reformation of the church — a recovery of the Gospel according to Ephesians 2:8-10.

I

On the left, our churches are being reduced to virtual social-service agencies. In these liberal churches, the gospel is equated more or less with doing good, being moral, helping the poor, visiting the sick and lonely and imprisoned, feeding the hungry, housing the homeless, sheltering the battered, teaching the illiterate. In this understanding of the gospel, being faithful Christians becomes the virtual equivalent of being faithful Democrats. This is not a bad thing to be, of course, as this lifelong Democrat can attest! God knows — and so do we — that services to the needy must be provided, if not by the church, then surely by the state. A society is measured largely by its care for those who cannot care for themselves: the poor and defenseless, the widows and orphans, as the Bible refers to them. A church or a nation that neglects such care has the wrath of God on its head. Yet such human caring is not the sum and essence of the gospel. The heart and soul of the gospel is salvation by grace alone through faith alone.

The order of grace and good works is ever so important. Indeed, we Christians are called by God to help the helpless in gratitude for his saving us from our own helplessness. Such acts of charity and gratitude are the glad and necessary consequence of the gospel, but they are not its burdensome and necessary condition. We do not seek to do good in order to earn God's favor. We do good works in sheer gratitude for the favor we could not possibly earn. This is why Paul says that we are God's workmanship rather than our own. Jesus Christ has redeemed us for the good works that will serve as signs of his salvation. This explains why Jesus says that we are to offer a cup of water to the thirsty in his name. For unless that cup of water is a sign of the water that slakes the ultimate human thirst, it can be a great deceit. Hence the potential danger in building houses for the homeless without ever helping them to identify and occupy their real home.

Martin Luther believed that such false good works serve as a roadblock on the path of salvation. "Works righteousness" is what Luther called this false notion that we can merit the mercy of God by our own good deeds. It is indeed a deadly doctrine. If we think God owes us anything, then we can know for sure that we do not know the God of the gospel. We are not saved by boastful works, says Paul, but by utterly unboastful grace. Only in Christ do we boast, the apostle declares elsewhere, by pointing away from ourselves to the Savior who hangs from the cross. In his famous *Isenheim Altarpiece,* Matthias Grünewald gets the order of things theologically right even if chronologically wrong when he depicts John the Baptist standing beneath the cross and pointing with his long index finger away from himself to Jesus, the man who has been nailed there for our sins. From the mouth of the Baptizer issue these words: "May he increase that I may decrease." Without the gospel of salvation by grace alone through faith alone, we get the order backwards: Christ decreases in order that we may increase.

Permit me two examples of works-righteousness. The first comes from an eminent Baptist religionist who likes to say that the word "Christian" should serve as an adjective more than a noun. He means by this claim that the ethical and spiritual quality of our lives is what makes us Christians: that is, how well or how ill we imitate the moral example Jesus sets in the Gospels, especially the commands set forth in the Sermon on the Mount. You will not be surprised to learn that this religionist has little use for St. Paul. In this man's understanding of the gospel, Jesus is not the one name given under heaven among men whereby we must be saved. He is more or less like every other great moral hero, from Buddha and Mohammed to Gandhi and Martin Luther King Jr. What my friend fails to see is that God first makes Christians into nouns in order that we might become adjectives. Jesus Christ makes us substantives capable of modifying the world in his name. The word *substantive* literally means "to stand under." It is not our good deeds that give us Christian substance. Jesus has transformed us into substantives by standing in our place on the cross and thus giving us a place to stand when we do our salutary works: before God, as forgiven sinners saved by grace alone through faith alone.

The second example comes from another Baptist minister, who reported to me how he had sought to give solace to a fellow preacher who felt that his own church had existed for fifty years without making any discernible difference to the city where it is located. "Why, of course you have made a difference," my pastor-friend sought to console his downcast comrade in ministry. "Look at the soup kitchen you built, the homeless shelter you erected, the school lunch program you instituted, the counseling hotline you set up." He is partially right: any faithful church should be rightly proud of such accomplishments. Yet he was listing such social services as the chief purpose of this Christian church, as proof that it had "made a difference" in its city. Not once did this Baptist preacher mention that for fifty years this church had

A Call for a Latter-Day Reformation of the Church 57

taught people to live the life of prayer, that it had enabled blacks and whites to be reconciled because they are brothers in Christ, that it had liberated women not by gender equality but by gospel equality, that it had proclaimed forgiveness of sins and newness of life, and hence that its members had been reconciled not only to each other but chiefly to the God who had wrought their salvation in Jesus Christ by grace alone through faith alone.

II

Lest we think that all evils lie on the left, let me make clear that our conservative churches are in no less need of Reformation, that they are no less guilty of abandoning the gospel of salvation by grace alone through faith alone. But here, instead of ethical works serving as the substitute, a sentimental personal piety is often made to replace the hard social realism of our redemption. I can make my case by citing a sign I saw in the office of two evangelical ministers. It read: "Christianity is a relationship." What this sign means, so far as I can tell, is that we are Christians by virtue of our having made a personal decision to enter a private spiritual intimacy with Jesus. It's a metaphor that implies two separate and autonomous creatures — Jesus and the solitary self — entering into a cozy and cuddly "relationship," a warm and fuzzy affair that more appropriately belongs to the old TV show called "The Dating Game." Certainly the gospel is relational through and through: it rightly relates us to God and to humans and the world. But its relationality is not essentially private. The gospel is socially embodied in the people called the church. As its members we are incorporated and engrafted into the body of Christ by our baptism, by our receiving of the Lord's Supper, by our hearing and doing of his Word, not by a chatty and sentimental private relationship with our divine buddy.

The first casualty of such conservative reduction of the gospel to sentimental piety is the bedrock Reformation doctrine of election. Whereas the Christ of the gospel makes all of the decisions that matter — choosing us to be included in his work called the Kingdom — the new conservative gospel leaves the essential decision to us. No longer is it God who elects us, but it is we who elect God. Instead of God choosing us from the foundation of the world, as Paul says in Ephesians, it is we who choose him.

Our Baptist forebears would have hooted in contempt over this decisionistic idea of Christian faith. Such an I-and-me-centered gospel is also reflected in the bumper sticker that reads: "I found it." What would Abraham or Isaac or Jacob, Amos or Jeremiah or Ezekiel, Peter or Stephen or Paul have made of such a slogan? They didn't find the God of the Bible: the Lord God chased them down like the hound of heaven pursuing his quarry. Abraham was tending sheep, Jeremiah was lying in his mother's womb, and Paul was persecuting Christians when God called them. Therefore, the motto of Christians should be something akin to this: "God in Christ has found us." And He finds us not so much by our personal religious decision and our private religious relationship as by the solitary thing that makes these other things possible: by God's grace alone given through faith alone.

This Jesus of the religious right is a sentimental savior because he makes no serious demands on us. He is not the Jesus of the Gospels, who bids his little flock to take up their cross and to come die with him. This false Christ is a success-oriented savior who calls Christians to be rich and good-looking and numerous. On the right, therefore, our churches are proclaiming a salvation not of ethical good works but of religious good works. The more you pray and read the Bible and attend church, so this false gospel goes, the happier and more prosperous you are guaranteed to become. This explains why the TV evangelists always have their phone number scrolling across the bottom of the screen: send us money and God will send you money. Theirs is indeed a prosperity gospel.

It follows that, just as most liberal Christians turn out to be Democrats, so do most conservative Christians turn out to be Republicans. No one has the courage to say that Jesus Christ is neither right nor left, neither Democrat nor Republican, but the radical critic and drastic transformer of every political and economic scheme. As the late Louisiana writer Walker Percy used to say, there isn't a dime's worth of difference between most conservatives and liberals. Yet Percy did spot one distinction between them. In his hilarious novel entitled *Love in the Ruins,* you can tell Christian liberals from Christian conservatives only because the liberals *require* their black maids to ride in the front seat when they are taking them home. Among conservatives, by contrast, one's faith is measured by the size of one's smile: the more blinding, the better. One of these conservative Christian pastors has a smile so wide that even his friends have named him Mr. Gleaming Gums. Yet

Scripture never records Jesus Christ as having exuded a beaming cheerfulness, though they surely record him as having wept over Jerusalem.

The false god of the false gospel of religious good works turns out to be someone rather like Santa Claus. He supposedly gives his followers whatever they want if they make their requests known in a sweetly pious way. Some of my super-pious Christian students tell me that they pray for Jesus to find them a parking place — and that he always comes through. In the Garden of Gethsemane, Jesus prayed that God would lift the bitter cup of absolute suffering and divine abandonment from his lips, but God said no. Please don't mistake me as ridiculing petitionary prayer. I do indeed believe that God answers prayer. I believe that he gives three answers to our prayers: Yes, No, and Later.

I once met a Christian lady in England who believes that God answers all prayers not only in the affirmative but also instantly. She announced that people who don't believe in Jesus always come to "a sticky end," as she put it. I replied to her that, so far as I could tell, our Lord himself came to a rather sticky end himself. I don't believe that God much cares whether we are at ease in the world; but I believe that he cares enormously whether we are faithful and thus joyful. Being at ease in the world is largely a matter of outward circumstance. You must possess certain things to live a life of ease: health, money, security, success, power. None of these things is required for joy. True joy lies in knowing — and thus in performing the drastic acts of witness that result from such knowledge — that we are saved by God's grace alone through his gift of faith alone. Here is the peace that surpasses all merely human happiness. We can have this joy and this peace no matter how grim our circumstances, amidst poverty and ill health, despite failure and weakness, and no matter how sinful we once were and may yet be again.

III

Permit me a single illustration of what I understand this true gospel of salvation by grace alone through faith alone to be, and thus what a work of true and godly righteousness looks like. It is a story so dramatic that I fear it might not seem relevant to you and me; but I hope you will see that it could also be your story or mine. It concerns a Vietnam veteran who suffers the worst effects of what we call the posttraumatic stress disorder. This man lives alone, and he spends much of his time drinking, trying to drown his memories of what he saw and what he did in Vietnam. He has horrible day visions and terrible nightmares about the children he killed there, wasting their lives with napalm and gunfire. He is convinced that he is going to hell, indeed that he already occupies hell. He is haunted by the verse of Scripture that declares, "You shall reap what you sow." On Christmas Eve of this year he went to a bar and got himself thoroughly plastered. This was not the best night but the worst night of the year for him. In the early hours of Christmas morning he came to his host's home not only drunk but also violent. His brother-in-law, a Methodist minister who is a friend of mine, sought quietly to talk him down from his drunken fury. At first the man wouldn't listen. In fact, he grabbed my friend by the throat and told him that he could kill him, that killing is the one thing he knows how to do well, and that the power to kill is what gives him real power over people.

Yet my friend was not afraid of this violent and drunken maniac. He did not cringe and beg for the killer to spare his life. My friend kept his calm not because he is a supremely brave man — though he is surely one of the bravest men I know — but because he is a faithful man, because he knows that he is saved by grace alone through faith alone. And so with a murderer's hands clutching his throat, my friend quietly made his witness: "I am not afraid of you, and I am not afraid of you because I love you, and I love you because I know that God loves you, and I know that God loves you for the same reason he loves me: because in Jesus Christ he has taken our sins on himself." Once the drunken man had loosened his grip in horror at the slaughter he had almost committed, my friend added statements such as these: "You will never find peace by trying to find some way of justifying what you did in Vietnam, not by calling it an act of war, not by excusing your deeds as mere obedience to the orders of your superiors. Nor will you ever be able to make up for what you did there. But Jesus Christ has already made up for it. If you go to hell, therefore, it will be for the same reason that I will go to hell: because you and I will have kicked and slapped away the outstretched arms of the man who has laid hold of us at Calvary. For in his cross he has reaped what you and I have sown. He has saved those children whom you killed, and he can also save you by grace alone through faith alone."

I am not here to report a sudden and complete conversion in this man, nor to promise that all will turn out well for him. If he finds his salvation at all, it will be through the long and rocky road that winds down from Golgotha. It is a path that will lead him straight past all liberal do-good religion and past all conservative feel-good religion. Like you and me, this man will find his salvation by being baptized in the slow red river of Jesus' blood. Like every one us, he will be called to make his witness to the world as he dwells among the people of God in the body of Christ called the church. There he will perform works of true righteousness such as my preacher-friend performed when he spoke the Word of hope that no counselor or social worker can speak. There he will find his forgiveness and redemption by grace alone through faith alone.

This, as I understand it, is the Reformation that both our liberal and our conservative churches need if they are not to become citadels of unbelief that crucify Christ afresh. This is the gospel according to Jesus Christ as it is summarized in Ephesians 2:8-10. This is the cross that is calling to you and to me:

> Come home, come home,
> Ye who are weary, come home,
> Earnestly, tenderly, Jesus is calling,
> Calling, O sinner, come home.

Wrestling Jacob and Being Named by God

Genesis 32:22-31

Paddington Chapel United Reformed Church
London
February 28, 1988

Mr. Ronald Reagan has said that he does not attend church because it is too dangerous. What he means, of course, is that his own presence there might put the congregation at unnecessary risk at the hands of assassins and terrorists. Yet it is a curious fact that this threat does not prevent the president from appearing in other public places, for example, at political rallies. At least it can be said in his behalf that he does not sponsor those dreadful White House services that Mr. Nixon so vigorously supported. I suspect the real reason Mr. Reagan does not attend divine services is that, like many of us, he is not a very good Christian, and thus does not understand that churchgoing is indeed a very dangerous business. We have not come this morning to this drafty old church in Central London in order to be safe and comfortable. The heating here militates against any such misunderstanding! We have come, instead, to praise and worship and glorify the living God, the God of whom Scripture says it is a terrible thing to fall into his hands.

The God with whom we have to deal is indeed a dangerous God. Worse things than petrol bombs and hand grenades can explode here. We have put ourselves at far greater peril, and we are wagering far higher stakes, than mere mortal danger. The risk we run in coming to this place at this hour is nothing less than the threat of eternal misery and the delight of eternal happiness. For we are gathered here for reasons entirely different from our civic duty or our nostalgic remembrance of things past. We are here to do what Jacob did at the River Jabbok: to wrestle with the angel of the Lord, to learn who God is and who he is not, to seek his blessing, and to acquire a new name. We have come to put away such childish things as malice and guile, insincerity and envy and slander. We have assembled ourselves in order to grow up to salvation, to become a holy priesthood, to be built into a spiritual house on Christ, the solid rock: the stone whom the builders rejected, but whom God has made the cornerstone for his new house and his new people.

Jacob is one of the wiliest characters in all of Scripture. As we have seen before, he is more a man of craft and cunning than of holiness and piety. He is the younger twin to his brother Esau who, being the first-born, is heir to his father's goods. And yet the two of them divide the affections of their parents. Esau the hunter and farmer is loved by his father, Isaac, while Jacob the homebody and gourmet cook is favored by his mother, Rebekah. It's a thick family tangle that no soap opera would dare to repeat — and that even Sigmund Freud could learn from. You will recall that Esau believes that his own manly strength counts far more than his birthright. Consequently, when he returns from the field utterly famished with hunger, he foolishly agrees to exchange his legacy as the firstborn for a mess of Jacob's pottage. Someone has wittily said that most of us moderns, hooked on this or that magic solution to our problems, sell our own birthright — not for a mess of pottage, but for a pot of message.

To compound his earlier trickery, Jacob fools the elderly and blind Isaac into giving him his final blessing. You will remember how, according to the instruction of his own mother, Jacob deceives the glazed eyes of the old man by wearing goat skins that would make him seem like the hairy-handed and rough-necked Esau. And because this second ruse also works, Jacob's name becomes the key to his character: he is the supplanter, the displacer, the deposer. Though born second, he becomes first by dint of his own scheming and devising. And yet he is the honored man of God: "Jacob have I loved, but Esau have I hated" becomes a virtual refrain echoing through Scripture.

The first real clue to the nature of this strange blessing laid on so unlikely a figure as Jacob is revealed in the scene at the River Jabbok. To understand it properly, we must read it in its larger context. So angry is Esau at all the devilment Jacob has done him that he has vowed long ago to kill his brother. Jacob is now returning from his lengthy sojourn in the land of Laban, whose two daughters, Rachel and Leah, he has married. Jacob fears that, though he has been gone for many years and is now the father of eleven children by these two wives, Esau will still keep his vow to kill him. And so he prepares a huge brotherly peace offering of goats and sheep, camels and asses. But before he can make his peace with Esau, Jacob has a life-altering encounter as he and his entourage camp by the River Jabbok.

There Jacob spends the night wrestling with an angel of God until dawn. Indeed, he almost defeats this heavenly combatant. Only by means of a blow to Jacob's thigh does the divine struggler survive, and even then Jacob will not let him go until the angel blesses him. The grace given to Jacob comes in the form of a new name: no longer will he be called Jacob, the supplanter or displacer, but Israel, the one who has striven with God and mankind and has prevailed. Jacob seems almost jaunty in his confidence about this victory and blessing. He renames the place Peniel, which means "the face of God." Heretofore, God had encountered his people only by letting them see him from the rear, for fear that anyone beholding his face would be obliterated by the sight of pure righteousness. Here at Peniel, however, Jacob has encountered God face to face and has not been destroyed.

What an odd story is this! It does not make Scripture a morally edifying book. I rather agree with the lady who wrote to the *Times* of London and demanded, not that television be censored for its corrupting influence on the young, but rather the Bible. Indeed, it does contain a multitude of exceedingly unscrupulous characters — like Jacob. And yet two small details of this Jacob story must not be overlooked before we turn away in disgust. The first is that, after Jacob has been given his new name, he asks the angel of God what his name is. Instead of an answer, Jacob gets something far more important — a blessing. God is who is he is, and God will be who he will be: that's what the name Yahweh means. We cannot name God because to name someone or something is to identify and even control that entity. Many of us have had the uncanny experience of feeling ourselves half cured when we learn the name of our illness, even if it be a deadly disease. So long as we don't know what's wrong with us, our pain is terrifying; but once the beast is identified, we feel immensely relieved and perhaps on the way to health.

"In names lies the significance of things" is a very old adage. It explains why language is so very important, why your British mastery of words is indeed one of the wonders of the world, why poetry remains the most important form of speech. For we cease to be animals when our breath becomes articulate, when we stop grunting and start speaking words and names. No longer are we mere creatures of our environment; we are also creators of it. And this is not our generally human so much as our specifically Hebrew heritage. Already in the first chapter of Genesis, we find God speaking the world into being: "And God said, Let there be light, and there was light." Adam's naming of all the created things is another crucial moment in the creation: Eden's plants and animals do not exist, in the very deepest sense, until Adam gives them names.

Yet what Jacob learns at Jabbok is rather a different lesson. For while God gives us the power to partially master experience through language, it is he who names and renames us rather than our naming him. We do not give titles to God and thus control him. God names himself and thus allows us graciously to know him, even to wrestle with him. Unless God remains radically other to us — as the one whom we cannot name and master to our own purposes — then we cannot encounter him as the personal God whom Scripture claims him to be.

The second thing Jacob learns from his all-night tussle with the angel of God is that we do not confront God without grave risk. Jacob receives a deep thigh wound that leaves him a permanent cripple. Not even the marvelous modern techniques of hip-replacement surgery would have healed Jacob, for his injury was clearly spiritual as well as physical. He will never be well again, limping through life as a maimed man. In an ironic sense, Jacob is damaged for good: in his disfigurement lies his real hope. To be wounded by God is to be set on the path toward new life. This is exactly what happens when Jacob at last faces the brother he dreads. Perhaps for the first time, Esau sees his injured brother as a figure worthy of pity rather than contempt. When at last the limping Jacob goes out to meet the twin whom he had wronged so grievously, his brother embraces him, falls on his neck kissing him, and they both weep.

They sob in the happy discovery that the real question is not who shall connive to be first in the kingdom of mankind, but who shall rejoice to be last in the kingdom of God. They have both found that real and lasting health is to be had only in the God of Israel, the "God who strives" with his people. This, then, is the huge hope held out by the Jacob story. God will not leave us to our own devices. The definition of hell is to be left utterly alone. Thanks be to God that he will not leave us to ourselves. He will bless us by wrestling with us, even by wounding us. The God who treats us roughly is the same God who will treat his Son with the terrible exactitude of his own justice. That son was wounded for our transgressions, and by his stripes are we healed. Amen.

PART III

SUFFERING AND SERVICE

The No-People Who Have Become God's People

1 Peter 2:1-10

First Baptist Church
Winston-Salem, North Carolina
July 2, 1989

The early Christians were often regarded as atheists. Not only did they refuse to worship the emperor; they would not offer homage to the many other gods in the pantheon of Roman religion either. It thus seemed that these Christians were atheists. To worship only one God was tantamount, in Roman eyes, to worshiping no god at all. And so we should remember that our Christian forebearers were not considered too religious but too irreligious, and that they were persecuted for not being good citizens in the way that Rome defined good citizenship.

The little letter called 1st Peter addresses this problem of the seeming hostility of Christians toward the government. The answer to the problem would seem obvious: we Christians can best serve our American nation by doing our civic duty, by shouldering the burdens that are common to all citizens. Yet the answer given by Peter is not obvious but startling. It says that we Christians minister to society and to the state by remaining, first and last, the church of Jesus Christ. It calls the church to be the church and not another thing, to be the people of God and not a no-people, to belong to Jesus Christ and not to our race or our country, not to our families or even ourselves. Christ and Christ alone is the living cornerstone upon whom God builds his kingdom. We are, in turn, but the pebbles and rocks with whom Christ builds his kingdom house called the church. Hence he calls us to be his witnesses, showing the world that its true hope lies in the God who is our salvation, that nowhere but on this solid rock does anyone have a place to stand, that all other ground is sinking sand.

I

The first Christians knew the cost of their redemption. They suffered persecution for their faith in the God who had suffered death upon the cross for our salvation. Few of us Americans know what it is like to suffer for our faith. Little, if at all, have we borne the cross of Christ's rejection. We should count ourselves blessed indeed that we are free to worship and serve God without fear. We should also remember, in prayer and gratitude, those Christian brothers and sisters around the world who, even at this very hour, are despised and persecuted for their faith in Jesus Christ. We ought to read, mark, learn, and inwardly digest the testimonies of Christian martyrdom that have come out of the Russian gulags and the German concentration camps, out of the Cuban political prisons and the Central American death squads and South African apartheid jails. These stories of Christian suffering are *Foxe's Book of Martyrs* for our time.

It was my great privilege, while on sabbatical leave in London, to meet the Ukrainian dissident Irina Ratushinskaya. She is a thirty-five-year-old poet whose parents raised her as an atheist so that their brilliant daughter could succeed within the Communist system in the only way possible — that is, as an unbeliever. Yet the seed of Christian faith had been planted in this fearless girl by her Polish Catholic grandparents, who had retained their faith despite the Communist denial of God. Why, this child asked, did my grandparents' faith make them go against the grain of the atheist state? Thus, as a young student in physics at the University of Odessa, Irina Ratushinskaya began to ask unscientific questions. If Christianity is as foolish and the Bible as false as the Communists say, then why are they so determined to stamp them out of existence? Why wouldn't the Christian faith simply collapse of its own imbecility?

Ratushinskaya was herself converted at the age of twenty-three after finding an eighteenth-century Russian Bible and reading the Gospels for the first time in her life. "All the pieces of my life fell into place" she says, "like a mosaic." And yet she confesses that she did not seek God. "God himself found me," she declares, "and helped me to endure, and nurtured my soul, because there was no one else to nurture my soul during my childhood and youth." This Christian convert was to spend four terrible years in a Soviet prison for the crime — I repeat, for the crime — of writing poetry. Though her work was completely unpolitical, she refused to submit her poems to the Soviet censors, so the KGB regarded her art as subversive to the Communist state. Indeed it is. Irina Ratushinskaya wrote not as a servant of the Soviet system but as a poet of the human condition. She will not blunt or blinker the truth about human sin and evil, nor about the human longing for freedom.

For her so-called crime of having an "unenthusiastic way of thinking" — that was the official charge — Ratushinskaya was subjected to horrible pain. She almost died from beatings she suffered at the hands of her guards, and she nearly starved to death on hunger strikes that she undertook to protest the unjust treatment of prisoners. Yet she was not deterred from her calling as a poet. She would scratch her poems on a bar of soap, commit them to memory, and then wash away the "incriminating" evidence. Fellow inmates memorized her poems, and by word of mouth they made their way beyond the prison walls, eventually to be published in the underground press. [They are now available in English translation under the title *Grey Is the Color of Hope*.]

The most remarkable thing about this remarkable woman is that she is free from all bitterness and anger about her frightful ordeal. The gospel has made her a truly liberated woman. When asked whether she had trouble obeying Jesus' command to pray for her persecutors, she answered forthrightly. "No," she said. "Even when I was so emaciated that it hurt to breathe, I never for a moment wished to change places with the prison guards who had made my life a temporary hell. For, as a Christian, I knew that my tormentors were in eternal hell — the hell of being unwilling to receive and thus unwilling to show mercy. And so I prayed for God to deliver them as well as me."

Irina Ratushinskaya gave a sardonic title to her speech in the chapel of King's College, London: "The Interference of God in the Internal Affairs of the Soviet Union." Against the Communist whine about Western interference in Russian affairs, she made it clear that God cannot be kept from intervening in *any* of the world's affairs. And yet Ratushinskaya ended her talk with a warning that stops all self-congratulation on our part. She said that the greatest need among Russian Christians today is, quite simply, for more Bibles. This statement prompted someone from the audience to ask why Western society is so faithless, why our churches are so spiritually dead, when we have access to dozens of Scripture translations and total freedom of worship? Ratushinskaya replied, with great spiritual discernment, that God has interfered with Soviet affairs in order to grant freedom as a *gift* amidst political repression, but that God has interfered with Western society to offer freedom as a *test* to see whether we will maintain faith in him when we have not been coerced. At one time nearly everyone was Christian almost as a matter of course; but now no one in the West is compelled to be Christian. Freedom is thus God's gift to the Russians, she concluded, but God's test to the Americans and the rest of the West.

II

The book of First Peter tells us how to pass the great test of our time. It calls the church to be the people of God enlivened by the incomparable gift of the gospel. This remains the indispensable answer, even though we Americans face quite a new question. Our problem is not persecution by the world but rather conformity to the world. Alas, we have largely failed the test of freedom. The church in our time and place is often indistinguishable from any good civic club. We have turned it into yet another means of upward mobility and social success and psychological comfort. No wonder our churches are sick unto death even when they are filled to overflowing. We have done many good things, but we have left undone the one thing needful: we have ignored the scandal and the offense of the gospel.

Jesus Christ is a stumbling stone to those who would run their own race, a roadblock to those who would make their own way, a millstone to those who would believe that God lifts those who lift themselves by the hair of their own head. The heart of the gospel is the Good News that none of us pull ourselves up by our own bootstraps. This is the human gospel of self-help and not the divine gospel of salvation. As Martin Luther and John Calvin and our Puritan ancestors never wearied of saying, we Christians are not saved *by* good works but *for* good works. Precisely because we can do nothing to save ourselves, we are freed to do everything in gratitude to God for saving us despite ourselves. It is his gospel alone that energizes us to lead lives of utmost thanksgiving and service, without fear of going unpaid. Christians know that Jesus paid it all. All to him we owe.

It is such a life-converting word that we hear in Jesus' command to love our neighbors as ourselves. This injunction must not be sentimentalized into mere politeness and vague kindness. It is no easy thing to love one's neighbor. G. K. Chesterton was no less wise than witty when he said that, while we make our friends and we make our enemies, God makes our neighbors. It is true of both the Old and New Testaments that God's people are enjoined not first of all to love the world, but rather to love the neighbor. They are literally the *nigh* ones, those who are near at hand, and we are commanded to love them as God loves us — as fellow sinners saved by grace. For if there be no community of the redeemed, if there be no people of God who have been shown mercy and who thus know how to show mercy, then the world is truly hopeless. Here in our worship of God, here in our fellowship with each other, here in the life of confession and prayer and praise, here alone can we do for the world the one thing it cannot do for itself. Here we proclaim and practice the salvation wrought by God in the Jews and Jesus Christ. Thus is the faithful church God's own answer to the world's wars and hatreds, a demonstration of how God means human life to be lived.

This explains why the short letter of First Peter declares it an outrage for Christians to draw knives and hurl daggers. With such enmity we not only violate each other, but we make a liar of Jesus Christ. How can the church of the Reconciler be filled with those who are unreconciled? Our real problem, says the author of our text, is not that we Christians are hostile to the government but that we are hostile to each other. Our refusal to be reconciled in Christ drives the world away from the church instead of welcoming it to God's great feast of salvation.

"Put away all malice and guile," cries the writer of this little epistle. "Get rid of all insincerity and envy, all slander." Drink the milk of your salvation, he summons us, that honey-laced milk that young Christians of the early church were given as they came out of the baptismal waters. This milk, says our author, is the very potion of paradise. Taste and see, he echoes the Psalmist, how good the Lord is. The meat and drink of the Lord's Table alone can fortify us to give our lives away in service, to become priests to each other, a holy nation of the redeemed, a people pleasing to God and thus of real service to our country.

Black preachers have much to teach us when they remark that 1 Peter 2:10 is the great galvanizing word to members of their churches: "Once you were no people, but now you are God's people." This does not mean merely that blacks who were once segregated and oppressed have been freed by civil rights legislation, though these laws certainly have meant a new day for black people. What the black preachers understand — and what we need so fully to learn — is that we are *all* no-people until we become God's people. The richest businessman is totally impoverished without God's grace. The most popular athlete or movie mogul or rock star is a nobody apart from God's recognition. The most learned scientist or professor is an utter ignoramus unless she knows the God whom she can truly believe. And the most powerful politician is a pathetic weakling if he does not get his strength from the gospel. You were a no-people, First Peter says to us, because you had not received mercy; but now you are God's people because you have received mercy.

My elderly maternal uncle can hardly read or write. He has never known anything but hard work, and he has never been anything but poor. He makes little if any "contribution to society," at least as the world measures it. And the world, in turn, accords him no honor whatsoever. He is a nobody. But this frail man and his wife attend, when they are able, a small Missionary Baptist church near Sherman, Texas, where something startling happens. "I don't amount to much," says my uncle, "and I give almost nothing to our little church. But there I'm treated like a king. I'm as important as the richest man present." His fellow Christians honor and care for him, not because he can repay their concern, but because he is indeed a son of the King, a joint heir with Christ. He is far richer than the world's richest.

This, I believe, is the Christian way of celebrating the Fourth of July: by celebrating the ultimate freedom to become God's people. We Americans will pass the terrible and wonderful test of freedom only if the church remains the church. Only in total allegiance to the God of Jesus Christ do we know how to give our partial allegiance to the flag. It was the horrible mistake of German Christians to give total allegiance to their nation as they sang their national anthem, *Deutschland, Deutschland über Alles* ("Germany, Germany above all others"). It was then that Hitler rose to power and turned the most civilized nation of the world into the most monstrous. Our one guard against such demonry happening here in America — as it very well could — is for

Christians to sing the very same tune, Haydn's "Prussian Hymn," but to the splendidly different words of John Newton:

> Glorious things of thee are spoken,
> Zion, city of our God. . . .
> On the Rock of Ages founded,
> Who can shake thy sure repose?
> With salvation's walls surrounded,
> Thou mayst smile at all thy foes.

The Call of the Crucified

Matthew 16:24

The declaration that Jesus Christ "suffered under Pontius Pilate; was crucified, died, and was buried" comes right at the center of the Apostles' Creed. This is altogether appropriate, because the cross is also the center of the Christian faith. The call to take up our cross and to follow the Lord all the way to death is the very heart of the gospel: it is the summons to suffer as Christ suffered, to be crucified with Jesus, to die and to be buried with him. Far from a dour and forbidding summons, this is the highest and gladdest of all privileges. The call to suffering and death and burial is not a summons that we grimly answer by our own unaided effort. Rather is it the new and glorious life that Christ himself grants to us as the gift of faith. Jesus is no heroic example, however noble, whom we are called to emulate. He is the crucified Son of God, who atones for our sin and enables our redemption through suffering for his sake and the kingdom's.

When we confess that our Lord "suffered under Pontius Pilate," we are dealing with concrete, visible reality. No other claim in the entire Apostles' Creed can be historically attested. Every other article concerns truth that is either invisible or undemonstrable. There is no proof, for example, that Christ was spiritually conceived and virginally born. We affirm these things by faith, and we cannot convince anyone to believe them who has not been granted the blessing of faith. About one matter, however, there is no doubt at all: Jesus "suffered under Pon-

---

This sermon was published previously in Roger Van Harn, ed., *Exploring and Proclaiming the Apostles' Creed* (Grand Rapids: Eerdmans, 2004), pp. 111-16.

tius Pilate." Even the Roman historian Tacitus confirms that the crucifixion was the ultimate public event of Christ's life and ministry.

There is no denying that our Lord experienced other kinds of suffering. He suffered the sorrows and disappointments that mortal flesh is heir to. He suffered the shame and scorn that good people always meet in evil times. He suffered the incomprehension of his own disciples, none of whom truly grasped the gospel that he called them to follow. Yet not one of these torments is mentioned in the creed. Jesus' real suffering was at the hands of the Roman prefect of Judea, Pontius Pilate, who colluded with the Jewish establishment to have him killed. Jesus' real pain was outward and public, and we do violence to his cross if we concentrate primarily on his inward and private suffering. The hard fact is that he ran afoul of Jewish and Roman authority, and that he suffered a cruel death for it.

Why was the rabbi from Nazareth such a severe threat to Pontius Pilate, and to those Sadducees and the Pharisees whom the local prefect dared not defy? And why should we Christians pose a real peril to the cultural authorities of our own time? The answer has to do with Pentecost and the birthing of the church. Once the early Christians had been filled with the Holy Spirit, their cross-centered faith revolutionized the world. They became unabashedly clear in their conviction that Christ's death had taken away the sin of the world, and that they participated in God's own life through baptism and the Eucharist. They astonished the pagans by their love for each other. And they showed hospitality even to aliens and strangers; they cared for the poor and the needy, the prostitutes and lepers. They forgave not only their friends but also their enemies. They refused to abort their babies or abandon them to death. They gave themselves over to a disciplined life of prayer and fasting — and often celibacy as well. Above all else, they were willing to die rather than renounce their Lord and his gospel of redemption.

The Romans assumed that they could readily suppress the followers of this Lord, whose crucifixion Pontius Pilate had engineered. They mocked the Christians as "atheists" because they had only a single God. To the Romans, with their many gods, worshiping only one God was tantamount to worshiping none. When the Christians also refused to offer sacrifices to Caesar himself, the Romans threatened them with death, believing that such persecution would put an end to these "Christers," as they were derisively called at Antioch. In fact, the Romans were already defeated when Christians fell to their knees in the

Coliseum, praying for the forgiveness of those who burned them to death or fed them to savage beasts.

No oppressive religious or political establishment can withstand such freedom, such strange liberty and power to become utterly alive, and thus to be utterly unpanicked by suffering and death. This is the one King whose kingdom runs athwart every nation and state, every demonic principality and power, every ethnic group and voting bloc, every worldly authority that claims final authority. It does not matter whether the demand for absolute allegiance occurs under the tyranny of a Roman emperor or the republican rule of a popularly elected president. Flannery O'Connor made exactly this point when she said that the death camps of Germany and Poland could also have been erected in her native state of Georgia.

I learned this unwelcome lesson when my family and I visited Dachau, the concentration camp located near Munich. With good cause, the Germans have not made it an easy place to find. Having finally located the train for Dachau, we discovered that it was loaded with American college students who were enjoying their European spring vacation as they, too, traveled to Dachau. It was the weekend of the NCAA basketball championship, and the train was full of raucous talk about the tournament. We might as well have been at a Wendy's or McDonald's in the United States. It was not a proud moment to be an American, much less a Christian — traveling to a Nazi death camp as if to a sporting event. Yet something surpassingly strange happened when we Americans entered the camp through the iron gates adorned with their mocking slogan *Arbeit Macht Frei* ("Work Makes Free"). Silence fell over everyone. Everything became eerily quiet. As we walked through the dormitories and past the crematoria, no one clucked confidently about the terrible thing that the Germans had done to the Jews. We all seemed to sense, in a subterranean and unconfessed way, that we also could commit such unspeakable crimes. I had no desire to shout, "*They* did this," but rather quietly to confess, "*We* did this," we human beings who killed the ultimate Jew named Jesus the Christ.

When a former student told his father my story, the man's reaction was completely negative and hostile. Because he can trace his ancestors back many generations and can cite their many noble contributions to human betterment, he gave this telling response: "*My* people would never do a thing like that." Understandable as such a sentiment is, it does not recognize the real meaning of evil nor the real justification that comes only through Jesus Christ. In slaying him, Pontius Pilate — together with the Pharisees and the Sadducees who persuaded Pilate that Christ must be killed — serves as our representative. The killing of Jesus reveals the horrible heart of sin. Sin, said Luther, is not lying and cheating; it is not slander and adultery; it is not even murder. These dreadful sins (in the plural) are the ugly manifestations of sin (in the singular): it is the rejection of God's mercy and grace. It is the refusal to entrust ourselves into Christ's keeping. It is the denial that the triune and incarnate God took upon himself the sins of the world, bearing the massive burden of evil and atoning for it by himself alone, that we might be released from the yoke of our bondage. Hence the call of the Crucified for us to take up our cross and follow him, to lose our lives for his sake and the kingdom's, to die in order that we might truly live.

The Crucified calls us to take up our own cross, to follow him, to suffer for the world's redemption as he suffered. I once believed, quite mistakenly, that our cross is to be found in the special burdens that we are all called to bear patiently and faithfully: perhaps an incurable illness, a mentally ill child, an unhappy marriage, a miserable work situation, a wretched old age. Such afflictions are real and often terrible, and we are in fact summoned to shoulder them without self-pity or despair. But Jesus' audience would not have pondered these mortal ills when they heard his command to take up their cross and follow him. What they knew is what we must learn: that our cross is our witness, our public testimony, even unto death, that we belong to the community of the Crucified, to the church of the suffering Savior, to this singular body that has been branded with the mark of the Nazarene.

It is no happenstance that the root meaning of the word martyr is "witness." Nor is it surprising that the early church identified those who had been killed for their faith as its most important witnesses. In fact, the church took the words of the second century theologian Tertullian and formulated a motto to describe the effect of their deaths. "The blood of the martyrs is the seed of the church." The slaying of the faithful is, ironically, the worst way to silence their witness. Far from stamping out the Faith, martyrdom gives it an odd kind of vibrancy. A persecuted church is, paradoxically, an honored church. Aleksandr Solzhenitsyn once said that the Communists paid Christianity the ultimate tribute when they tried to exterminate it. He added, ever so harshly but ever so truly, that we Americans offer Christ the ultimate insult by seeking to domesticate him.

The sayings of Tertullian and Solzhenitsyn are truer for our time than ever before. It is a staggering, a chilling fact that more Christians were killed for their faith during the twentieth century than in all of the previous centuries combined. Nearly 40 million were martyred during the past one hundred years, compared to roughly 27 million in the prior nineteen hundred years. Approximately 12 million Christians perished in the Soviet Union alone. Though such martyrdom may seem to be a remote likelihood for American Christians, we should be prepared to suffer under modern Herods and Pilates — even as we must also be prepared to reject their violence. To be the friends of God is, alas, to have adversaries in the world.

Christians whose souls and bodies have been transformed by a Messiah who himself could not be turned back from his Cross will make enemies. Yet it is important to remember that we are called to suffer not primarily as individuals but as a Christian community. A church that does not bow down to our contemporary idols will be persecuted. It will not be allowed freely to follow its Lord. The community of the Crucified will inevitably clash with a culture that despises suffering and worships what it calls "freedom of choice" — whether in amassing untold wealth or in aborting unwanted babies. A church that refuses to offer sacrifices to these and our other gods of comfort and convenience will surely incur the wrath of the cultural police force — whether from public pressure or governmental power, whether from the educational establishment or the therapeutic priests of our time. If we refuse to participate in our culture of death, as Pope John Paul II rightly calls our deadly moral climate, we must be prepared to suffer as members of Christ's crucified body.

Allow a single illustration to suffice, even if it requires a necessary verbal violence, lest we sanitize sin. The Watts Street Baptist Church in Durham, North Carolina, served as a powerful Christian voice during the racial crisis of the 1950s and '60s. Its minister, Warren Carr, was not ashamed of the gospel. He had the courage to proclaim its Good News that, in the atoning life and death and resurrection of Jesus Christ, we have all been reconciled to God. Having one Lord and one faith and one baptism, we are brothers and sisters without regard to skin color or social class. In the midst of a rigidly segregated society, this Baptist congregation stood with its minister in extending these claims to the race question. As a result, the church came under periodic attack. On a certain Thursday morning, an ugly message appeared on the doors of the church: "Go to hell, Warren Carr." The minister ordered this crude insult to be scrubbed off immediately. On Friday, there was another racist slur scrawled on the church entrance: "Go to hell, you nigger-loving Warren Carr." Again, the minister ordered that it be quickly removed.

On Saturday, still more racist invective had been sprayed across the front of the church. Yet the vilifiers had slightly shifted their attack: "This church loves niggers." Reverend Carr ordered that the accusatory sentence be left visible for a few days. Despite their odious slur-word, the hatemongers had advertised the church's real business. In their blind fury, they had at last got the gospel right. It is not about a courageous individual defying an unjust social order and being attacked for his keen social conscience — although a firebomb was in fact thrown against the front window of the Carr parsonage. The call of the Crucified concerns the witness of the entire church. Jesus summons us to live as a redeeming and atoning community. We are to invite everyone — young and old, rich and poor, divorced and married, gay and straight, red and yellow, black and white — to receive forgiveness of sin, to suffer and die and be buried with Christ. There alone lies the Way to abundant, joyful, lasting, eternal life.

Stanley Hauerwas rightly observes that our culture has only a single fundamental belief — namely, that we are to fear death above all else. So fully have even we Christians lost sight of the Cross that we have become terrified of dying. Yet there is a subtler dread also at work here: we are afraid of being raised from the dead by the risen Christ. We fear our own transformation, knowing that its blessings will cost us no less than everything — our souls, our lives, our all. Blessed are the dead who die in the Lord. If we have died with Christ, we shall also live with him. Such unfathomably simple claims explain why the church commemorates its saints, not on the day of their birth, but rather on the day of their death. Our coming into the world matters far less than our going from it — our passage into eternal life. In our death, our lives are meant to reach their completion and fulfillment in Christ. Hence these final words of Dietrich Bonhoeffer as he was hanged at Flossenberg prison just a few days before it was liberated by the Allies in 1945: "This is the end — for me, the beginning of life."

Whether our witness brings us suffering great or small, our death is the one thing that no one can take from us. Though Jesus suffered and was crucified under Pontius Pilate, he was no unwilling victim:

Christ gave up his life freely, if also amidst agony. Even if we are never called to suffer "unto blood," as the author of Hebrews says, we remain Christ's witnesses in both our living and our dying. We are called to testify that, because in our baptism we have been buried with him, so in our death will we rise with him. "It is not the suffering," said St. Augustine, "that makes genuine martyrs; it is the cause." So it is with us who are called to be living rather than dead witnesses of the gospel. We have the right cause and the right man on our side — the kingdom and the Crucified. Amen.

The Suffering That Makes for Character

Romans 5:1-11

North Park Presbyterian Church,
Dallas, Texas
February 24, 2002

Mount Tabor United Methodist Church
Winston-Salem, North Carolina
March 3, 2002

Nowhere more clearly than in Paul's letter to the Romans, and especially in Romans 5, do we learn why mercy and grace and forgiveness and reconciliation lie at the center of what the apostle calls "the gospel of God." Paul faced a severe split in the church at Rome. It was an ugly rift between the Jewish Christians, who still practiced the ceremonies of traditional Judaism, and the Gentile Christians, who had come into the church without having first become Jews. Each side held the other in great suspicion. Neither felt that the other was worthy of forgiveness. Both had committed sins of mutual accusation that seemed to put their relation beyond repair. As a Jew who was perfect in all things regarding the law, Paul was prepared to side with the Judaizers; yet, as one who believed that Christ had perfectly fulfilled the law, Paul also knew that Christians are not bound by Jewish ritual practices. Thus could he have joined either faction, and he could have done so with integrity. Yet he refuses to take sides. Instead, Paul calls the Christians at Rome to the one and only thing that could heal their deep division, namely, to the mercy of God made real in Jesus Christ. Notice well that the apostle does not urge them to be nice to each other. Nor does he summon them to a vague and unspecific love. Instead, he commands them to the suffering that makes for character.

The Greek word for "character" means a mark or a sign. For Christians to have character means that we are people marked by the Cross, that we are branded with the gospel, even that we are tattooed with the Good News. These are our distinguishing characteristics. To be Christian is to live so that our lives could not be explained apart from the gospel. If others can account for our existence in any other terms than the Cross and Resurrection, then we lack Christian character. Lest this call to character seem stern and forbidding, we must recall that Paul roots it in the mercy of God.

The church is not constituted by strong-willed and self-made people. Nor is it even proper to say, as I once was inclined to say, that our character is the sum total of all our choices. Better and more Christian by far to say that our character is the sum total of all the gifts that we have not sinfully refused but graciously received, both from God and others. The chief of these gifts is the forgiveness of sin in Jesus Christ. And since forgiveness comes from the Cross, Paul also links character to suffering and endurance and hope. Hence my desire to proclaim the strange Good News to be found in three kinds of suffering: physical suffering, spiritual suffering, and the suffering that comes when we are attacked for making faithful witness to Jesus Christ.

I

We need to be clear about this matter of suffering, lest it come to grip us with a false fascination. There are two distinct kinds of Christian suffering. The first kind has to do with what philosophers call natural evil. Human existence has troubles built into its very makeup. The world is full of snakes; we do not need to seek them out. Suffering will find us soon enough. It found Christ from the very start, when Herod ordered his death no sooner than he had been born. The Russians have a wise saying about the inevitability of suffering. "We start to grow up," a Russian proverb holds, "when we stop saying 'It won't happen to me.'" It will happen, and sooner more often than later. The phone call and the doorbell and the lab report bring all too many tidings of woe. They call us to give up things we love dearly. In his novel *Till We Have Faces,* C. S. Lewis describes our lives as a series of farewells. The chances and changes of time make us constantly bid adieu. We say farewell first to our youth, then to our home, later to our parents and friends, later still to our health, perhaps even to our wealth, and finally to life itself.

The danger of suffering, even of suffering rightly borne, is that it can turn us in upon ourselves. It often makes us sad and self-centered rather than glad and joyful. We all know people whose troubles and illnesses make them talk about little but themselves. Søren Kierkegaard, the strange suffering saint of nineteenth-century Denmark, thus tells of the man who was offered happiness on the proverbial shining platter. "How dare you take away my misery!" the man shouted. "Would you rob me of my one reason for living, my unhappiness?" The answer is, Yes, of course. Jesus Christ is indeed the robber of all inward-focusing self-pity. He turns us ever more outward and away from ourselves. He frees us from the suffocating snail-shell world of the Merely Me. He welcomes us into the spacious and airy realm of his kingdom. There he invites us to concentrate our minds and our lives on him and his world and his people, there to find our joy. "Rejoice in the Lord always," Paul commands us. "Again I will say, Rejoice."

Let us be clear that suffering and misery are not the same thing. Many of us are miserable because we have made a mess of our lives. We are petty and small-minded; we are snappish and ill-tempered; we are self-absorbed and unloving, and we have spurned the grace of God. Even our physical misery is often self-induced. I'm deaf, in part, because I stupidly used a chain saw without ear-protection. When Paul urges us to rejoice, even to boast, in our suffering, he does not have such misery in mind. He means that, by the grace of God, we can find redemption amidst the physical suffering that he himself suffered. Paul spoke of his "thorn in the flesh." Yet while he prayed thrice for this thorn to be removed, he never became embittered at having to bear it. Paul knows that Christ nowhere declares his disciples exempt from physical ordeal. On the contrary, the book of Job declares that "man is born to suffering as the sparks fly upward." Yet ours is a world obsessed with the avoidance of suffering, and thus with sundry pills and programs that offer quick fixes for suffering. George Will refers to the self-help books that line our bookstore shelves as our Do-It-Yourself Instant God Kits.

There is a terrible irony at work here. Thomas Merton argues that most of the world's suffering is caused by our attempt to avoid suffering, and thus to find substitutes for the endurance that suffering requires. The more we try to avoid suffering, the more we actually suffer. For we begin to dread injuries that are so small, to imagine hurts so trivial, that our very existence becomes a constant torture. We cushion ourselves with comforts that make us miserable, forgetting Chesterton's wise warning: "There is only an inch of difference between the padded cushion and the padded cell." We become wretched precisely to the extent that we believe we were born to find pleasure, and that our pleasure consists in constantly being amused and entertained. Aleksandr Solzhenitsyn taught us the precise Christian counter-truth: "If a man were born only to be happy, he would not be born to die." The Beatitudes call us to blessedness rather than pleasantness. And blessedness is linked to faithfulness — to suffering patiently borne by the mercy of God.

Many of my elderly friends have had their latter years marked by physical suffering almost without relief. I can attest in their behalf that they have borne their bodily misery so faithfully that they have made a mighty witness to the gospel. I also know an elderly lady who confesses that the hardest thing about old age is not only her bodily aches and pains but also the terrible tedium of waiting to die. My next-door neighbor in Winston-Salem was a faithful Methodist who lived to be more than 100. I would often take him to local nursing homes to see his friends on Sunday afternoons. With a twinkle in his eye, he would say, even when he was himself approaching the century mark: "Let's go visit the old folks." Yet, by the end of his life, it had become a terrible weariness. He thus asked me whether it was a sin for him to pray every night that God might take him, so that he might not awaken. I replied that I believed it wasn't sinful for him thus to pray for death, since he had lived such a long and faithful life. But I also told him that he was giving testimony to the grace of God by his gracious endurance of his old age. His Christian character had been formed by suffering mercifully endured.

At Baylor, one of my favorite students is paraplegic. She has spent her entire life in a wheelchair. It's especially rending to see her propelling herself down the sidewalks when it rains, for of course she can't hold an umbrella while she wheels herself about. This attractive young woman has, at least to my knowledge, never had a single date. The average American male, whose taste in women has been formed by hypersexualized television commercials, cannot discern this woman's beauty, for hers is a beauty of character as well as body. I learned the depth of both her beauty and her character when I asked her a hard question. I asked whether, if it were possible, she would choose an ambulatory existence. Would she leap at the chance to walk like everyone else? She paused for a long while and then answered that she is not sure. Her life as a paralytic has proved to be so strangely blessed that her suffering has become God's surprising character-making gift.

II

There is also a spiritual suffering that we are called to endure for the sake of the gospel and for the building up of our character. This is the suffering that has little to do with our bodies because it primarily afflicts our souls. It's a suffering far harder to bear than physical pain. It comes when friendships are broken, when children spurn everything their parents have given them, when the schools and churches and companies to which we have dedicated our lives prove faithless and corrupt. It's ever so tempting, when such calamities come, to conclude that we have wasted our lives, that we have indeed lived for nothing. How could Paul dare ask us to rejoice in sufferings of this terrible spiritual kind?

What could be worse than losing a child — whether to death or to disease, whether to alienation or betrayal? Children are supposed to bury their parents, not the other way around. Friendships are made for life, not for temporary convenience. As C. S. Lewis says, friendship is the one love that is not diminished in being divided; it wonderfully increases when it is divided. To be rejected by a friend without cause thus makes for almost unbearable pain. What about those Enron employees who had given their lives to their company, only to discover that their bosses had bankrupted their retirement funds? Their cynicism and disgust must be overwhelming. What about those teachers who have given their entire lives to their schools, only to see all of their moral and academic standards collapse, as the schools have become a sad shadow of what they once were? What about those pastors who have dedicated their ministry to churches that then forsook everything they once stood for? No wonder one of my friends made this remark about a mutual friend: "There are two things she won't talk about: the death of her son and the failure of her marriage." They are the marks of her spiritual suffering.

There is simply no accounting for much of our spiritual suffering.

But there is a strange kind of sense to be found in our failures. Most of us learn very little from success. When we make notable accomplishments, we assume that it's because of our diligent effort or our brilliant strategy or even our worthy character. Vince Lombardi put the American creed well when he said that winning is not the most important thing — it's the only thing. Paul is profoundly un-American when he declares all his successes to be mere dung. He says that his strength lies in his weakness, that his wisdom lies in the folly of the gospel, that he counts nothing as gain except the privilege of dying with Christ.

We usually learn more from our failures than from our successes. Failure teaches us, among other things, to sympathize with the losers. It keeps us from boasting about our own achievements. The athletes who pound their chests and point to the skies after scoring a winning goal would do better making such gestures after they have committed a huge error, thus asking God's forgiveness rather than congratulating themselves under the guise of humility. I confess that I am a better teacher and scholar for having learned the meaning of defeat. It has taught me to seek out the shy student who can't make eye contact, to befriend the colleague whom others ostracize, to go against the grain of the popular and the accepted way of doing things. It's a lesson I first learned from my chief collegiate professor, Paul Barrus. I'll never forget the day when, quietly and without any dramatic sense of self-importance, he explained the deep lines in his face. He said that these creases of care were his battle scars. They were the marks of his spiritual suffering. They are what gave him true Christian character.

III

When the apostle Paul speaks of suffering, he also refers to the political persecution that had befallen the Christians in Rome, especially under the emperor Nero. Such suffering may seem utterly irrelevant to our own situation, since most of us will never have to suffer publicly for our faith. Yet we must never forget that there were more Christian martyrs in the twentieth century than in any other century in history. And if our own witness were radically Christian, it would also produce public suffering, even here in America. If our churches were communities of character, the world would be breaking down the doors to get in, or else it would be committing arson to burn us out.

To be the friend of God is necessarily to court opposition. If we love God and our neighbors and our enemies as Christ commands and enables to do, we are sure to make other folks scorn us. Nor are our enemies always far off. Chesterton says that the Bible commands us to love our neighbors and our enemies because they are usually the same people. It's hard to love the person next door, or even the one in the next room. In *The Brothers Karamazov*, Dostoevsky's character Katerina Ivanovna says that she can love humanity with no problems. But when she's put in the same room with another person, she climbs the walls. The neighbor is the one who is near rather than far — the one who knows our faults even as we know hers.

After September 11, 2001, many people have become numb with unconcern about their neighbors. A friend wrote me recently to say that he no longer trusts anyone or anything; the whole world seems full of serpents. Terrorism is now a permanent threat to our existence. Fear overwhelms our peace, dread stamps out our hope. A cousin who lives on Long Island tells me that his neighborhood remains devastated by the destruction of the World Trade Towers. We, too, would certainly be spiritually flattened if scores of our own neighbors had stepped out their doors that morning never to return. Yet we Americans remain a desperate and hopeless people exactly to the extent that we have lost hope in the God who has already established eternal life in our midst.

George Orwell, the eminent social critic who was no sort of Christian, said that loss of belief in immortality has done more damage to modern life than any other thing. Hoping for nothing beyond this world, we cannot "hope beyond hope." It is St. Paul, once again, who reminds us whence comes our hope that life and not death shall finally prevail. If Christ be not raised from the dead, he declared, and if we have our hope only in this world, we are of all people most desperate. My favorite minister has requested that, if ever a tombstone is erected over his ashes, it contain but a single declaration: "Nothing matters but the Resurrection." For it is the risen Lord who alone grants the mercy that produces character. He alone gives us the character that is built upon suffering. He alone enables us patiently to bear our suffering through endurance. And this endurance rests on the single hope that does not fail us: the love of God in Christ Jesus that has been poured into our hearts by the Holy Spirit. Amen.

Christians as the Little Ones, the Hobbits of the World

Luke 17:1-10

Good Shepherd Community Church
Toronto, Ontario
September 19, 2004

Valley Covenant Church
Eugene, Oregon
October 10, 2004

First Baptist Church
Winston-Salem, North Carolina
September 11, 2005

Our world worships bigness, largeness, grandiosity. We Americans — especially we Texans! — like things that are outsized. For us denizens of the world's most powerful nation, the biggest is always best: the biggest economy, the biggest military, the biggest profit, the biggest salary, the biggest résumé, the biggest house, the biggest automobile, even the biggest church. Unless your membership numbers at least five thousand, you belong only to a medium-sized church in Texas. Rarely do we ask why our Christian ancestors did not idolize but scorned bigness. To them, largeness of size often meant smallness of mind and spirit. By contrast, the small and the weak, those who are nothing in the world's sight, turn out to be God's chief instruments.

I

In the Old Testament, for instance, we read of the Anakim and the Nephilim, "the mighty sons of old" who strike fear in the Israelites who go to scout out the Promised Land. These monstrous men make the Israelites look like mere grasshoppers in comparison. Yet the wrath of Yahweh, to our great surprise, does not fall on the evil giants who have defied God by cohabiting with the daughters of men. God's fury falls on the Israelites who have refused to trust him to defeat such colossal creatures (Num. 13-14). The heart of the gospel is that God triumphs not by coercion but attraction, not by brute force but by subtle persuasion, not by sword and spear but by cross and resurrection, not by accusation and indictment but by forgiveness and reconciliation, not by the high and mighty but by the small and humble — by the least and the lowliest, by the little people of the kingdom. "The least of these" is a phrase that appears, in fact, throughout the Gospels. "Truly I say to you," declares our Lord, "as you did it to one of the least of these my brethren, you did it to me" (Matt. 25:40). Here Jesus refers, despite popular opinion, not chiefly to the weak and the vulnerable and the helpless — the suffering masses yearning to be free. Instead, he is speaking about the ordinary humble believers who are his followers, his little brothers and sisters. Unless we feed and visit and comfort Christ's "little flock," as he called it, the world has no hope. For it is through these little ones, these ordinary Christians, that God works, not through the swaggering Anakim and Nephilim. Surely, Christ has in mind these same obscure and unnoticed disciples when he declares, in our text for today, that woe and wrath will come to anyone who causes "these little ones to sin": "It would be better if a millstone were hung 'round his neck and he were cast into the sea."

II

Why this biblical obsession with the last and least, with the little people of the kingdom? Why this harsh warning that anyone who leads them astray will meet a terrible judgment, a fate akin to that of a drowning man who is thrown a millstone for a life-jacket. It's for the same reason, I believe, that Tolkien made hobbits the heroes of *The Lord of the Rings*. They, too, are the little ones of Middle-earth. They are the nobodies whom the great ones of the world don't bother to notice, or else whom they scorn as useless and irrelevant. The hobbits' small bodies seem to indicate their insignificant character. And yet it is mainly through these diminutive hobbits — not through the mighty wizards and the kingly men, not through the brilliant elves and the stubborn dwarves — that the demonic Sauron and his orc-forces are finally defeated.

We can surely discern in the hobbits something of a parallel to the little ones who are Christ's witnesses. Unlike such a brave man as Boromir, or even such a brilliant wizard as Saruman, the hobbits have no grandiose ambitions. Neither Bilbo nor Frodo, not Sam nor Merry nor Pippin, wants to be a ruler over others. Worldly power and position mean nothing to them, nor are they driven by aspirations of bigness and control. They do not desire to dominate anything. Neither are the hobbits gadabouts; instead, they remain quite contented in their own little corner of creation called the Shire. There they cultivate their gardens and exercise their crafts. Even their modest homes are low-slung and tunnelly, the smallness of their scale befitting the modesty of their inhabitants. Nor are the hobbits wasteful consumers, since they throw away nothing that has potential use. They do not label their saved-up stuff as mere "junk" but rather *mathom,* the Old English word for "treasure." On their birthdays the hobbits do not receive gifts; they bestow them on others. Thus is their chief delight found in humble things: families and friends, poetry and stories, singing and dancing, hot baths and fresh bread, pipeweed and brown ale, slabs of ripe cheese and cuts of cold meat. The hobbits are such lovers of food, in fact, that they enjoy six meals a day. Not an ounce of SlimFast is to be found in all of Hobbiton!

Someone is likely to protest that is it sheer foolishness to liken Tolkien's undersized creatures to the little ones about whom Jesus speaks. We Christians are called, after all, to be strong and not weak, to fight evil courageously instead of cultivating our gardens contentedly, to sacrifice everything rather than to live pleasantly in the world. That is, we are called not to sing and dance and make merry but to take up our cross and follow Christ, even to the bitter end, which is called death. Yes, these things are indeed the chief requirements of the Christian life, but so are they the same things that Tolkien's hobbits are called to do. Their modest and unpretentious lives enable them, when the crunch comes, to be strong, to fight bravely, to sacrifice everything, to take up the Ruling Ring, and to journey all the way to the bitter end found at the Cracks of Mount Doom, whose volcanic fires alone will melt that fatal band of gold. Yet Frodo and Sam, Merry and Pippin, hear and heed this summons to follow this quest and to destroy the Ring of demonic power, not because they are adventurous but because they are willing to be last and least, the smallest and most obscure, the little people of Middle-earth.

III

Since the world's salvation depends on the little ones who are his disciples, Jesus speaks harshly about anyone who occasions their downfall. Yet who are these unnamed deceivers, these condemned creatures who lead the little ones into sin? Again, Tolkien offers us a clue. Saruman is such an enormously learned wizard that Gandalf holds him in great honor. To his horror, however, Gandalf discovers that Saruman is willing to join forces with Sauron, believing that he can redirect Sauron's vicious power toward noble ends. Initially, Gandalf is impressed with Saruman's argument. How can anything large and permanently good be won in alliance with these weak little halflings called hobbits? Thus is Saruman a believer that good ends justify evil means, and thus is he one of those who will have a millstone hung 'round his neck in the midst of the sea. In fact, Saruman doesn't have to wait for final judgment. One of his own followers, a creep named Grima Wormtongue, cuts off his head.

In the brave warrior Boromir we have an even subtler betrayal of the little ones. Yet Boromir is one of Tolkien's most admirable characters. Rather than cooperating with Sauron, he wants to slay him. Boromir is willing to give up everything, even to die, in order to save the Shire from the assaults of Sauron. But by what means? Boromir wants to seize the Ring with brute force from Frodo in order to use it against Sauron. Unlike Saruman, who wanted to cooperate with evil in order to accomplish good, Boromir is determined to defeat demonic power by means of demonic power: to overcome evil things by evil means. Alas, he thus becomes the analogue of Peter among Jesus' followers. The Fellowship's solidarity is broken not by orc or warg or troll — not even by the wicked wizard Saruman — but by one of their own friends, by a member of the Company, by Boromir.

How many of our churches, I ask, are being led astray by Sarumans and Boromirs? How many Saruman-like pastors are urging their congregations to use evil means to accomplish allegedly good ends? How many Boromir-inspired leaders are urging their congregations to fight evil with evil? Who is dangling these enticing temptations before ordinary humble Christians, the little ones who are Jesus' flock? Who will thus have a millstone for his necklace as he tries to swim in the sea? At the risk of offense, allow me to be specific. Certain church leaders are saying, for example, that if we Christians do not gain political power and national prominence, our witness will be in vain. Many of those leaders clearly believe that Christ's Kingdom will not come unless George Bush is reelected to the presidency, and yet there are almost as many who believe that it will not come unless he is defeated and John Kerry is installed in the White House.

So it is with many of the other hot-button issues of our time. I hear Christian leaders declaring, for example, that if we do not put a stop to homosexual marriages and stand up for traditional family values, both our churches and our culture will collapse. We must organize ourselves into a political movement, they say, and thus take back our country. I confess that I find these sentiments alarming. They sound all too much like something that Saruman might advocate. We Christians never had control of the country in the first place — or if we did, we shouldn't have! The church is not a political organization of either the left or the right. We Christians are not meant to manage the nation-state but to serve as a radical alternative to those who measure things by size and force, even if they are our own elected leaders. God's people are not the Sarumans and Boromirs of the world. We are the little ones, the hobbits whose power lies in our weakness, whose strength lies not in spear and sword but in the quiet force of the gospel.

IV

Notice well that Jesus doesn't attack the godless pagans; he orders his disciples to put their own house in order. The church orders its own house, according to Jesus, when we Christians do not condone but rebuke sin — and then when we forgive those whom we have rebuked, even seven times a day. The apostles are so astonished by this command to forgive unendingly that they cry out for Jesus to increase their faith. They cannot believe that such radical and repeated forgiveness is possible. Instead, they want the evildoers to be cast out and punished. They want a church that lives not by faith but by works, not by grace but by condemnation. Jesus replies that such cold-hearted contempt is the cold core of unbelief: "If you had only the faith that is the size of a mustard seed," he says, "you could perform miracles that are miniscule when compared to the forgiveness of sins: you could pluck up a sycamine tree and make it flourish in the midst of the Mediterranean. And if so little faith could produce so great a feat," he asks, "how much more magnificent would be your power to forgive sins if you had real faith?"

Such forgiveness is not a spectacular accomplishment, says Jesus. It is the ordinary duty and responsibility of every Christian. The mercy and grace of God are the means by which God's little ones work the salvation of the world. Again, Tolkien can help us. When Boromir dies after having slain many orcs in order that Merry and Pippin might escape, Aragorn does not hover over him in angry judgment, condemning him for trying to seize the Ring from Frodo and thus betraying the Company. On the contrary, Aragorn forgives Boromir and enables him to die in peace. Tolkien the Christian is telling us that the world will not be shamed into salvation. Unbelievers will not be saved by our condemnation of their evils. Sin makes nobody truly happy, however much pleasure they may temporarily enjoy and however much power they may briefly possess. Evil punishes and eventually destroys itself, even if it also destroys much good in the process. This solemn fact requires Christians to exercise enormous patience. We must not turn the church into a huge political party that attempts to wrench the world back into shape, accomplishing such alleged good by the swaggering power of votes and elections. The Lamb of God conquers not by slaying but by being slain for the sins of the world in order that we might live by the miracle of forgiveness.

The chief quality of Christ's miraculous forgiveness is that it is meant for those who don't deserve it. Tolkien makes this Christian truth plain in a character named Gollum, a hobbit who deserves death rather than mercy. For Gollum once happened on the all-controlling Ring — the Ring that rules all other rings and gives him the power of invisibility and unending life. Gollum has used it rather modestly, mainly to feed his ravenous appetite for raw fish. But because the Ring enables Gollum to get what he wants by illicit means, by taking advantage even of fish, it has corrupted him. He has come to worship the

Ring. He talks to it as if were an actual person, constantly uttering words of endearment to it: "My precious, my precious." Indeed, Gollum gets his name from his perpetual throat-muttering. Having cut himself off from everyone else, Gollum talks to himself in the language of "we." Thus has he created a pseudo-community of himself and the Ring. Gollum has lost his character, his ability to engage with and to care for others. He lives in total isolation: he is a shadow and parody of himself. He has lost his character, broken his integrity, and thus damned his soul.

Just as Gollum talks to the Ring as if it were his beloved, so does he refer to everyone else as an "it." The Ring has made him depersonalize and even dehumanize others. We, too, have our equivalents of this one ruling Ring, and they make us behave in a similar fashion. Our cars and our homes, our careers and our vacations, our accomplishments and our reputations become our "precious." They cause us to treat others as if they were an "it." These false gods that we worship make us almost invisible to others, so well do they hide us behind their façade. We fear that these substitutes for God that constitute our lives will be taken away from us, and out of this fear we commit most of our evils. It's fear that often causes us to compromise our most basic convictions: fear of not being accepted, fear of not being successful, fear of not belonging, fear of becoming poor.

Having lost possession of the Ring, Gollum is willing to regain it at any cost whatsoever, even if he must kill his fellow hobbits. Gollum is a creature not to be readily trusted; he is indeed an evil hobbit. When Frodo learns that Bilbo has spared him, even though he could easily have killed him, and thus been rid of this palpable menace, Frodo is furious. It is then that the wizard Gandalf declares this crucial truth to Frodo that governs the entire story: "Deserves [death]! I daresay [Gollum] does. Many that live deserve death. And some that die deserve life. Can you give it to them? For even the very wise cannot see all ends. I have not much hope that Gollum can be cured before he dies, but there is a chance of it. And he is bound up with the fate of the Ring. My heart tells me that he has some part to play yet, for good or ill, before the end; and when that comes, the pity of Bilbo may rule the fate of many — yours not least."

This mercy, this radical forgiveness of sins is what enables the little ones of Middle-earth to triumph over Sauron and his fellow Anakim and Nephilim. Such pardon for sin is also our one hope as Christians.

It alone can set the church's own house in order and thus save the world from its grace-denying destruction. The pity of Jesus Christ rules the fate not of many but of all, for God rules the whole world from his Son's cross. And we are the little ones who serve humbly as God's hobbits. Amen.

A Farewell Sermon to a Faithful People

Deuteronomy 32:48-52; 34:5-12; Philippians 4:4-9

Paddington Chapel United Reformed Church
London
June 19, 1988

"I've been to the mountaintop. . . . Like anybody, I would like to live a long life. Longevity has its place. But I'm not concerned about that now. I just want to do God's will. And He's allowed me to go up to the mountain. And I've looked over. And I've seen the promised land. I may not get there with you. But I want you to know tonight, that we, as a people, will get to the promised land. And I'm happy, tonight. I'm not worried about anything. I'm not fearing any man. Mine eyes have seen the glory of the coming of the Lord."

Thus did Martin Luther King Jr. confess his faith, as though in premonition of his own death, only a few days before he was assassinated in April 1968. Five years earlier he had given perhaps the most stirring oration in the history of American religion. He delivered it at the high point of the civil rights movement in 1963, when blacks and whites joined — more than a half a million strong — in front of the Lincoln Memorial in Washington. It was called the "I Have a Dream" speech. For there, like Moses peering into the Promised Land, Dr. King described his own dream-vision of racial reconciliation and liberty in America.

To the thronged thousands, and to the millions more watching on television, he declared in the name of God that the American people would no longer tolerate a political and social system that denied Negroes their fundamental freedoms. "Free at last, free at last," he trumpeted. "Thank God Almighty, I'm free at last." It was indeed a decisive moment. For all the many troubles that would follow, and for all the problems that still remain, this was indeed the turning point. Down would come many of those demeaning barriers that said, either covertly or overtly, "For Whites Only." They had kept black people out of hotels and restaurants, out of schools and universities and churches, even away from public restrooms and drinking fountains.

It was a moment that many of those gathered at Wembley Stadium two Saturdays ago must have hoped to repeat. The evil system of apartheid has done to South African blacks what segregation did to American Negroes: it has made them seem not just inferior and second-class but also subhuman, as if they were not people but animals. Up went a mighty cry of one hundred thousand souls that such evil must be put to an end. And yet something seemed to be missing in the Wembley celebration of Nelson Mandela's seventy years on earth, more than a third of which he has spent in prison. Well-intentioned as they may have been, these rock stars and movie stars lacked Martin Luther King's Moses-like vision of the Promised Land. For King had seen something beyond politics: he had already beheld the land flowing with milk and honey. His eyes had seen the glory of the coming of the Lord. And so he was truly free, free even amidst segregation and discrimination, free because God Almighty had released him from the chains of condemnation. It is thus to the final farewell visions of Moses and Paul that we must we turn if we are to understand what it means to be God's free people in this time and this place.

I. Weep Not for Moses

The Scriptures are unrelenting in their honesty about human sin and divine promise. More than such founding fathers as Abraham and Isaac and Jacob, more even than mighty King David, Moses is the true prophet of Israel. He has led his people out of Egyptian slavery and through their forty years of wandering in the wilderness, now to the edge of the Promised Land. He has been taken up on the mountain and allowed to survey the place of Israel's deliverance. But he has not been allowed to enter it because he broke faith with God. The offense seems so trifling that one can almost miss it. It has to do with Moses' smiting of the rock at Meribah in order to draw forth water for the starving Israelites. Moses' sin is that he takes credit for this miraculous deed as if he had performed it himself, rather than enabling the people see it as the gift of God. But in the world of biblical faith, it is never a trivial matter to claim for oneself the glory that belongs to God: indeed, such is the heart of evil.

When Moses claimed the miracle at Meribah as his own act, he did a deadly thing. He deflected to himself the honor that belongs to God alone. From the greatest to the least, all things are God's and we are but his stewards. George MacDonald once said that the motto of hell is: "We are our own." The counterproposition of heaven is: "We belong to God." Therein lies all the difference that faith makes. To live as if one belonged to oneself is the most massive presumption one can commit. Yet it is, alas, the rule under which our world seeks to live. We want everything to serve our own pleasure and profit, to make us comfortable and contented, to bring us credit and honor. So to live, no matter how cultured or moral or even religious we are, is to break faith with God. It is to sin and thus to die. And it was what prevented the great prophet Moses from crossing over Jordan into Campground.

Yet we are not to weep for Moses. Though he cannot enter it, he is allowed to see the Promised Land and to know that his people will find their blessing there. He has been their leader, and so he remains their exemplar even in his sinfulness. God redeems Moses while denying him fulfillment. Though Joshua is appointed as the successor who will lead Israel to her promised destiny, the Bible is unabashed in declaring that Moses is the greatest of all Israelite prophets. And so we have to be very careful in feeling sad and sorry about Moses going to his death: he is indeed sad, but not despairing; he is unhappy, but not wretched.

Again, there is a great difference. Scripture puts no premium on happiness as the world understands the term. "Happiness" usually means that all is well, that one has no worries or fears, that one is in control of one's life. I can think of no biblical character whom such terms describe. Never do all things go swimmingly for Isaiah and Daniel; never do Amos and Jeremiah live without fear or worry; never do Paul and the disciples claim control of their own lives. John Newton comes much closer to the heart of biblical faith in the third stanza of his great old hymn:

Through many dangers, toils and snares,
I have already come;

'Tis grace has brought me safe thus far,
And grace will lead me home.

It is such divine grace that also leads Moses home. He is not swept up
to heaven in a chariot of fire like Elijah. He resembles both John Calvin
and Wolfgang Mozart in having an unmarked, unknown tomb. This is as
it should be. There is something unseemly about a shrine where people
come to worship dead heroes. Better to praise our forefathers in the faith
by taking up their vision and extending their work than by doing homage at their gravesites. They are not there. They are with God. The Israelites wept thirty days for Moses, but then the time of mourning was
ended. There is a biblical statute of limitations set on tears. We do not
honor our dead by keeping their memories alive with our grief, but by
keeping their faith alive with our belief. Thus did the Israelites enter Ca-
naan without Moses, leaving him behind in his unmarked grave.

II. We Shall Come Rejoicing

St. Paul bids much the same kind of farewell to the church at Philippi.
There are no tearful good-byes. He urges his people instead to rejoice in
the Lord always, to have anxiety about nothing, to make all things
known to God in prayer and supplication. His valedictory contains no
nostalgia. The word "nostalgia" means homesickness, and there is little
room for it in the Christian faith. We are not a backward-looking people. We cannot be homesick in a world where, as Hebrews says, we have
no abiding place. It's not where we've been that counts so much as
where we are going. Satchel Paige, the great pitcher in the Negro
Leagues during the 1930s, said, "Don't look back. Somebody may be
gaining on you!" That's not quite the motive we Christians have for re-
jecting the backward glance. We recall the things God has done yesterday — both his blessings and his judgments — only because they are
signposts that lead us forward today toward the Promised Land. Any
other remembrance of things past produces a sweet melancholy that is
both pernicious and paralyzing.

This is a lesson especially important for a church such as Paddington Chapel. Your former greatness may tempt you to a wistful nostalgia
about the past, and to great grief over the little thing that you have now
shrunk to. But I would be unfaithful if I encouraged such nostalgia.

My duty in this final sermon is to encourage you with the hope and the joy of the gospel. If there is one memory to which you should hold fast, I would propose the following one. During the terrible years of World War II, you canceled only a single service: it was on the dreadful Sunday of September 3, 1939, when war was first declared. Yet some of you have confessed that the Paddington congregation later regretted this suspension of worship. You vowed not to suspend worship again, even though large assemblies were discouraged because they would be vulnerable to massive loss of life. A nearby church at worship did in fact suffer a direct hit by a German bomb, which killed more than a hundred. Yet you Christians at Paddington Chapel gathered every Sunday for worship throughout the Blitzkrieg. You knew that the church is never a place for safety and security; rather, it is always a place of danger because it is first and last a house for the confession of faith and sin, and thus for the praise and service of God.

You have also confessed that your worship was charged with a life-and-death vitality you had never known before. Instead of sentimentally singing, "He speaks and the sound of his voice is so sweet, the birds hush their singing," you rang out the great hymns of gospel substance: "How firm a foundation, ye saints of the Lord, is laid for your faith in his excellent Word." In November 1940 a bomb did indeed strike the church's Mission Hall: it cracked the main wall, collapsed ceilings, and left holes in the roof. Yet the very next week, when the roads were clogged with an early winter snow, the Women's Missionary Society gathered there for regular fellowship. Though an air-raid alert had been sounded, and though a cold wind was blowing through the bomb holes, these women were undaunted. A passerby overheard them singing, "Count your many blessings, name them one by one; count your many blessings, see what God hath done."

Suzanne and I have experienced nothing so dramatic during our six months in your midst. Yet you have been a wondrously receptive and redemptive community: renting to us your lovely manse, inviting us into your homes, taking us on country rides, telling us about your troubles and your triumphs. You have let us bear your burdens and share your joys, even as you have healed our own wounds and given us great happiness. You have treated us not as the strangers whom we would seem to be but as the brother and sister in Christ whom we are. And so you have meant far more to us than all the monuments of culture and art that we have seen.

Such faithfulness as a community of the gospel is your real hope for the future. Such constancy is what will sustain you both personally and congregationally. You are not a dwindling social club but a remnant of the faithful people of God. You are thus empowered by a strength infinitely greater than yourselves — namely, by God's own grace. He is the real source and basis for all of those virtues that Paul lists at the end of his letter to the Philippians: forbearance, freedom from anxiety, peace, prayer, honor, justice, purity, loveliness, graciousness. Note well that Paul does not command us to exemplify these virtues by dint of our own strength. Such would be the counsel of despair, for who of us could ever fulfill even one of these commands? These things surpass all understanding and are thus humanly impossible. But remember the great promise of the gospel: with God all things are possible. And so when Paul commands us to think on these things, he is not talking about idle meditation but about total concentration. And to concentrate means to have but a single center, focusing everything on him who stands at the core of the core: Jesus Christ.

This surely is why Paul heads the list of Christian virtues with the command to rejoice always. There is no final sadness in faith, no tragic resignation to the chances and changes of time. Life surely works its alterations in our lives. Every day brings new difficulties. We are not the same people today that we were yesterday. But there is never an occasion that does not permit rejoicing. Not old age nor the loss of our powers, not the decline of the church nor the decay of society, not even the death of friends nor the end of life — nothing can separate us from the love of God in Christ Jesus. His death has put an end to death. Now there is no looking back. We have seen the Promised Land even if we haven't entered it. The one command that must ring always in our ears, therefore, is the injunction to rejoice and to rejoice again. There is much seed yet to be sown, many fields yet to be harvested. Our promise lies in the hope voiced in the declaration of the old gospel hymn that Suzanne and I grew up singing in our small-town Baptist churches of northeast Texas: "We shall come rejoicing, bringing in the sheaves." Amen.

The Rock That Springs with the Water of Life

Exodus 17:1-7; John 4:5-30; Romans 5:1-11

DaySpring Baptist Church
Waco, Texas
February 24, 2008

It is reported that Karl Barth, the greatest theologian of the twentieth century, was asked what he would have said to Hitler if he could have encountered the monstrous man who was destroying Europe and who would likely ruin the whole world if he were not stopped. Barth's interlocutor assumed that he would offer a scorching prophetic judgment against the miscreant's awful politics of destruction. Barth replied that such accusations, though true, would have caused Hitler to defend himself. "Germany lies in financial ruin," Hitler would have replied. "We were dealt with unjustly in the Treaty of Versailles ending the First War. And the Jews are destroying our sense of national identity." And on and on.

Barth knew all too well that the Reichschancellor was just like us: we can justify every sin that we have committed. To accuse someone of evil is almost always to get a diatribe of recrimination in response. When we pummel them, they pummel us. But to the word of forgiveness there can be no self-defense. Instead of offering a vigorous counterargument against Hitler, or even assailing his many barbarous acts, Barth said that he would have simply quoted Romans 5:8: "While we were yet sinners, Christ died for us." To my mind, these are the most precious ten syllables in our native tongue. Nothing less than God's mercy could have prompted a fiend such as Hitler — just as it can also prompt sinners such as you and me — to repent and be redeemed.

When friend or enemy forgives us, or when we forgive enemy or friend, there are only two responses: either acceptance or rejection. And if we accept forgiveness, it's not because we humiliate ourselves in groveling shame. It's because the gracious act enables our gracious response. Theologians call it "prevenient grace," the grace that comes before and makes possible our very embrace of it. Receiving and embracing God's forgiveness leaves us nothing to do but the most important thing of all: to correct the evils for which we have been forgiven. This is the point that we are meant to learn again in Lent. Though we deserve nothing, God provides and enables everything necessary: "While we were yet sinners, Christ died for us" — the ten most precious syllables in our mother tongue.

I. We Are a People Thirsting for More Than Water

The first lesson from Exodus 17 deals with the Israelites as a faultfinding people. They grumbled at God. They murmured and whined. They wearied of wandering for forty years in the wilderness, eating nothing but manna, even though it tasted like wafers with honey. They grew so tired of God's way with them that they sought their own way. They would eventually fashion themselves an idol, an image of the god whom they wished they had followed: a snorting, pawing, horn-thrusting bull, a brute male deity of sheer potency. No wonder Moses smashed it to dust.

Yet we must not judge the Israelites too harshly. Like them, we also want deliverance now — not tomorrow, much less sometime in the far future. God has sent us into these forty days of repentance, asking us to feed off nothing but the manna of contrition. The color of this season is purple, the hue of the bruised conscience, the tint of the battered heart. Thus should we remember that we are indeed like the Israelites, a guilty people. Like theirs, ours is a barren world, ours a dry and barren time. The narrator in Evelyn Waugh's *Brideshead Revisited* (1945) describes our plight with a telling analogy: "When the water holes are dry," says Waugh, "people seek to drink at the mirage." We Texans know that, when the brilliant summer sun would glint off the old concrete highways, it would give the appearance of a lake at the bottom of the hill we had just topped. Then it would vanish as we approached it. Yet we're trying to drink there.

I need to name only a few of the many mirages from which we are seeking to drink: our titillating escapism built largely on violence and pornography; our deadly boredom during a singularly unedifying political campaign; our massive greed for creature comforts and technical gadgets, when much of the Third World starves or else dies of malnutrition as well as curable diseases; and, perhaps worst of all, our moral numbness to the genocide in Darfur, the violence in Iraq and Afghanistan and Pakistan, the endless strife between the Israelis and the Palestinians. These are the waterless mirages that Lent calls us to abandon. We are called to turn, instead, to the true water that nourishes our parched lives and deserted culture.

Unlike us, the Israelites were dying of literal thirst no less than spiritual thirst. Unlike our forty days of Lenten penitence, they would eventually wander for forty years in the wilderness of Sinai. Having been delivered from Egyptian slavery, they had been promised a land flowing with milk and honey. Instead, they had come to a place called Horeb, which means "barrenness." Surely God's people had cause for their complaint, and surely we must sympathize with their lament against Moses their leader. "Why did you bring us up out of Egypt," they cried, "to kill us and our children and our cattle with thirst?"

Yes, God hears Israel's plea. Yes, He supplies his people with their most immediate need — water, the source of life. Yet we must note ever so well that God does not act on Israel's terms. Indeed, Yahweh is angry that Israel has demanded that he demonstrate his faithfulness, as if he would not otherwise have made good on his promise. And so, to remind Israel that his provision is always miraculous rather than something obvious and thus to be taken for granted — a mere matter of stopping long enough to dig a well — God has Moses strike a solid rock, the least likely place to find a hidden spring of water. Such is always the nature of our complaint, and such is always the nature of God's grace. He grants us not what we want so much as what we need: he quenches our spiritual no less than our physical thirst. Therefore, Lent reminds us of the real miracle: "While we were yet sinners, Christ died for us."

II. We Are a Well-Watered People

The question is not whether the Horeb event, like most other biblical events, can be proved or disproved via the tools of science and history.

Be assured that St. Paul used no such addle-pated literalism when he interpreted this story. The real question, as he understands it, is not whether it happened but what it means? Paul asked the question that almost all of our ancestors in the faith have asked: Where is Christ mysteriously figured in this event? How is the whole pattern of salvation already present here? Listen to these words he addresses to the church at Corinth in order to distinguish between an apostle and a professor:

> I want you to know, brethren, that our fathers were all under the cloud, and all passed through the sea, and all were baptized into Moses in the cloud and the sea, and all ate the supernatural food, and all drank the supernatural drink. For they drank from the supernatural Rock which followed them, and the Rock was Christ. (1 Cor. 10:1-4)

How remarkable! The crossing of the Red Sea was Israel's baptism. The daily manna on which Israel fed was the body of Christ. The water that gushed from the side of the rock was the blood of Christ. And the rock that Moses struck was none other than Christ himself! And that's not all. Christ, the new Moses, was not only leading Israel under the guise of the old Moses; he was also following them like the Hound of Heaven, making sure that they arrived in the Promised Land of salvation. Other ancient commentators also link the day-cloud and the night-fire to the Holy Spirit's guiding presence. Thus are we Christians none other than the original Israel in contemporary form as the ecclesial people of God! Yet we know it only because our foreparents in the faith were not afraid of allegory. Indeed, it was their spiritual meat and drink. They read Scripture through types and antitypes, through foreshadowings and fulfillments, through analogies and likenesses — not to play a mere game but to make us messengers of the good news that "while we were yet sinners, Christ died for us."

Our lectionary texts make a similar link between Moses' striking water from the rock at Horeb with Jesus' encounter with the Samaritan woman at the well of Jacob. It may have been the well where Jacob met his long-awaited wife Rachel and drew water for her. Except here the roles are reversed, though the gender difference remains at the fore. The nameless woman is startled that Jesus would approach her. Ancient rabbis did not speak to women in public, especially not to despised Samaritan women. What is going on here? We must not jump too quickly to a figural reading of this encounter. For it's blazing noon, Jesus has traveled far, and he's both weary and thirsty. He wants a deep drink of refreshing water from this well that is no mere cistern but an opening to underground springs. So must we remind ourselves that the needs of the world are rarely spiritual alone but also physical. Jesus warns sharply against our failure to feed the hungry, to give drink to the thirsty, to visit the prisoners and the shut-ins. We do not belong to Christ's people unless we do these things, as Matthew 25 makes clear.

Yet we must also be clear about the distinction between the two kinds of water and thus the two kinds of ministry. The Samaritan woman learns it slowly but clearly. At first she thinks Jesus is a prophet because he knows that she has been married five times but is now living out of wedlock. Thus has she added adultery to her outcast character. Yet Jesus does not scold her — either for failing to recognize that he is more than a prophet, or for living in a state of sin. Instead, he reverses roles, from being the one who asks for water to the one who gives. "Those who drink of the water that I give," says Jesus, "shall never thirst again." Instead, they shall become springs of "water welling up to eternal life."

Perhaps sensing that her kindness to him will make her receptive to the Good News, Jesus eventually informs the Samaritan woman that he is the long-expected Christ, the Messiah of Israel. We are told only that she left her water jar and went about asking whether it could be true that the Water of Life actually springs from this man Jesus? Yet we can surmise that she did something else. Having received the living water of transforming forgiveness, we can be assured that she also brought an end to her adulterous life, not in guilt but in gratitude. So are we called to do as she did — to live according to the Good News. For no matter how arid our culture, no matter how great our guilt and thus our thirst, we are offered the water of life, the cup of salvation, the sign that "while we were yet sinners Christ died for us"?

III. We Are Meant to Serve as Living Water for Others

With every divine blessing comes a divine command. There is no cheap grace, no quenching of our thirst that doesn't prompt us to quench the thirst of others. Salvation is free precisely because discipleship is so costly. Because we pay nothing for it, we give everything in return. Francis Cardinal George, the archbishop of Chicago, put the matter well when he said, "Our job as Christians is to spend our lives trying to convince ourselves and others that suffering and death are good for us." This surely is the heart of Christ's promise to the Samaritan woman. Those who drink from his cup shall gladly suffer and even die in order that others might not suffer and die of physical or spiritual thirst.

What would it mean for us, in this time and this place, to become springs of water welling up to eternal life? Remember that, for Jesus, "eternal life" does not mean pie-in-the-sky-by-and-by. It means God's kingdom beginning here and now, even as it shall be made perfect and complete there and then. Let two examples suffice, both of them personal and local. I know that preachers aren't supposed to use personal illustrations, but then, I'm not a preacher. And I have permission to use these stories.

Celina Varela, as her name indicates, is Hispanic. Her parents worked very hard to see that she would receive a good education. She did. In fact, after attending Baylor University, she finished at the top of her class at Truett Seminary, where I had the honor of teaching her. With such a fine academic record, Celina was poised to pursue virtually any kind of ministry that God might lead her to, perhaps to some prestigious place where her salary would be commensurate with her fancy title, and she would "make her parents proud," as we like to say. And yet the Christ standing at Jacob's well led Celina to drink a different cup of water. He led her to get rid of all the possessions that would not fit into her second-hand clunker and to strike out for Chicago. There she lives communally with a mainly Mennonite group called Reba Place, an inner-city ministry that seeks to bring both kinds of water to the down-and-out of Evanston, Illinois. Her parents understand, I might add, that Celina is paying them the highest possible tribute. For they did not rear her "to make a name for herself," but to be a servant of Christ, doing work that the world doesn't bother to reward.

Matt Waller is also a Baylor alumnus, the son of Baptist missionaries to South America, an honors graduate who could have easily made his way to graduate school or to a well-paying job in the business world. Instead, Matt has spent this year teaching the poor people of Bolivia and Ethiopia how to dig wells, so that they may literally have fresh water to drink — but also to let them know that the ground water is a sign of the Spring that wells up to eternal life. Instead of grumbling about the low pay and the hard conditions, Matt has recently written to say that he almost feels guilty about having so great a privilege. I quote him: "At the moment, this trip is almost purely selfish. I love the well drilling, the tangible hard day's work, the rural setting, [the] rural people, and so forth. I don't think that I could say, in good conscience, that I'm making any sacrifices. I grew up in a third-world country, and I've missed the lifestyle. . . . Surely the yoke is too easy, the burden too light, for this experience to be a sacrifice."

Neither Celina nor Matt asked God to promise rewards in exchange for their service. God forbids such selfish deals, such faithless tests of his goodness. Instead, these young people are doing what Lent calls us all to do: to drink from the crystal fountain that will never run dry, from the Spring of living water that wells up to eternal life. Lent calls us to bypass mirages, to tap this Rock from whom our salvation pours forth, to remember that, "while we were yet sinners, Christ died for us." Come, let us eat of this manna and drink from this cup. Amen.

PART IV

DOCTRINE AND THE MORAL LIFE

Christians and Jews: Wayfarers through the Wasteland

Genesis 17:1-4, 7-14; Ephesians 4:1-7

St. Charles Avenue Baptist Church
New Orleans, Louisiana
January 23, 2003

Highland Park Baptist Church
Austin, Texas
May 16, 2004

Frederick the Great, the Prussian emperor in the eighteenth century, was not only a fierce skeptic in general but also a cultured despiser of religion in particular. Hence the doubting king's tart question to his personal physician, a Swiss doctor named Zimmerman: "Give me even a single proof for God's existence," asked the king. Zimmerman instantly answered: "Your majesty, consider the Jews!" The Southern writer Walker Percy shares this same conviction that the Jews constitute a divine sign. Repeatedly in his novels and essays, Percy confesses his fascination with — rather, his astonishment at — the presence of Jews, especially Jews in America. Binx Bolling, the protagonist of *The Moviegoer*, says that his neck prickles whenever he passes a Jew in the streets of New Orleans. Zimmerman and Bolling are astonished for the same reason: there is simply no accounting for the survival of this tiny company of persecuted (and sometimes, alas, persecuting) tribe except as the chosen people of God.

The same should be true of us Christians. There should be no way to account for our existence except as a people who belong to Jesus Christ. Both our friends and enemies should have no other means of explaining our lives except as we are members of Christ's community called the church. Take away our Christianity, and our lives should make no sense. Take away the gospel and the church, and we should remain an enigma both to ourselves and the world. So it is with our Jewish friends and neighbors. They share our most basic conviction. Against the modern secular assumption that we belong first and last to ourselves, Christians and Jews believe that we belong to a divinely constituted community that exists to show the world its true way and to remind the world of its true story. And this means that we will never be entirely at home in this world. Instead, we will remain lifelong wayfarers and pilgrims on the pathway to the kingdom of God. The synagogue and the church have completely reoriented our lives, giving us a new identity both outwardly and inwardly.

I

Until 1948, the Jews had no land, no temple, no constitution, no government, no monarch or president — virtually nothing at all, except their identity as Jews. Yet they had somehow survived. There are some Jews, and not Gentiles alone, who believe that the Palestinians were done a considerable injustice when the Western powers seized their land and homes in order to create the state of Israel. Those powers made it into a homeland for the Jews whom these same American and European governments would not give eager refuge either before or after the Holocaust. However that may be, one fact about the Jews remains virtually uncontested: every other human tribe and nation has risen and fallen and eventually disappeared, from such eminent civilizations as the Etruscans and Minoans, the Aztecs and the Incas, to such obscure ones as the Amorites and the Jebusites and the Hittites. "Where are the Hittites?" Percy has one of his philo-Jewish characters sardonically ask. The Jews are the one exception to this dread rule governing all peoples and even civilizations: they rise and then fall, they flourish and then wither like leaves of grass. All smaller cultures are eventually assimilated into the larger ones that surround and overwhelm them. But the people Israel are the astonishing exception to that rule, and thus do they constitute a divine sign, perhaps the one proof of God's existence. The reason is clear: the covenant that God made with Abraham has never been broken, and the Jews have never been destroyed, not even by Hitler's massive and nearly successful attempt to exterminate them.

Yet it's a Covenant that is sealed in a strange way that we moderns must not lightly dismiss. The male Jew becomes a son of the covenant by circumcision, the removal of the foreskin of his penis. To be a Jew — and I will argue that the same is true of us Christian — is not therefore to cultivate some inwardness of soul, some hiddenness of heart, some secret spiritual essence. Jewish life is an outward and visible life that begins with this quite bodily ritual of circumcision. A Jew is, in the simplest of definitions, a person born of a Jewish mother. Before DNA, it was not possible to prove a child's paternity; but there can be little doubt about the womb from which we issue forth, however dubious our paternal origin. Except in the case of conversion, one doesn't elect to be a Jew. Jewish faith is God's totally unbidden gift to his people called Israel. God's summons came not to a great and mighty nation like the United States, not to a high civilization such as the Greeks or the Romans or the Babylonians. Rather, it came to a wandering Aramean shepherd named Abraham and to his descendants. The Catholic wit Hilaire Belloc put the matter into a neat little ditty later to be popularized by Harry Emerson Fosdick: "How odd of God to choose the Jews." A Jewish wag surmised that God asked every other tribe and clan on earth to be his people, but that they were all smart enough to refuse such a dubious blessing. Then when Israel finally and foolishly accepted, Yahweh gave them the only Middle Eastern country that has no oil.

Far more seriously: since a Jew is a person born of a Jewish mother, the maternal-linking navel is a theological no less than a biological marker of Jewish identity. As inheritors of God's covenant, Jews perform a radical act of faith by bringing children into the world. The birth of a Jewish baby is, by definition, a renewal of the covenant first made by God with Sarah and Abraham, with Rebecca and Isaac, with Rachel and Jacob, perhaps even with Leah. No wonder Elie Wiesel, the Jewish writer and Holocaust survivor, confessed his great reluctance to have children after he lost his entire family in Hitler's concentration camps and after barely surviving himself. If God would not spare six million of his own people, why isn't the covenant irreparably severed, the world wholly abandoned by God, and thus life itself rendered unworthy of propagating? That Jews do indeed give birth to children and thereby extend the covenant thus remains a remarkable thing.

It means that real Jews are people who cannot be defined in any other way than by their Jewishness. Their covenanted faith gives their existence angularity and bite. They should not be mistaken for anything other than Jews. A Jewish friend of mine named Michael Goldberg refuses to deny the central tenets of his Judaism in order to be nice and polite and inoffensive, that is, "just to get along." Goldberg insists, for example, that the letters O.T. do not stand for Old Testament but Only Testament. He also maintains that the initials N.T. are not short for New Testament but for Not True. Goldberg also confesses his hope to become rich enough one day to buy the New York Yankees away from George Steinbrenner. When that day comes, says Goldberg, he will give the Yankees a new name: the New York Jews! Goldberg, I submit, is a serious Jew. He does not want merely to be tolerated but to be engaged and taken seriously. Nor does he want us Christians to repudiate our own core convictions for the sake of interreligious etiquette. For him, as for other serious Jews, the messiah has not yet come, and we Christians are thus deluded in believing that a crucified second-rate rabbi named Jesus is the one uniquely and finally anointed by God.

What, then, could make Goldberg and all other Jews our companions in faith? It does not mean that, like them, we have enjoyed such a new birth of freedom in this country that we are sharers in the American success story. Manfred Vogel, a wise professorial rabbi once put the matter to me with appropriate sharpness: "While America has been good for Jews," he said, "it has been bad for Judaism." What he meant is that the United States has, on the whole, provided Jews a splendid haven from persecution, giving them a marvelous new birth of both political and economic freedom. Alas, he added, many Jews have mistaken such freedom for the ultimate good, and thus they have left off the practices of their faith. They have forgotten that Judaism is not a vaguely spiritual but a concretely practical religion.

By "practical" I mean the outward and visible practices that make Jews both become and remain Jews. The kosher laws are the most obvious examples, but there are also strict provisions for sexual practices as well. They determine, for instance, the times of the month when sexual intercourse is permitted. Stanley Hauerwas is fond of quoting a Jewish friend of his who says that he would never take seriously any religion that didn't tell him what to do with his pots and pans and his genitals. For it is by such odd notions about cooking and eating and having sex that Jews remain strangers and wanderers in the world, pilgrims and wayfarers through the wasteland of modern American culture. No wonder, then, that the author of the book of Hebrews declares that the people of Israel are seeking a new homeland, a better country, a heavenly city, one with true foundations because its builder and maker is God. "Therefore, God is not ashamed to be called their God, for he has prepared for them a city."

It remains a simple but astonishing fact that the Jews have never been totally assimilated. They have never been absorbed by their host cultures like countless other ethnic and religious groups — like so many water drops falling into the all-absorbing ocean. Our observant Jewish friends have often been unwilling to bow down and worship the tin gods of capitalism or socialism, of nationalism or materialism. These Jewish worshipers of the one true God have refused to genuflect even before the golden god of toleration. They have sought to honor the high and noble achievements of our nation's founding fathers and mothers only within proper limits. America has indeed given the world a new birth of freedom: the political freedom to participate in the governance of our lives, the economic freedom to prosper from the labors of our hands and minds, the religious freedom not to have our conscience coerced in matters of faith. Great and splendid gifts are these we enjoy here in America, and it is right and good to honor and praise these immense achievements on this weekend of the presidential inauguration. But it is also right and good to recall and give thanks for our Jewish colaborers in biblical religion for teaching us that America must never become our deity, but rather that we and they shall never have any other god but God.

II

It is little wonder that Hitler hated the Jews. They would not be assimilated into becoming "good Germans." They would not idolatrously sing "Deutschland, Deutschland über alles." Their religion was far too thorny and particular for it to be absorbed into such high "spiritual" ideals as *Blutbrüderschaft*, the brotherhood of race and nation. Karl Barth, the Swiss theologian and enemy of Hitler, insisted that every anti-Semite is, by definition, a hater of Jesus Christ: to despise Jews is to despise the Jew named Jesus. The rabbi born to Mary and raised in Joseph's carpentry shop is, for us Christians, the ultimate Jew. If Hitler had been consistent in his anti-Semitism, he would have sought to exterminate not only the Jews but also the Christians. Alas, he didn't need to. Most German Christians had already conformed their faith to their politics. There was little if any difference between being German and being Christian. I fear that this may be our condition as well. Many — perhaps even most — of us think of ourselves as Americans first and as Christians only second, if not third or fourth. We largely equate American democratic ideals with the bedrock claims of the Christian faith, forgetting that, while they do often overlap, they also conflict with and contradict each other.

Perhaps more than any other modern Protestant theologian of the twentieth century, Karl Barth grasped these conflicts and contradictions. As the author of the Barmen Declaration, a joint Protestant statement protesting Hitler's attempt to suborn the church to the state, Barth was ousted from his teaching post at the University of Bonn in 1939. He had refused to take an oath of loyalty to Hitler, and he had preached a sermon whose present-tense verb in the title, though it is a biblical phrase, was deemed outrageous: "Salvation Comes from the Jews." Returning to Bonn in 1946, Barth helped his students understand that the attempted extermination of the Jews was the *necessary* and not the *incidental* consequence of Nazi politics:

> A nation which . . . chooses itself and makes itself the basis and measure of everything — such a nation must sooner or later collide with the truly chosen people of God. In the proclamation . . . of such an elect nationality there is already . . . a basic denial of Israel and therewith a denial of Jesus Christ and therefore, finally, of God himself. Anti-Semitism is the form of godlessness beside which, what is usually called atheism . . . is quite innocuous.*

So it is with us. To declare that the United States of America is God's exceptional nation, "the last, best hope of earth" — as if we were immune from the sins that afflict nations and peoples — is to practice the ultimate atheism. It is to deny not only Israel as God's unique people but also Jesus Christ and his church as the only objects of our absolute allegiance.

Surely someone will say, "But we Americans are in no danger of any such hatred or scorn for Jews, much less persecution of them. The Holocaust could never happen here." Alas, it is not so. It could indeed hap-

---

* *Dogmatics in Outline* (Harper and Row, 1959), p. 77.

pen here. Wendell Berry, the Baptist poet and prophet from Port Royal, Kentucky, declares that it has already happened here. Our removal of the First Peoples from their native lands was the first American holocaust, and I would add that our enslavement of black people was the second. We will commit such outrages yet again if we fail to join the Jews in practicing the outward and visible life of faith, thus making the church of Jesus Christ stand as concrete evidence for God's existence. As Zimmerman said to Frederick the Great, "Your majesty, consider the Jews!" so must it be said to the world rulers of this present evil age: "You benevolent tyrants and wicked terrorists, consider the church of Jesus Christ!"

What is our chief visible marker as Christians? What identifies us unmistakably as bearers of the cross? Just as the Jews (at least the men!) are religiously marked by their circumcision, so are we Christians sacramentally marked by our baptism. We are the people whom God has inducted by water and the Spirit into the unique community. Baptism has been, after all, the very essence of our Baptist tradition. We have not baptized everyone automatically, but only those who seriously understand that, in baptism, they have died and risen and been sealed with Christ. Even so, baptism remains the church's act and gift, and we remain its recipients. We ourselves assent to live the life of faith, but we do not baptize ourselves. Therefore, the baptistery is not a washing basin so much as it is a watery tomb, a liquid grave into which we plunge believers into a death by drowning, only to raise them up again like newborn children, their wet hair stuck to their scalp as if from their mother's womb.

The church of Jesus Christ is the extension and fulfillment of the promise God made to Abraham that he would be the father of a great nation and a blessing to all the peoples of the earth. And just as the command was given to Abraham to circumcise all Jewish males on the eighth day, so does Christ command us to go into all the world in order to teach and preach and baptize in his name. Let me be as lucid as I can: baptism is the Christian equivalent of circumcision. It is the outward and visible sign that God has adopted us as his people, that our ultimate allegiance has been transferred from family and friends, from nation and culture, to the kingdom of God. It is in those waters that we are given the armor necessary to combat the principalities and powers, the world rulers of this present darkness, and thus to remain wanderers and pilgrims in the wasteland of modern pagan culture.

This is the single truth that I have the most difficult time persuading my Baylor students to take seriously. For them, Christian faith is largely a Lone Ranger affair (forgetting that even he had Tonto as his companion). The Christian life often means little more than a private and individual relationship to Jesus as it is cultivated through prayer and Bible study and fellowship. Now these things can all be good things, but there is no reason to call them distinctively Christian. For these things also are dangerously subjective and thus delusory — as when, for example, students believe that Jesus finds them parking places. Against such subjectivist belief, I offer my own original but succinct formulation: to be a Christian is to belong to Christ's body that is called the church, and thus to observe its outward and visible practices. And the chief public act that makes us Christians — the one that gives us a new name and a new identity — is the act of baptism. Our real name is no longer Ralph Wood or Steven Meriwether, George Bush or John Kerry, but . . . Christian. Nor is baptism a temporary pledge. It's a permanent and irreversible thing. We cannot divorce the church. Our names are inscribed in the Lamb's Book of Life.

This, then, is the Good News that makes us Jews of a different order: we are not first of all male or female, not homosexuals or heterosexuals, not Republicans or Democrats, not Asians or Americans, not Caucasians or Cajuns, not rich or poor, not black or brown, not handsome or homely, not even sick or well. We are first and last and always Christians whose allegiance has been transferred from this world to the kingdom of God. What unutterably good news this is! The body of Christ is the world's only multicultural, multiethnic, multinational community: the kingdom ruled by the Jewish Savior named Jesus, the one in whom God has reconciled the world unto himself. Through it alone can we come to our true homeland, our abiding city. Through it alone can we escape the culture of death. And through it alone can we find the culture of life and thus finally cease our wandering. Amen.

The Scandal of Our Redemption

Luke 7:18-23

First Presbyterian Church
Kerrville, Texas
March 21, 1999

Jesus utters one of the strangest sayings in the New Testament when, in Luke 7:23, he declares: "Blessed is he who takes no offense at me." What makes this saying so strange is that Jesus has just been reminding the disciples of John the Baptist about the mighty and miraculous deeds they have seen him perform: how he cleansed the lepers, how he made the blind see, the lame walk, the deaf hear, the dead rise up, and the poor hear the gospel. Then he adds those odd words about the blessedness of those whom he does not offend. Jesus' baffling sentence can be translated even more literally: "Happy are those who are not scandalized by me." Such a rendering makes things even worse. Who would be scandalized at Christ's wondrous works of goodness and grace? Aren't Jesus' saving acts of rescue and release the very things we all want and need? Why would anyone take offense at them? Isn't it the mark of a confused professor — indeed, the sign of an egghead whose brains have been fatally scrambled — that he should come to declare "the scandal of our redemption"? Shouldn't we insist, instead, that salvation in Jesus Christ is something soothing and comforting, something consoling and cheering, something inoffensive and unscandalous?

It is the mark of the courage of your pastor, Tom Currie, if not his foolhardiness, that he has invited this layman to give lectures about a scandalous Southern writer named Flannery O'Connor and to preach a sermon on what is outrageous and offensive about our redemption in

Jesus Christ. If there is any excuse for the double whammy to which you are being subjected, you can blame it on John Calvin. I confess that I have taken my own theological bearings, at least indirectly, from this first and most original and incisive of all Presbyterians. Yet Calvin has suffered the worst press of any theologian in the history of the Christian church. He is remembered chiefly for burning Servetus at the stake, and for setting up a rigid theocracy in Geneva, where both public and private life was strictly governed. Yet we should remember that, by the standards of the sixteenth century, Calvin's measures were actually quite mild, though to explain is not to excuse.

Many people persist in regarding Calvin as so joyless a creature that he must have chewed grass for breakfast and crunched dirt for dessert. Calvin's portraits do indeed depict him as a dour and glum figure, with his narrow face and pointed beard making him look quite formidable. No wonder that the American satirist H. L. Mencken defined Calvinists (i.e., Puritans) as those gloomy souls who go about in the dread fear that somewhere, somehow, somebody might be happy. One of my atheist friends says that he doesn't believe in God because all our Christian gabbing about the love of God seems to him but so much wishful thinking, the desire of lonely and desperate people to find comfort and hope when there is none. Yet this same atheist friend has also confessed to me that, if he ever is converted, he will become a Calvinist. "Why?" I asked in puzzlement. "Because," he replied, "nobody could have thought up anything as crazy as Calvinism!" The notion that God predestined some of his human creatures for salvation and others for perdition, even before they were created, much less fallen, is indeed a fiendishly difficult doctrine, though we should make sure that we have understood it before we dismiss it, much less ridicule it.

I have come to declare that, appearances to the contrary, John Calvin is preeminently a theologian of grace. Few people know that Calvin described Christians as *les débonnairs,* the good-natured and glad-hearted. Calvin was so debonair, in fact, that when his friends urged him to join Luther and the other Reformers in breaking the rule of priestly celibacy by marrying, Calvin instructed them to go pick out a wife for him. They did so, and he married this widow with a child. Calvin was also debonair about death. So little was he concerned about his personal legacy that he didn't bother to designate a burial place or to set up a monument. Even until this day, we don't know where Calvin is interred in the Geneva cemetery. Hence my contention that John Calvin was the debonair apostle of Jesus Christ because he proclaimed the redemption that is supremely happy because it is supremely scandalous.

I. The Twin Parties Scandalized by God's Grace

Why does Jesus warn that he is likely to give offense? I believe that it is precisely because he performs mighty works of deliverance. We resent these miracles of transformation because they represent a terrible threat to our own sufficiency. We want to save ourselves. We don't want anyone else to liberate us. We dread the wonder of restored sight and hearing, the miracles of ambulation and healing and newness of life, and above all, the staggering surprise of the Good News being preached to the poor. All such deliverances put us and the world in utter dependence on Jesus Christ. This is what we don't want, and thus are we scandalized and offended when he makes these things the very marks of his kingdom.

There are two chief kinds of offended and scandalized folks. First, there are those many souls who seem to get along quite well by themselves: we call them humanists and secularists. Surely, we all have friends who are not worshiping God on this Sunday morning because they see no need to confess sin or to seek redemption. They have made their way through life by their own wits and gumption. Henry David Thoreau was one of these folks. A minister is supposed to have asked the dying Thoreau whether he had made his peace with God. Thoreau gave the preacher a supremely witty and pagan answer: "I'm wasn't aware that we had ever quarreled." Our secular neighbors have no quarrel with God because they have no concern with God. They find sufficient satisfaction in their friends and families, in their homes and gardens, in their movies and sports, in their volunteer work at the schools and in the civic clubs.

One of my friends recently confessed that his own "church of choice" is Habitat for Humanity. To such humanists, all of our God-bothering is a foolish extravagance, a huge waste of money and time. They argue that our massive expenditures on preachers and teachers and musicians, on lovely sanctuaries and elaborate services, could be much better spent on the hungry and the homeless, those who have real material needs as most of us do not. The poor don't need to have the gospel preached to them; they need bread and jobs. The moral and self-sacrificing humanists who make such claims are rightly scandalized by the Christian claim that their lives have lasting worth only in re-lation to Jesus Christ. They are justly offended by the declaration that he alone is the way, the truth, and the life. They are understandably outraged at the command to get off their Habitat for Humanity lad-ders and to come crack their knees at the altar of God.

Lest we Christians take any comfort in the discomfort of our hu-manist neighbors and friends, we should remind ourselves that there is a second set of folks who are offended by the radical redemption wrought in and by Jesus Christ. I refer, of course, to us Christians. We are scandalized in subtle, even deeply religious, ways. We believe that our religious works can compel God's grace and favor, thus allowing us to earn our salvation. And so we read our Bibles diligently, we pray reg-ularly, we go to church frequently, we volunteer for committees and ac-tivities, we even tithe our gross rather than our net income — all in the confident conviction that, since we have been good, God had better be good to us. This is called the pietist ploy: the more pious we are, the more we are tempted to think that God owes us something. We usually think that God owes us prosperity and health and happiness.

Unless we Christians are ever so careful, our faith becomes a strangely selfish proposition. We are tempted to think that, because we have made considerable sacrifices for God, surely he will spare us the ails and ills of mortal flesh. Surely our marriages won't fail, surely our health won't fail, surely our jobs won't end, and surely our children won't cause us endless trouble. When such things happen, as they inev-itably do, we are often offended, even scandalized, at the Christ who has not spared us. One of my former students who was considering giv-ing herself to a religious vocation changed her mind when one of her best friends died from the injuries he had suffered in a freak accident — even after she had prayed for him long and fervently. Why should she serve a God who would not intervene to save this young life full of so much goodness and promise? Thus do we Christians who are scandal-ized by the gospel join Rabbi Kushner in asking why bad things hap-pen to good people.

II. Prevenient Grace

Though the book of Job and the Psalms of Lament ask this question ever so insistently, it is not really the profound question. The rightly offensive question is this: "Why do good things happen to bad people?" Why, indeed, has the supremely good thing, the unbounded love and mercy of God in Jesus Christ, happened to such utterly undeserving creatures as us? It was Calvin who, among the Reformers of the sixteenth century, had the clearest answer to this question and thus the clearest mind about the scandal of our redemption. Following St. Paul and St. Augustine, Calvin taught that God's grace is always prevenient. This a fancy Latinate word that means simply that God's grace comes before and thus enables every good thing that we can imagine or perform, even as it constrains us from the evils that we in our sinful nature would otherwise do.

Permit me a personal instance of prevenient grace. I confess that, insofar as I escaped the usual temptations and torments of adolescence, it was not because I was a pious and righteous youth, the proverbial goody two-shoes. As my childhood friends can copiously attest, I was just as mean and selfish as the next brat. Yet if I managed to avoid some of the more obvious teenage calamities, it was for one reason only: I had a large regard for my parents. I knew that they were such good and generous people that I did not want to violate them. I was not afraid of them so much as I respected them and thus wanted to honor them. It is true, of course, that there were other youths in my hometown who also had good parents and who yet dishonored them. Grace never coerces; it always urges our glad response. No one forced my acts of filial reverence. Yet my freedom to be faithful came not from myself; it was enabled by my parents' free gift of themselves. Unless their goodness had "prevened" and made possible my own, I would not have sought a similar sort of grace for myself. As St. Paul puts it ever so sharply, there can be absolutely no boasting — except through the giver of all grace, Jesus Christ.

John Calvin made a similar point when he observed that the New Testament records both Jesus and John the Baptist as having called to their followers: "Repent, for the kingdom of heaven is at hand." But what the New Testament really means, Calvin candidly added, is exactly the opposite: "The kingdom of heaven is at hand; therefore, repent." The difference is subtle but huge. We are not forced to repent in order to receive God's grace and forgiveness as a consequence of our contrition. We want to repent because Christ has taken our sins upon himself that we might be freed from them. We do not work and worship in the expectation that God will reward us because we have been righteous.

The Scandal of Our Redemption 127

We seek to live in faithful obedience to Christ — glorifying God and enjoying him forever — because he has already made us righteous for his own sake. What divides us from our humanist and secularist friends, therefore, is that they do not know the real source of either their delights or their duties. They believe that these delights and duties are of their own doing; by contrast, we Christians are convinced that they come from the prevenient grace of God.

III. Predestination

It should be evident that I am emphasizing the utter priority and prevenience of God's grace because I believe it lies at the heart of our scandalous redemption in Jesus Christ. "You did not choose me," Jesus says to his disciples in John 15:16, "but I chose you." Paul is even more emphatic: "Those whom he foreknew he also predestined to be conformed to the image of his Son. . . . And those whom he predestined he also called; and those whom he called he also justified; and those whom he justified he also glorified" (Rom. 8:29-30). Here lies the true north of the Calvinist doctrine called predestination, the dreaded P-word that even Presbyterians have become loath to use. It is not difficult to understand why Calvinists have fallen silent about their central dogma. We live in a culture of personal choices, and we worship at the throne of individual preferences. The shopping mall and the cafeteria line are our ideal images of what freedom means: we believe that we are free whenever we can choose for ourselves whatever we want, without anyone telling us what we ought to do. It should come as a shock to us that our Christian ancestors thought this notion of choice to be the very definition of damnation. Our foreparents believed that to choose and to get whatever one wants is not freedom but slavery, not liberty but death.

Why so great a reversal? Our Calvinist forebears understood that the human will is crooked at its core. The human heart, said Calvin, is a factory for the perpetual making of idols. He thus joined Luther and Augustine in speaking of original sin, the disease that we cannot cure by trying harder and doing better. Catholics and Protestants are agreed that we are fallen and sinful creatures at the very center of our being. This does not mean that we are utterly worthless wretches; on the contrary, we remain essentially good because we are made in God's good image. Yet we have forfeited the good that God provided us in creation. Even the best of us has made Adam's sin our own. Like lost sheep, we have all gone astray and awry. There is none righteous, not even one. We are all guilty lambs who have made ourselves helpless prey before the ravenous wolves of sin. We have entered upon a dreadful path that permits no U-turns. Sin is both irreversible and incurable by our own powers. St. Paul says that we are dead in our sins and trespasses. St. Augustine reminds us that corpses don't eventually get tired of their graves and then decide to rise up out of them. We lie dead, alas, in the Procrustean bed of sin that we have so sorrily made for ourselves.

Sin is as pervasive as a blood disease: nothing remains uninfected by our own selfish will. With his typically graphic imagination, Luther said that leprosy is not cured pustule by pustule. Like a crimson stain, sin taints everything that we do. As I tell my students — to their considerable relief! — we commit sin not only from the waist down but, far more fatally, from the neck up. Therefore, to give our fallen human wills unconstrained free choice is not to emancipate but to entrap ourselves. Such sinful "preferences" enable us merely to spin ever more elaborate spider webs of our own bondage. The American shopping mall serves as a convenient image of hell as Dante envisions it in the *Divine Comedy*. As in the thirteenth century, so now: the damned often circle about in an endless sameness, their eyes not blazing in agony but glazed in boredom and emptiness.

Agreeing again with Paul, Calvin taught something even more drastic and scandalous. He taught that we sin against God even more heinously in our good deeds than in our evil acts. Whenever we do generous things, we are tempted to do them for our own gratification. I have a pastor friend who confesses that he gets an adrenaline rush from solving people's problems. Reinhold Niebuhr warned that we are never in such great danger as when we have done something good, for it is then that we are most tempted to smugness and self-congratulation. I remind my students that the one who is leaving her dormitory for church, but stopping to wag a finger of righteous reminder at the student who is bent on her knees at the commode, barfing out the sins of Saturday night, stands in much greater danger of damnation than the pathetic hung-over creature.

The real scandal of God's prevenient and predestining grace is that God refuses to give us what we deserve. He has acted in Jesus Christ to do for us what we could not possibly do for ourselves, namely, to free us from the cocoon of sin and self-interest. These wondrously glad tidings mean that our hope and our worth, our present and our future, our dignity and our honor and destiny are not dependent on our own goodness but on God's grace. It is God who in Christ chooses graciously to dispose himself toward us, and in that gracious divine choice lies our only freedom.

President Clinton seemed not to have understood this great glad news. He felt compelled to make a public act of contrition for his sexual sin in order for God and his countrymen to forgive him. Here is what he confessed: "It is important to me that everybody who has ever been hurt know that the sorrow I feel is genuine." As the culture-critic Jean Elshtain has pointed out, Mr. Clinton was far more concerned that his audience feel his pain than he was willing to admit his sin. Had the president understood the scandalously good news that he is already forgiven, I believe that he would not have made his statement at a national prayer breakfast but before his home congregation at the Immanuel Baptist Church of Little Rock, and with no television cameras or reporters present. There he would have confessed his great gratitude for God's forgiveness, his true sorrow at having violated his Savior as well as his family and friends and indeed the American people. There he might also have promised to perform genuine acts of repentance, namely, by resigning his office and spending his remaining days doing charity and church work in his native Arkansas.

The inevitable question arises: What about those who misuse their freedom, who turn away from grace, who are either contemptuous or indifferent toward God? Doesn't their sinful unbelief cancel God's gracious gift? Paul asks the same question in Romans 3: "What if some are unfaithful? Does their faithlessness nullify the faithfulness of God?" Paul's answer is as unequivocal as it is emphatic: "By no means! Let God be true, though every man be false." Paul does not make sin unserious. Quite to the contrary, sin is now made all the more serious for being committed in the face of God's goodness. As Karl Barth liked to say, hell should be reserved chiefly for Christians! We are the special recipients of divine mercy, and yet we often live as practical atheists, that is, as if God doesn't matter.

Even so, sin and damnation are not the first or the final reality. The one unchangeable fact is God's prevenient and predestining grace. Nothing can separate us from it. What if everyone on earth, Paul asks, were to deny the grace of God? Would it then be negated, rendered null and void? Paul knew that this supreme denial had happened already. It occurred at Golgotha. As the old Negro spiritual makes clear, we *all* were there when they crucified our Lord. There every man and woman, every son and daughter of our original parents, declared themselves utterly false. Yet God remains true now even as then. He answers our graceless No with his own gracious negation of it. And this double negative makes for the grandest of affirmatives: the unbounded Yes of the gospel.

It follows that predestination and prevenience do not chiefly concern who's in and who's out. They are not mainly about the accepted and the rejected. These doctrines declare that God is utterly free and gracious, and thus that he wills for us to be utterly free and gracious. They tell us that God elects us rather than we him. They teach that God chooses us, not for a life of privilege and ease and self-satisfaction, but for a life of service and charity, of abundant joy and true liberty. Karl Barth clarifies this complicated matter in two staggering paradoxes. God condemns us, says Barth, by acquitting us. God imprisons us by flinging wide the cell door. What Barth means by these mind-bending analogies is that we discover the real extent of our guilt when we have stood at the foot of the cross, the very place where God abandoned his Son to our sin in order that we be made innocent. We know the real extent of our freedom when we see that we have imprisoned ourselves in sin, but that God has sprung us free in order to re-enslave us to a joyful life of obedience and gratitude and humility.

This, then, is the happy scandal of our redemption. It is not easy to see, and it is even harder to enact. The call of the cross is not to be pious or to do good, but to throw our lives away into the bottomless well of gratitude to the God who has given us so great a salvation. Freedom lies not in doing what we sinfully and selfishly want, but rather in doing what we faithfully and generously should — namely, in giving ourselves gladly to God and our neighbor. Blessed are those who are not offended at Jesus Christ, for they have happily surrendered all desire to save themselves, seeking and finding their only worth in him. Amen.

Loud, Dogmatic, and Certain: Three Good Christian Words

FACULTY CONVOCATION SERMON

Truett Theological Seminary,
Baylor University
Waco, Texas
January 14, 1999

The best sermon ideas often come from unlikely sources. Matthew Schobert, a seminarian just beginning to feel his own theological oats, recently explained to me why the theology of Karl Barth is an impossible option for a pluralistic and multicultural age such as ours. Barth, said Schobert, renders Christian faith loud, dogmatic, and certain. This young theologian assumed that, like all other civilized souls, I would eagerly agree with him. At a time when diversity and inclusiveness and tolerance are the sacrosanct words, we think it bad taste as well as bad religion to be loud, dogmatic, and certain. The seminarian made it clear that Christians should not be loud but quiet, not dogmatic but open-minded, not certain but tentative. He was properly shocked when I confessed that an authentic witness to the gospel of Jesus Christ is necessarily loud, dogmatic, and certain. I have come, therefore, to defend these good words, not in the name of Karl Barth, but in the name of the good God.

I

I was surprised to find how often the Bible uses the word "loud" in a positive way. The Psalmist calls all the earth to "make a joyful noise unto the Lord," to "make a loud noise, and rejoice, and sing praise" (Ps. 98:4, KJV). Solomon dedicates the newly built temple in Jerusalem by addressing all the assembly of Israel with a loud voice, saying "Blessed be the Lord who has given rest to his people Israel, according to all that he promised; not one word has failed of all his good promise, which he uttered by Moses his servant" (1 Kings 8:55-56). We find more of the same loudness in the New Testament. In Luke's Gospel, Elizabeth greets the news of the Annunciation to Mary with a loud voice, declaring, "Blessed art thou among women, and blessed is the fruit of thy womb" (Luke 1:42). And the Gadarene demoniac cries out to Jesus in a loud voice: "What have I to do with thee, Jesus, thou Son of God most high? I beseech thee, torment me not" (Luke 8:28). Our Lord himself dies by crying out in a loud voice, "Father, into thy hands I commend my spirit" (Luke 23:46). And in the book of Revelation, the twenty-four angelic elders gather around the throne of heaven, declaring in a loud voice: "Worthy is the Lamb who was slain, to receive power and wealth and wisdom and might and honor and glory and blessing" (Rev. 5:12).

Why all this biblical emphasis on loudness, when loudness is usually a sign of stupidity? The less sure we are about our arguments, someone has observed, the higher we ratchet our voices. And everyone dislikes a loudmouth. How blessed is the assurance that we can silence the loudness of evangelists such as Kenneth Copeland and of sports commentators such as Dick Vitale with the mute button. There are some Baptists, I suspect, who wish they had mute buttons for the preachers in their pulpits. Perhaps the only benefit of being deaf is that I can shut off my hearing aids and thus silence anything I do not want to hear. Yet the chief characters of the Bible do not stop their ears. They are eager hearers of the Word. Having heard it, they spend a good deal of their time shouting it, and the reason seems obvious enough. The Good News of Jesus Christ is utterly extraordinary: it is "what no eye has seen, nor ear heard, nor the heart of man conceived" (1 Cor. 2:9). To be quiet about this one Word that gives true life, to mute this singularly joyful noise, is to commit a terrible violence against it.

I contend that we are all shouting one kind of message or another, if not with our voices then with our lives. Even the mousiest of wall-flowers and wimpiest of geeks are making clear and dramatic statements about what they stand for. To stand for nothing is to take the worst of all stances. It is to believe that there is nothing ultimately worth living and dying for — and shouting about. It is also to announce the antigospel called nihilism. Dante understood this antigospel well. When he came to imagine the various gradations of hell, where sins are punished according to the damage they do both to God and the world, he reserved the severest punishment for the neutrals. The neutrals are those souls who stood for nothing larger than themselves, who were silent and acquiescent in the face of evil because they also denied that there was any good to shout about.

Unlike the many other damned creatures we encounter in Dante's hell, these small-souled men and women are all nameless: their sins were not large enough to give them true personal identity or to merit real damnation. Dante thus places them outside hell, in its anteroom or vestibule, in order to mark their utter unworthiness. There in that terrible outer circle, they are stung by wasps and flies. Thus pricked and goaded by biting insects, these Neutrals run furiously in pursuit of a creature who carries a white flag that has no insignia. Their banner is as blank as their lives are void of all devotion and passion. Having laid down their lives for no cause or commitment in this world, they are thus condemned to die for nothing in the eternal world. T. S. Eliot says that the fate of these crimped creatures will be the fate of most moderns as well. In one of his most chilling phrases, Eliot declares that "we are not men enough to be damned."

When we look at the empty faces that inhabit the shopping malls and the sports arenas, or that stare back at us from the bathroom mirror, we are made to wonder whether our souls are too miniscule to merit even God's wrath. Somebody needs to shout at us, loudly declaring that we are creatures made not for ourselves but meant for communion with God and thus also with our neighbors. Our culture and our churches need preachers who will disturb our spiritual slumbers, calling us to live and fight and die under the banner of the cross. If not, we shall die before we die. The fear that we are dead before we have been buried prompted the novelist Graham Greene to liken this present generation to Pontius Pilate. Asked to render a clear judgment on Jesus, Pilate sought a safe and self-protecting neutrality. He refused to declare himself either for or against Jesus — to shout out either a Yea or a Nay. Pilate was not loud but quiet, even silent. He didn't have to wash his mouth out because he had first washed his hands. Hence Graham Greene's stark staying: "It is better to have blood on our hands like Judas than water like Pilate."

Better still — infinitely bette — is it to be loud-mouthed fools for

Christ's sake. To be vocal about the gospel is to draw stares and to cause comment. It is to be thought odd, eccentric, even "crazy" — good Christian words all. Jesus' first disciples thought he was deranged for shouting his message so relentlessly. William F. Buckley says that he can't imagine the apostle Paul attending a Manhattan dinner party. If you mention God on such an occasion, says Buckley, the other guests will stare at you; if you mention God twice, he adds, you won't be invited back. "It is better to speak wisdom foolishly, like the saints," said G. K. Chesterton, "rather than to speak folly wisely, like the dons." Paul was a rabbi but not a don. He was too strangely obsessed with salvation in Jesus Christ to indulge in polite prattle. He had a thorn not only in his flesh but also under his saddle. It caused Paul to buck and rear up, to snort and bellow.

Like Paul, we are called to be not only loud but also eccentric in the literal sense of the word: to be "off-center." We are not meant to have the world as our point of reference, but the cross. Flannery O'Connor is supposed to have given John 10:10 this slight but splendid emendation: "You shall know the Truth, and the Truth shall make you odd." It sounds like her, though I can find no place where she says it. There is no doubt that she described her own grotesque fiction as a sort of literary shouting. In an ear-wadded age such as ours, there are few other options: "To the deaf you must shout," she declares, "and for the almost blind you draw large and startling figures." Most of our preaching, like most of our literature, constitutes a terrible quietness, a drawing of small figures, and thus a virtual silencing of the Word.

Being a radical Christian gave Flannery O'Connor a great regard for Karl Barth. "I like old Karl," she said, "because he throws the furniture around." In one of his furniture-throwing early sermons, Barth smashed the flimsy chair of Protestant liberalism over the heads of his old teachers. "You cannot speak of God," Barth reminded them, "by speaking of man in a loud voice." There is only one reality that requires us to raise our voices, and it is the God of the gospel. God may speak to us as he did to Elijah, in "a still small voice," but he commissions us to shout the gospel from the rooftops. Barth was not vain but honest when, after declaring the truth loud and clear, he would say of himself: "Well roared, lion!" So did our nineteenth-century Baptist ancestors refuse to remain quiet about their source of hope and courage amid the hardships that would make us lesser Christians quail and fail. They sang and they shouted the victory that inspired their own struggle:

Sing the wondrous love of Jesus
Sing his mercy and his grace;
In the mansions bright and blessed,
He'll prepare for us a place.

While we walk the pilgrim pathway,
Clouds will overspread the sky;
But when traveling days are over,
Not a shadow, not a sigh.

Onward to the prize before us!
Soon his beauty we'll behold;
Soon the pearly gates will open,
We shall tread the streets of gold.

When we all get to heaven,
What a day of rejoicing that will be!
When we all see Jesus,
We'll sing and shout the victory.

II

If loudness is something intrinsic to the gospel, I believe that being dogmatic is even more germane to it. Yet "dogmatic" has become a dirty word among Baptist moderates: it is their favorite term for describing fundamentalists. God knows that the fundamentalists deserve all the ugly adjectives that they have earned — mean-spirited, knot-headed, rationalistic, literalistic, dishonest, and just plain evil. But why should we grant the fundamentalists such a good title as "dogmatic"? I discovered the reason only recently, when I referred favorably to "orthodox Christianity" in a Sunday school class. I was immediately asked why we would want to use such an adjective in a moderate Baptist church and at an enlightened Baptist university such as Baylor? Being a confessed contrarian as well as dogmatist, I asked, "Why not?" My interlocutor replied that "orthodox" is a word that describes those who have tunnel vision, those who are narrow- and close-minded, who indeed are "dogmatic." And so at last I figured it out: The word "dogmatic" is our moniker for those folks of whom we surely want to say,

"We thank thee, O Lord, that we are not as they are." I must confess that I didn't overcome my friend's worry about those who are dogmatic when I confessed my own worry about Christians who are so open-minded that their brains have fallen out. His consternation was only increased, I fear, when I also quoted G. K. Chesterton's splendid aphorism: "The purpose of an open mind is like that of an open mouth: to shut it on something solid."

Dogma is the solid truth that the triune God has shut our hearts and minds on, even as he closed the door on Noah so that the ark might stay afloat with life and hope. In Israel and Jesus Christ, God has enclosed us in the virtuous circle of his own self-disclosure. Dogma is thus linked to revelation, to truth that we could not know on our own but that must be shown to us. We know, of course, that dogma develops, that it is not fixed and frozen, that it can go wrong, and that it is tainted with human self-interest and historical limitation. Even so, "dogmatic" remains a very good Christian word. It refers to the teaching that lies at the very heart of Christian faith. But it is teaching that human ingenuity cannot invent by mere thinking, any more that we can increase our height by wishing it so. To be dogmatic, therefore, is to be rooted in dogma, in such Christian doctrines as creation and sin, justification and sanctification, election and atonement, reconciliation and glorification, even in what someone has called both the perseverance and perspiration of the saints. As preachers and teachers of the gospel, we will have something worth saying and hearing only if we are dogmatic in this precise sense, only if we are declaring the doctrines of the faith.

Far from being outmoded and irrelevant and stultifying, dogmas are truly freeing. They enable us to confront truths that we cannot exhaust. Flannery O'Connor puts it well: "Dogma is about the only thing left that preserves mystery." *Mysterion* is a word that can be translated "sacrament" as well as "mystery." Baptism and the Lord's Supper are both *mysteria* in the biblical sense. We will never fully fathom either our baptism in the watery grave of sin and death or our communion at the sumptuous feast of the Lord's Table. For in Scripture, mystery is not synonymous with "puzzle" and "riddle," not the equal of "conundrum" and "enigma" — those things that balk the mind and stifle understanding. Nor is mystery a convenient screen for a soupy sort of spirituality. "To St. Paul and the early Christian thinkers," writes the Catholic biblical scholar Claude Tresmontant, "[mystery] was on the contrary the particular object of intelligence, its fullest nourishment. The mysterion is something so rich in intelligible content, so inexhaustibly full of delectation for the mind, that no contemplation can ever reach its end. It is an eternal delectation of the mind."

The need to be dogmatic lies at the heart of Luther's debate with Erasmus on the bondage of the will. The real issue between them was not whether we are free to ask someone to pass the salt, as C. S. Lewis wittily remarked, or whether such a common request has been somehow foreordained from all creation. The issue was whether there are truths that we human beings cannot construct or discover on our own. Luther thought that there were, and that they are called doctrines; Erasmus, he feared, would strip the gospel of all such dogmatic truth. Erasmus would reduce Christian faith to ethical common sense, to the noblest doing of good, to the moral obligations that would require Jesus to be, not the crucified and risen Savior, but rather the exemplar and model whom we are meant to imitate by our own ethical powers.

It is not natural and obvious, said Luther against Erasmus, to understand that we are sinners. It is immensely hard and difficult to grasp so simple a thing as sin. There is only one place where it can be discovered: at Golgotha. There we are shown that sin consists not in committing such evil acts as lying and whoring, as stealing and murdering, not even in something so heinous as genocide. These terrible things are sins plural, and they are spelled in the lower case. They are the evils that we can fathom on our own, and thus that we think we can cure on our own. Sin singular and spelled with a capital *S* is something quite different. It is a fundamental distrust of God, a basic refusal to yield our lives to the love of God, a bitter determination to fend for ourselves, even if it means slaying God's own Son. All our large and small sins derive from such primordial and persistent Sin. Therefore, to be dogmatic about so central a Christian dogma as original sin is not to be close-minded, but truthful. And to be dogmatic about the Lamb of God who takes away the sins of the world is not to be exclusive and insensitive but to announce the most inclusive truth of all. Again, our ancestors knew better and thus they sang better.

> I know not why God's wondrous grace
> To me He hath made known,
> Nor why, unworthy, Christ in love
> Redeemed me for his own.

I know not how this saving faith
To me He did impart,
Nor how believing in His Word
Wrought peace within my heart.

I know not how the Spirit moves,
Convincing men of sin,
Revealing Jesus thro' the Word,
Creating faith in Him.

I know not when my Lord may come
At night or noonday fair,
Nor if I'll walk the vale with Him,
Or meet Him in the air.

But "I know whom I have believéd
And am persuaded that He is able
To keep that which I've committed
Unto Him against that day."

III

In a pluralist age such as ours, uncertainty has become one of the chief virtues. Lesslie Newbigin, an evangelical Christian theologian, is willing to confess, thanks to his work as a missionary in India, that all truth is perspectival and cultural. No one stands outside the universe as a solitary soul viewing it *sub specie aeternitatis.* We are not Olympian gods but finite women and men. We all wear filtering lenses and stand on axiomatic suppositions. Even the scientists who seem to investigate the natural order with naked eyes and thus with unbiased certainty are severely limited by the assumptions that they bring to their enterprise. They can see and understand only what their paradigms and presuppositions permit. No single human perspective, whether individual or corporate, can transcend and thus trump all the others. We are historically contingent creatures through and through. We see through a glass very darkly and uncertainly indeed.

Even the now-fashionable multiculturalism that attempts to synthesize the various miscellaneous truths into a new and definitive whole is itself a culturally conditioned enterprise. Who gets to do the synthesizing and on what basis? The currently reigning model for dealing with the problem of pluralism is diversity. It's the old Enlightenment notion that if all truths are treated as equal and given equal airing, then the larger, capitalized Truth will both emerge and prevail. But why should it? Isn't it more likely that advocates of the competing truths will draw guns and fire on each other — as they are doing in Bosnia and Israel, in Ireland and Yemen? Were it not so bloody, wouldn't such multiculturalism be comical? Kierkegaard disdained such a notion as "truth by vote"; Nietzsche more accurately called it "truth by power." What, therefore, are the criteria for our vaunted inclusivity? Can anything be excluded if all truths and all cultures are considered equal? Is Santeria, the Caribbean blood cult now popular in Cuba and in much of Miami, to be considered a religion having the same status as Christianity? Should Wicca, the latter-day practice of witchcraft, be given membership in the National Council of Churches, right alongside the Metropolitan Community churches? Are Nazis and Skinheads, racists and abortionists, to be included in our much-hallowed diversity?

In the name of such diversity, a rigid uniformity now rules much of the American academy. We tolerate all points of view except those that take truth seriously enough to believe that some things are intolerable. "Tolerance," said Chesterton, "is a virtue to those who believe nothing." Hospitality is the far more Christian way of engaging and forbearing persons and groups who are inimical to our own purposes. Unlike the tolerance that declares, "We will put up with you," hospitality declares, "We will put you up." Christians are willing to take seriously the practices and convictions of their opponents, engaging them in a setting that confesses that we, too, are sinners. "The people who are the most bigoted," Chesterton thus added, "are the people who have no convictions at all." Some of our seminaries and colleges are promoting this kind of bigoted and convictionless diversity. They profess not to care what use their students and professors make of their liberty, so long as all are free to maximize their personal preferences, and so long as they do no harm to others. When asked what constitutes "harm," one of the new diversity mongers answered "tissue damage" — as though people could not be harmed in many ways other than bodily injury.

Newbigin candidly assesses the futility of our multicultural pretensions: "A variety of relative truths do not become absolute by being combined." In *The Abolition of Man,* C. S. Lewis warns of a far more frightening prospect. Already in 1947 he was prophesying that the political managers and the thought police would shape these miscellaneous truths into social and political schemes that would serve the managers while turning the rest of us into slaves. Surely, diversity is a great virtue, but it is a great virtue only when our various talents and perspectives have a single purpose and focus. Unless we are joined in devotion to a common good, a Hobbesian war of all against all is the real likelihood. Paul puts it this way: "There are varieties of gifts, but the same Spirit. There are varieties of service, but the same Lord. And there are varieties of working, but the same God who inspires them all in everyone . . . many members, but one body" (1 Cor. 12:4-6, 12).

I do not have the answer to the vexed question of cultural pluralism. To discern whether truth is invented out of our own subjective interests and thus multiplex in character, or whether it is discovered within some objective realm of natural law and thus unitary in character, or whether it is an inextricable mixture of both — this is the enormous theological and philosophical task of our time. We Christians are interested in this debate largely because it might help us discern precisely how and why the gospel of Jesus Christ is neither our invention nor our discovery, but God's own act of radical self-identification. Our ministry as teachers and preachers is surely premised on this certain and unshakable foundation: "God was in Christ reconciling the world to himself" (2 Cor. 5:18).

Therefore, the gospel is not a relative and contingent truth confined to the dying culture of the West. Jesus Christ is not Savior just for us, but for everybody. As St. Augustine wisely taught, something that is true only for me is not true at all. The gospel is not the center of our little bourgeois circle; it is "the still point of the turning world," as T. S. Eliot called it, the centripetal and centrifugal focus of the entire cosmos. The Bible is not a tribal anthology of interesting folktales that illustrate universal and timeless truths. It recounts the one Story that lays certain claim upon every human life and culture, calling them all into radical question and thus demanding their radical transformation into God's new people.

This means that we cannot dodge the scandal of certainty and particularity. God's choosing of Israel from all the nations is exclusive in the extreme. Over all other nations and cultures, God privileges what Newbigin wryly calls "one of the minor ethnic communities of the

Near East." In Jesus Christ, there is even greater offense. He is the Messiah who looks like a deluded and defeated man: he is the Lord who declares, with utmost outrageousness, that he has chosen us rather than we him. Yet in Christ's very choosing of us may lie the real answer to the problem of cultural multiplicity and uncertainty. Jesus summons his followers not to privilege but to witness — to the bringing of salvation to all peoples: "I chose you and appointed you that you should go and bear fruit" (John 15:16). The salvation that we are charged to go and shout out brings true reconciliation with God and between individuals and among peoples. Ironically, the stone of stumbling is the solid rock on which every culture and people can stand. If we do not summon others to stand there with us, we shall all sink into the abyss of our own self-interest. Women and men, rich and poor, gay and straight, first world and third, red and yellow, black and brown and white — we all have our one hope in the singular certainty that we are precious in God's sight.

Let it last be said that to belong to Jesus Christ is a very strange sort of certainty. St. Paul forbids our boasting about any certainty other than the certainty of Christ's cross. A. W. Tozer explains why: "The man with the cross no longer controls his own destiny; he lost control when he picked up the cross. That cross immediately became to him an all-absorbing interest, an overwhelming interference." The cross of Christ brings with it the certainty that we will have doubts, fears, struggles, and troubles. To be Christ's loud, dogmatic, and certain witnesses is a calling at once blessed beyond all presumption and dangerous beyond all control. The gospel is the one truth worth living and dying for, the one privilege beyond all adequate thanksgiving. But it is also the one certainty that will require us to give offense, to make enemies, even to be persecuted for righteousness' sake.

The Irish theologian Herbert McCabe sums up this cruciform certainty ever so well: "If you do not love you will not be [truly] alive; [and] if you do love you will be killed." The cross of Christ is certain to cost us nothing less than our lives — if not in actual martyrdom, then surely in our daily dying to sin, and finally in the courage and grace required to face the death and resurrection that await us all. Amid such perils and wonders, only one thing remains absolutely certain: that nothing can separate us from the love of God in Christ Jesus, that we stand on the one solid rock, that all other ground — all other ground — is sinking sand.

My hope is built on nothing less
Than Jesus' blood and righteousness;
I dare not trust the sweetest frame,
But wholly lean on Jesus' name.

When darkness seems to hide His face,
I rest on his unchanging grace;
In every high and stormy gale,
My anchor holds within the veil.

His oath, His covenant, His blood
Support me in the whelming flood;
When all around my soul gives way,
He then is all my hope and stay.

When he shall come with trumpet sound,
Oh, may I then in Him be found;
Dressed in His righteousness alone,
Faultless to stand before the throne.

On Christ, the solid Rock, I stand;
All other ground is sinking sand,
All other ground is sinking sand.

Thou Shalt Not Slay either Bodies or Souls

The Society for Evangelical Anglican Doctrine
Christ Episcopal Church
Plano, Texas
February 28, 2003

There is no better beginning for a sermon on the Decalogue's sixth commandment — the prohibition against killing — than to recall the obvious: that we live in a culture of killing, a culture of death, as Pope John Paul II has rightly called it. Though we all know the grim statistics, they nonetheless bear repeating: More people were slaughtered in the twentieth century than in all of the previous centuries combined — roughly 180 million. A lesser-known fact is there were also more Christian martyrs in this century of gore than in all of the prior centuries: nearly 40 million, compared to "only" 26 million in the preceding nineteen centuries. The ratio between civilian and military deaths has also been exactly reversed in our time — from 1:9 to 9:1. Ours is an epoch of blood, an age of carnage.

We are tempted to comfort ourselves with the assurance that the atrocities of our age can be laid to the charge of the Nazis and the Communists and the followers of Osama bin Laden. But Christians must confess, on the contrary, that our churches have helped to create this ethos of butchery. Rather than merely lamenting this sorry fact, my aim is to set forth three ways whereby we might offer radical Christian resistance to our culture of mayhem and murder. The first is to recall the church's basic teachings concerning peacemaking and the necessary conditions for declaring a war to be just. The second is to deal with the two kinds of killing that afflict our churches perhaps most directly, namely, abortion and the neglect of the elderly. Finally, I want to argue that our churches should be worried about their complicity in a new and worse kind of death than anything we've ever experienced before, namely, the death of our souls.

I

Karl Barth begins his treatment of the sixth commandment with Albert Schweitzer's claim that we were not meant to kill at all, that we were meant to eat the fruits of the earth alone, that the blood of life belongs only to God. Ever so hesitantly, therefore, do we take animal life as God's reluctant concession to our fallen condition, as kosher practices serve to remind orthodox Jews. This will not be the last compromise that Israel and the church have made with God's original intention for his people. However, there is one abandonment of the primal divine will that we should never have made. It is the death penalty. Even though it can be justified from Old Testament texts, the same is not true of the New Testament. When Jesus himself died for the sins of the world — the one and only person who did not deserve the death penalty thus receiving it — he surely lifted the burden of our punishing anyone else with such a sentence. This was the real message of John Paul II's letter that protested the execution of Timothy McVeigh, the terrorist bomber who killed 168 people in blowing up the Alfred P. Murrah Building in Oklahoma City (partly as revenge for the death of 73 people at the Branch Davidian compound two years earlier, outside my own city of Waco, Texas). The pope's point was not that no one deserves execution — and certainly McVeigh was a despicable killer — but that none of us is pure enough to put anyone beyond the bounds of redemption. Rather than dealing with the killing of animals or criminals, however, I want first to wrestle with the worst carnage of all — war.

In a freshman religion class at Baylor this semester, I walked my students through the basic New Testament texts concerning war and peace. It was not difficult to show them that there is a clear presumption against violence and killing everywhere in Christian Scripture. The grace note can hardly be mistaken: turn the other cheek, walk the second mile, give back good when you have received evil, refuse to take up arms and fight, become peacemakers if you want to be called the sons of God. My students gladly acknowledged that these commands lie at the heart of the gospel message. Yet they insisted that the summons to nonviolence applies only to our individual treatment of fellow Christians, not to our corporate relationship with non-Christian people or with enemy nations. Jesus, they said, is setting up a golden ideal that he perhaps wants us to strive for; but he knows that we cannot possibly reach it. For in the real world, they concluded, we must defend ourselves against enemies. We cannot let our freedoms be jeopardized, our American way of life be threatened.

It would be all too easy to demonstrate the inadequacy of my students' response to the most fundamental teachings of the New Testament. But I must confess, instead, that these young Christian collegians are making the same deadly mistake that I myself have made, the same mistake that the vast majority of other Christians have also made: we have declared the "real world" to be the world of slaughter, while we have consigned Christ's peaceable kingdom to the realm of the artificial and unreal, the merely "ideal." This is to get matters exactly and dreadfully backward. The reconciled and transformed life that Jesus both proclaimed and enacted is not an impossible goal but an eschatological reality in the precise sense of the word. Christ's peaceable kingdom is not of this false world ruled by Prince Satan, but it is of the true world ruled by God, the radically reordered future that the incarnate Lord has already begun right here in our midst through his people. We who do not live in this kingdom of peace here and now, I should add, cannot expect to live in it hereafter.

Martin Luther King Jr., John Howard Yoder, James Wm. McClendon, Stanley Hauerwas, Richard Hays, and a host of other Christian preachers and teachers have shown that a totally reconciling kind of nonviolence lies at the core of the new community that Christ inaugurated with his life and death and resurrection. Yet it is important to be clear about why Christians have refused to kill their enemies. They were not prompted by a universal pacifist ideal shared and sustained by all people of good will. Christians repudiate violence, not by means of their own fallen will but by the power that the Crucified himself works in and through his church: its preaching and sacraments, its prayers and practices. Christians are opposed to war, therefore, for the sake of the world's redemption in and through Jesus Christ. The faithful church is the real answer to our culture of death, for only in this community can God's people find the grace and forgiveness to sustain our obedience to the sixth commandment, as well as the other nine commandments. For an Alabama federal district judge to post them in his courtroom, by contrast, is to conscript them for the cause of American civil religion. Thereby are they robbed of their theological intention, even as they are removed from the two communities essential to their fulfillment, namely, the synagogue and the church.

Just as it is the original divine intention that we not kill animals, so is it the primal will of God that we not kill our fellow human beings. Yet, while many believers eat meat in concession to the Fall, so have certain Christians felt it necessary to modify the Decalogue's sixth commandment. Their fallback position is called the Just War argument. It is also my own position, since I remain unpersuaded that the killing of Osama bin Laden and the killing of unborn children are of the same order. Its chief premise is that Christians have the obligation to protect the lives of the innocent, even by recourse to violence. The best recent Just War advocates have been Paul Ramsey and Jean Bethke Elshtain, though it was first broached by St. Augustine in the fifth century. Because the seven Just War criteria have been clearly formulated by the U.S. Conference of Catholic Bishops, I asked my students to determine whether the coming war with Iraq could meet this most basic Christian test.

(1) A preemptive strike against Iraq satisfies the requirement of a "just cause" insofar as it will be aimed at correcting "a grave public evil, that is, aggression or violation of the basic rights of a whole population." Saddam Hussein is a grave public menace, not least of all to his own fellow Iraqis, perhaps a million of whom he has killed. (2) It also meets the test of "right intention," again if we concede that our troops will use "force . . . only in a truly just cause and solely for that purpose." It is unforgivably cynical and libelous to accuse President Bush of wanting war for the sake of oil. Peter Beinart, among other liberal columnists, has pointed out that the cost of oil will sharply increase if we go to war with Iraq. (3) The coming war also passes the requirement of "comparative justice." This test insists that the injustice committed by the offending tyrant and his followers must "significantly outweigh" the injustice that would be inflicted on them. Again, this criterion is met: the suffering that Saddam has inflicted on the people of Iraq, and on those whom he would attack with the nuclear and biological weapons he is said to possess, are surely greater than the suffering we will inflict on him and his supporters.

(4) Yet our proposed war fails the test of "legitimate authority" if we take the United Nations as a serious body of international law. Pres-

ident Bush has argued that we can no longer grant it such authority, but this is not a conclusion that either the U.S. Congress or the nations of the world have themselves arrived at. Thus would an attack on Iraq, carried out in direct defiance of the United Nations, turn us into a rogue nation making its own laws and abiding by its own will. (5) The war also fails the test of "equal measures," since the bombing of civilian populations greatly outweighs the retaliation that the Iraqi army is capable of making against our forces. And if they resort to biological weapons, they will kill thousands of their own people as well as our soldiers. (6) The war also fails the test of "proportionality," since the estimated 500,000 lives that will be lost in this war hugely overbalance whatever good may be achieved by it. And, finally, (7) it fails the test of "last resort," which holds that "force may be used only after all peaceful measures have been seriously tried and exhausted." Manifestly, they have not, even if Saddam has cynically manipulated the weapons inspections process to his own advantage. There is still reason to keep the inspectors at work, because, even at best, the threatened war passes only three of the seven criteria, and because it fails four of the most important ones.

I asked a former student who is also a former army officer to read a draft of this speech. He complained that, according to these seven criteria, very few if any wars in human history could be justified. I replied that he had got the point exactly right: Christians have remarkably few occasions to sanction war. There may be purely political and pragmatic ways of supporting the coming attack against Iraq, but the Conference of U.S. Catholic Bishops, alongside every major Protestant group in America, have all unanimously agreed that there are no Christian grounds for going to war. There is one exception to this ecclesial unanimity: the Southern Baptist Convention has been notably absent from the list of denominations condemning the coming war. SBC leaders would argue, of course, that these other Christian groups who condemn the forthcoming attack on Iraq are but politicized liberals seeking allegedly Christian grounds for justifying their own spinelessness: their compassion is so sappy that they cannot stand up to a monster like Saddam. Yet, surely the onus lies on the SBC leaders to prove that they are not themselves a set of warmongers seeking sanction for their own bellicose self-righteousness. At the very least, the SBC leaders ought to pause before declaring the present pope an invertebrate liberal!

To my considerable surprise, I found that all but one of my thirty-two students, most of whom would describe themselves as conservatives and/or evangelicals, were convinced that the proposed attack on Iraq does not meet all seven of the Just War criteria. And the one student who remained unpersuaded now confesses, to her considerable worry, that she is wavering. More alarming than surprising was the confession of my students that none of them had ever heard of the Just War tradition. Their urban and often nondenominational churches have failed to give them even the rudiments of Christian instruction concerning war and peace.

Here I am completely at one with them. As a Baptist youth growing up in rural northeast Texas during the 1950s, I was never exposed to anything akin to it. On the contrary, I can still remember my saintly mother warning me against the one thing that would bring total shame on her and my father and our larger community: a refusal on my part to go to war if I were drafted. She was not merely reflecting the Texas way of life, though to be a sissy about fighting with either one's fists or the army's guns is, in this rough-and-tumble state, to declare one's unworthiness in the most fundamental way. No, my dear and gentle mother was hardly a blustering combatant; on the contrary, she was upholding one of the noblest of human virtues, namely, the nobility of being willing to die in defense of one's country. Yet one does not need to be a Christian to make this noblest of human sacrifices. And my mother wanted me to be a Christian above all else. Therefore, I blame our church rather than her: it had never taught us that Christians believe that there is a nobler virtue than the courage of armed battle, and that Christians call it martyrdom. This highest form of courage is the strength to die rather than to repudiate our faith in the triune God, especially if such a repudiation of Christ requires us to kill others.

These are not abstract theological concerns. The Methodist minister in an East Texas town has recently been dismissed because she refuses to say the Pledge of Allegiance to the flag at the local Lions Club. Far from being anti-American, this young preacher of the gospel is trying to order her loves faithfully: she is trying to make it clear that her allegiance to Jesus Christ and his kingdom takes precedence over everything else. Yet her own church has not only repudiated her brave witness; it has also granted her even less freedom as a Christian than her country grants her as a citizen, because no American is *required* to say the Pledge of Allegiance. The flags placed in our churches, if they can be justified at all, should reflect the order of Christian judgment: the Christian flag should stand at the center, high and lifted up; to the right and somewhat below it, the flag of the denomination; to the left and lower still — making clear that we judge the nation by Jesus Christ and his church — the American flag should take its subordinate place.

I recognize that there are real tensions between the Just War and the pacifist traditions in Christian thought. In fact, the two cannot be reconciled. However, our chief problem is not only that we have ignored the call to Christian pacifism and martyrdom. Our chief problem is that many — I would wager, most — of our churches have failed to teach and thus to shape the lives of their parishioners according to the Just War tradition. Thus, it is perhaps neither impolite nor impolitic for me to ask whether the Episcopal parish in Midland, Texas, where the young George W. Bush was nurtured in the Christian faith, or the Methodist church in Austin, where he now holds membership, has offered him any serious grounding in such basic Christian teaching?

II

It is not only concerning war that we Christians have violated the sixth commandment. We have often colluded with our culture of death in sanctioning abortion. It is true that the Bible does not condemn abortion, just as it does not condemn pedophilia and necrophilia and masturbation. Some things are too obviously wrong to need prohibiting. (I should add, parenthetically, that a former student who is now the senior warden of his Episcopal parish in Virginia told me about an interesting new phrase he picked up at a national church conference in Pittsburgh recently. He discovered that masturbation has a newly approved name: "self-massage.")

But where Scripture itself remains silent about abortion, Christian tradition is astonishingly vocal about it. From the very beginning, Christians were known as the people who set themselves apart from their pagan neighbors by not killing their so-called unwanted babies. By the time of the *Didache,* the early summary of Christian doctrine and practice recorded in the late first or early second century, the church had made explicit the rule that had always been implicit: "You shall not murder a child by abortion nor kill that which is born." Convinced that they were meant to live against the grain of the "culture of death" in which they lived, these early Christians repudiated the common Greco-Roman practice called "exposure." Even casual readers of Sophocles' *Oedipus the King* will remember that, in the ancient Mediterranean world, unwanted babies — in Oedipus's case, a club-footed infant — were taken to remote places and left to die from exposure to the ravages of either wild animals or inclement weather. In writing his *First Apology* sometime around 155, Justin Martyr is vehement in commanding Christians to reject infanticide in all its forms, especially exposure. Justin points out that the sex-traders of his day, like those of our own time, were seizing abandoned babies and raising them to become prostitutes.

It is not difficult to measure the extent of our hypersexualized culture. Four of every five American eighteen-year-old males have already had sex; three in five females have done the same. Millions of babies are being conceived out of wedlock, and abortion has become the standard means of dealing with such pregnancies. The practice of teenage abortion does not happen in secular circles alone; it is also the common practice among many church families as well. One of Baylor's most illustrious Christian alumnae, a woman made famous for having been captured by the Taliban (and later rescued) in Afghanistan, has sorrowfully confessed that, even before she arrived at Baylor as a freshman, she had undergone an abortion. Many middle-class Christian couples also resort to abortion as their preferred means of birth control. Yet, sadly, the church often remains silent about this rampant recourse to the killing of our babies,

It is a major scandal that we Christians even debate whether unborn babies are human beings. Such debate shows how desperate we have become to justify our desire to enjoy convenient and unbothered lives. A faithful church would not only encourage its married couples to bring their babies into the world; it would also find ways to sustain the pregnancies of their teenagers, even as they would help the poor and the outcast be able to celebrate the glad gift of life. Allow me an illustration. I happened to be in the office of a Baylor colleague when one of his students called on the phone. It became evident that this young man was distressed over his girlfriend's pregnancy, that he wanted to talk with his professor about their terrible mistake, and that he sought his professor's approval for an abortion. I quickly excused myself and began to leave the room, but my colleague signaled for me to stay. It became one of the most important moments of my life, for I shall never forget what I heard my friend reply. "Yes," he said to his student, "you have made a terrible mistake in failing to practice sexual discipline before marriage. You have violated each other, you have violated your families and friends and churches, and you have also violated God. Come to my office immediately, therefore, so we can make plans for your girlfriend to carry this baby to term. But let's be very clear about something far more important: no baby is ever a mistake. Every baby is a creature made in the image of God."

We Christians make fools of both ourselves and of our Lord when we speak of abortion as a reproductive right and merely as an individual choice — as if the taking of human life were the equivalent of shopping for clothes or selecting an automobile, as if our moral existence were a consumer's existence. All the things that count in this world, especially the Christian things, are matters of communal obligation and obedience, not of private choice. There is no better place to comprehend our culture's idolatry of subjective choice than in Justice Anthony Kennedy's majority opinion in the 1992 *Planned Parenthood v. Casey* case before the Supreme Court, a decision that upheld *Roe v. Wade*. Justice Kennedy is to be commended for his awful clarity in articulating the privatism and subjectivism that have produced our culture of death. "At the very heart of liberty," wrote Justice Kennedy, "is the right to define one's own concept of existence, of meaning, of the universe, of the mystery of human life."

I cannot imagine a more succinct definition of madness than Mr. Kennedy's contention that every person should define the moral meaning of the universe for himself. Worse than madness, this privatized and utterly subjectivist idea of freedom is precisely what Christians have defined as slavery. We find liberty — as Christ and all the saints have reiterated relentlessly — not when we define reality for ourselves but when we live in utter obedience to God and in unstinting devotion to our neighbors. Only there lies liberty, in what the Prayer Book so memorably calls "the service which is perfect freedom." And let us not be mistaken about Cranmer's use of the word "service" in its early Latinate sense: It does not mean dutiful civic club work, but happy slavery to God.

We need also to be unmistaken about the fact that our culture of death has put the very old in no less terrible peril than the very young. I recall my Roman Catholic professor rattling my self-imposed cage, shaking my flimsy moral foundations, when he made the following declaration: "While we hear a great deal about the injustices suffered by blacks and women, we hear almost nothing about the most abused and neglected members of our society — the old." Ours may be the very first culture in the world's history not to honor the elderly, but to exalt the young instead. Though we have not yet begun to euthanize them, such a practice may not be far off. If you think this prospect unlikely, I urge you to read *The Children of Men*, P. D. James's stark prophecy of the world that lies ahead of us. In the meantime, rather than euthanizing them, we murder the elderly by neglect. Seventy percent of all nursing and retirement home residents receive not a single visitor in an entire year.

Those whom we do care for somewhat more humanely, we often insult by treating them as if they were children. My own dear mother, if I may cite her yet again, belonged to the XYZ Club sponsored by her local Baptist church. Most of the members of this organization were in their late seventies, and some were already in their eighties, even their nineties. Yet the acronym XYZ indicated not that they had reached the end of life's symbolic alphabet, but rather that they possessed "Extra Youth and Zest." What a cynical affront! What a crass denial of my mother's aged humanity! What a cold-hearted refusal to take her seriously! Like most of her friends, she had lived a long and often hard life. Far from being youthful and zestful, she once confessed to me (only because I had asked) that there was never a moment when she did not know pain — though she never complained about it.

An elderly friend who recently suffered a broken pelvis laments that, while we make an extraordinary expenditure of time and money to keep the elderly alive, our society has no idea what to do with these old folks now that they can be kept alive longer than ever. I believe that our churches should be drawing on the rich experience of people such as my mother, learning from their deep wisdom and being chastened by their difficult lives. When we leave them to rot in nursing homes, they often become senile almost overnight, since their minds and souls have been deprived of their real vitality.

No imaginative writer has helped us confront the crimes we commit in killing both the young and the old more vividly than has the Louisiana Catholic novelist Walker Percy. He includes one of our allegedly well-cared-for senior citizens in his apocalyptic novel of 1971 called *Love in the Ruins*. There we briefly encounter a character named Mr. Ives. His name is perhaps reminiscent of the folk singer Burl Ives as well as the composer Charles Ives, both of whom remained creatively alive well into their old age. Percy's Mr. Ives is a retired archaeologist. He has been sent to live out his last years in a luxurious retirement home in Tampa, a place that amply meets his every want and need. Yet Mr. Ives is so miserable in this paradise for the elderly that he becomes totally uncooperative and bitterly rebellious. At the New Orleans hospital where he has been sent for treatment, therapists and psychiatrists descend upon Mr. Ives to decipher what is wrong. Their cold objective account of Mr. Ives's offenses reveals that the old codger has a wonderfully profane wit:

> "The subject has not only refused to participate in the various recreational, educational, creative, and group activities but has on occasion engaged in antisocial and disruptive behavior. He refused: shuffleboard tournament, senior softball, Golden Years gymkhana, papa putt-putt, donkey baseball, Guys and Gals à go-go, the redfish rodeo, and granddaddy golf. He refused: free trip to Los Angeles to participate in Art Linkletter III's "the young-olds," even though chosen for this trip by his own community.
>
> "Did on two occasions defecate on Flirtation Walk during the Merry Widow's Promenade.
>
> "Did on the occasion of the Ohio Day breakfast during the period of well-wishing and when the microphone was passed to him utter gross insults and obscenities to Ohioans, among the mildest of which was the expression, repeated many times: 'Piss on all chickenshit Ohioans!'
>
> "Did in fact urinate on Ohio in the Garden of the Fifty States."

Mr. Ives is angry because he has been treated like a child — as if he needed to be entertained with "recreational activities," as if he had no dignity of his own. Ives regards the retirees from Ohio whom he has met in Tampa as the epitome of all that is bland and mediocre and spiritually dead in contemporary American life. Not even periodic behavioral conditioning in the hospital's Skinner Box can cure Mr. Ives's anger at the sacrilege that has been visited on him. At last one of the physicians gathers enough common sense to recognize that Mr. Ives wants simply to be sent home. Released at last from his prison of alleged comfort, Mr. Ives is free to return to his farm called Lost Cove in

Sherwood, Tennessee. Asked what he plans to do there, Ives replies: "Write a book, look at the hills, live till I die." This man who had been spiritually assaulted with an insulting kindness was brought back to life by quite an ordinary act, a willingness to acknowledge that, like other human beings, he had his own life-project. He did not want to be suffocated with false care.

Whether by cruel neglect or by insulting condescension, we stand accountable to God for having violated the sixth commandment as it applies to old people: killing them off well in advance of their death.

III

Whence comes our culture's wholesale contempt for the sixth commandment, "You shall not kill"? How are our churches complicit in creating our culture of death? A partial answer is to be found, I believe, in identifying another and subtler kind of death that lies at the core of our malevolent world. Again, it is Walker Percy's *Love in the Ruins* that provides us with a clue. In a revealing scene, a Catholic priest named Father Rinaldo Smith approaches the lectern at his New Orleans church, prepared to deliver his weekly homily before saying Mass. To his horror, Smith discovers that he cannot come forth with his sermon. "Excuse me," he declares after a long and embarrassing silence, "but the channels are jammed and the word is not getting through."

Father Smith's congregation nervously titters, assuming that there must be a problem with the church's speaker system. Alas, it is not so. Still unable to talk, the priest is led away from the chancel to the sacristy, where he collapses. There again he mutters "something about 'the news being jammed.'" In the hospital, Smith recovers his speech well enough to be quizzed by the attending psychiatrist, a nonobservant Jew named Max Gottlieb. At last the priest clarifies the nature of his religious aphasia, his theological wordlessness. The gremlin interfering with Father Smith's speech is not electronic. The demonic principalities and powers of the air, Smith explains, have silenced the Good News. "Their tactic has prevailed," he elaborates. "Death is winning, life is losing." Father Smith refers not only to the massive outward holocausts of our time and place, but also to the demonic inward collapse of those who remain alive. "Do you mean the living are dead?" asks Gottlieb. "Yes," answers Smith. "How can that be, Father? How can the living be dead?" "I mean their souls," replies the priest. "I am surrounded by the corpses of souls. We live in a city of the dead."

This, I suggest, is the canker eating at the core of culture, turning it into a culture of death. There is something unmistakably demonic about our time. That we fail to recognize the demonry all around us is not surprising. As Charles Baudelaire declared in the nineteenth century, the Satan's cleverest trick is to convince us that he does not exist. Perhaps it is our denial of the demonic that accounts for our pusillanimity, our smallness and deadness of soul. Many modern writers have remarked it. Franz Kafka said that most of us are not men enough to be damned. Perhaps Kafka was remembering that most of the souls in Dante's hell possess a certain magnanimity, a greatness of soul that they maintain even in their damnation. They have enough depth and substance to be clear about living in brazen denial and defiance of God. Yet, in the outer circle of the Inferno, in the region reserved for those who are not worthy even of damnation, are the Neutrals. They are those men and women who stood for nothing, the ones who had no character at all. They are Laodiceans — like us.

In our blithe ignorance of the demonic, we have failed to discern the link between the deadness of our own souls and the more obvious forms of death that surround us. This point came home to me as I watched a recent installment of the PBS program *Nova*, which was devoted to the development of biological weapons of mass destruction. From 1943 until 1989, our own nation operated a laboratory in Fort Detrick, Maryland, where we designed a series of deadly toxins meant to kill millions. In the early 1980s, hundreds of these dread vials of death were sold to Iraq and Syria and North Korea. Many more of these toxins were manufactured in the gigantic death-labs of the Soviet Union, which possessed enough poison to kill the entire human race nine or ten times over.

The PBS interviewer visited the scientist who for many years headed our own germ warfare operation at Fort Detrick. He is a jolly good fellow, a jovial soul who uses an ordinary garden sprayer to demonstrate how easy it would be to disperse deadly anthrax spores over an entire city. Yet PBS's allegedly hardheaded investigative reporter never bothered to ask this scientist how he could give the best years of his life, not to combating but rather to manufacturing diseases. I kept wondering whether this man is a Christian, and if so, what church he attends, and whether he ever performs acts of worship and service there that might shake him from his moral torpor. Nor could I fail to be reminded of the Nazi officers who operated the concentration camps, came home to their wives and ruddy-cheeked children, listened to Mozart in the evening, attended church on Sundays, and then went back to Dachau and Tegel on Monday morning.

When Father Smith confesses that he is "surrounded by the corpses of souls," he doesn't single out wicked secularists for blame. He clearly implies that an insidious and invisible kind of death has overcome our churches no less than our culture. Walker Percy himself expressed a similar kind of distress about the dead souls who sit in the high places of governmental and cultural power. Only two years before his death in 1990, Percy wrote a letter to the New York *Times* that it refused to publish. That our national "newspaper of record" refused to print a plea voiced by one of our major novelists makes the letter all the more worth our hearing:

> The most influential book published in German in the first quarter of [the 20th] century was entitled *The Justification of the Destruction of Life Devoid of Value.* Its co-authors were the distinguished jurist Karl Binding and the prominent psychiatrist Alfred Hoche. Neither Binding nor Hoche had ever heard of Hitler or the Nazis. Nor, in all likelihood, did Hitler ever read the book. He didn't have to.
>
> . . . I would not wish to be understood as implying that the respected American institutions I have named [The *New York Times,* the United States Supreme Court, the American Civil Liberties Union, the National Organization of Women] are similar or corresponding to pre-Nazi institutions.
>
> But I do suggest that once the line is crossed, once the principle gains acceptance — juridically, medically, socially [and I would add religiously] — [that] innocent human life can be destroyed for whatever reason, for the most admirable socioeconomic, medical, or social reasons — then it does not take a prophet to predict what will happen next, or if not next, then sooner or later. At any rate, a warning is in order. Depending on the disposition of the majority and the opinion polls — now in favor of allowing women to get rid of unborn and unwanted babies — it is not difficult to imagine an electorate or a court ten years, fifty years from now, who would favor getting rid of use-

less old people, retarded children, anti-social blacks, illegal Hispanics, gypsies, Jews. . . ."*

This may seem to be a grim note to end on. But there is something strangely salubrious about telling the truth, even when it is unpleasant. Our dead souls might be shocked back into life. Rowan Williams, the new archbishop of Canterbury, puts the matter ever so well when he reverses the old chestnut that "truth is the first casualty of war." "Peace," replies Archbishop Williams, "is the first casualty of untruthfulness." Instead of war's being a necessary evil that kills off the truth, Williams is suggesting that we start to kill each other whenever we fail to tell the truth — about ourselves, about the world and, above all, about God's will both for us and the world.

The great glad news is that the church is called by Jesus Christ to become his community of truth and thus his culture of life. Its liturgical worship centered on the Word and sacrament, together with its practical and prophetic teachings about war and peace — especially as they derive from the sixth commandment — are meant to form our character and to shape our souls. Here alone, in the church, can we Christians find the courage to give our lives justifiably rather than to take the lives of others unjustifiably. Here alone can we find the compassion to care for the unborn and the elderly, especially when society regards them as "devoid of value." Here alone can we find the Spirit of truth that enables us to become a community of living rather than dead souls. Amen.

* *Signposts in a Strange Land,* pp. 350-51.

Hurrying Toward Hell

Isaiah 40:27-31; Mark 14:32-42; Hebrews 12:1-3

First Baptist Church
Washington, D.C.
May 23, 1993

When a friend asked about my sermon subject for this Sunday, I told him that I planned to preach on the devil. Because we will be discussing C. S. Lewis's *Screwtape Letters* in these next few days, it seemed appropriate to address the question of the demonic in my sermon. "Well," replied the friend, "you've chosen the appropriate place." I was a bit troubled at such a suggestion, fearing that my colleague knew something about this church that no one had bothered to tell me. Then the truth of my friend's cryptic saying became evident. Washington is a microcosm of our country's larger life. The vices that plague our churches and our society (no less than the virtues that redeem them) come to their clearest focus in our capital city.

But clear does not mean obvious. Genesis calls the serpent "the subtlest beast of the field." Because the devil is the great impostor, it takes the probing light of the gospel to fathom his dark deceits, especially in this place. I believe that the prophet Isaiah and the evangelist Mark and the author of Hebrews give us such light. They teach us that one of Satan's slickest tricks is to make us hurry. The call of the gospel, by contrast, is not to hurry but to wait upon God, not to scurry madly but to watch keenly for the deceptions of the devil, not to grow weary and faint from dashing about doing good, but to run with perseverance the race that Christ has set before us.

I

Scholars tell us that chapters 40–60 of Isaiah were written a good deal later than the first thirty-nine chapters. Written by the hand of a "Second Isaiah," they come near the end of Judah's long captivity in Babylon. In 539 BCE, the Assyrian tyrants were at last defeated by Cyrus, the Persian king. And so Israel's release seemed at hand. Yet many of the Jewish exiles were impatient with God's slow deliverance: they wanted freedom now — not sometime soon, but right now. "How are we to go on living?" asks Ezekiel. "There is none to comfort me," cries the author of Lamentations. "How shall we sing the Lord's song in a strange land?" the Psalmist demands to know. To all of these Hebrew prophets and poets, God seems tardy. He does not do things quickly enough. He takes too much time. A wag has said that when we wish someone "Godspeed," we are sentencing them to travel at the rate of approximately three miles an hour.

Yet Scripture teaches that patience is the essence of God's nature and action. His mill grinds slowly, as the old proverb has it, though exceedingly fine. God is not in a hurry. He has all the time both in the world and beyond the world. The ancient immemorial past stands before God as a mere moment: "A thousand ages in thy sight are like an evening gone." The vast stretches of the future unfold before God like so many chapters in a book. He is Alpha and Omega, the first and the last, the beginning and the end. And so God is not in a rush. He has all the time he needs. God is patient, and thus slow to anger. He can wait without panic. He does things in his own good time and according to his own calendar, not ours. As one of the psalmists says, "My times are in thy hand." "So teach us," another psalmist declares, "to number our days that we may get a heart of wisdom." Our God is a patient God.

The devil, by contrast, cannot wait. He is ever the busybody. Indeed, he is the author of the quick fix. The serpent beguiles Eve by promising her instant knowledge and wisdom: "Eat of this tree," he says, "and you won't have to labor patiently in God's garden. You won't have to wait for God gradually to teach you the meaning of good and evil. You shall be suddenly wise. Yes, you shall be divine. Indeed, you shall not die." It sounded good then and it sounds good now. Who wants to grow old and die like a mere mortal? Who wants delayed gratification? Why take the slow road of suffering, up the steep hill of the cross, when there are so many shortcuts and easy downhill slopes? Why wait on the slow working of the Lord God when the world offers instant power and pleasure?

This is not to say that all waiting is virtuous. There is an urgency about the gospel that will now allow us to sit at ease in Zion. Christians are indeed commanded to be about the business of "making the most of the time" (Eph. 5:16; Col. 4:5). Martin Luther King Jr. rightly complained, therefore, that the white moderate Christians of Birmingham counseled him falsely to slow down in his drive for black equality, as if they would then get around to granting it in their own good time. King was wise enough to see that their waiting was not a delay so much as a rejection of the clamant need for radical racial reform.

To make the most of the time is not a contradiction to waiting patiently. For true waiting is a preparation for right action. The demonic temptation not to wait but to hurry is especially acute in this nation of ours. We Americans are a people who cannot wait. Our whole history makes us want to do things quickly. Europe was too slow in granting political and economic and religious liberty to our ancestors, and so many of them left in a hurry. To our enormous credit, we Americans have remedied many of the ancient wrongs that other people thought to be irreparable. This country remains, for all its many faults, a beacon of freedom for those who are bound in the chains of the past. To deny this great truth and to trash America is to speak for the author of all lies. Worse still, it is to miss the devil's subtlest trick, that is, his power to convert our great American virtue into our terrible American vice. He is the perverter who twists and distorts our strength into our weakness. Because we are the people who have done so many good things, he makes us believe that we are the people who can do everything. Finally, he convinces us that we can fix even the Fall.

II

Both politically and personally, our refusal to wait on God is the essence of our sin. Politicians are constantly tempted to cut corners, to get elected by crooked means, to stay in office by promising to fix things quickly. Judas Iscariot was such a politician, and his party was called the Zealots. They wanted to overthrow the Roman oppressors instantly, to drive the rascals out in a hurry. Therefore, Judas was impatient with Jesus' refusal to take such coercive power into his own hands.

He wanted his Lord to establish a kingdom of this world, and thus to insist that his disciples take up arms and fight.

As often happens, the political zealot became the political cynic. Since Judas couldn't have everything his way, he would have nothing at all. Selling his soul for a bribe, he betrayed Jesus to the religious authorities. Even in his guilt, Judas could not wait. Like Peter, who also betrayed Jesus, Judas could have been forgiven and restored to faithfulness. But Judas was determined to be in a rush, to die even as he lived — hurriedly. Judas could not wait patiently for his redemption. He would not take the slow road toward salvation, and so he ended by dancing the desperate jig of a man hanging in midair, or else by running off a cliff into a gully or gorge, where his moral bloatedness burst like a watermelon.

It is not only politicians who are in a desperate hurry. When others ask us how we have been doing, we have a standard one-word reply. "Busy, busy, busy." It's a terrible and vicious cycle, a demonic gerbil-wheel that we are all spinning on. We first create for ourselves a set of supposedly necessary activities, and then we wear ourselves out busily performing these tasks that we ourselves have invented. Multiply this circular make-work pattern by a thousand times, and what we get is a bureaucracy — governmental, commercial, educational, ecclesiastical. Our work thus becomes our only source of meaning. Why else do we go back to our offices at night and on the weekends? Why else is there so little time for our friends and families, for our thoughts and, above all, for our prayers?

From the White House to my house and your house, we are a desperately busy people. This furious busyness is the surest sign of our apostasy. We do not believe — as the Negro spiritual so simply says, and as Mahalia Jackson sang so beautifully — that God has the whole world in his hands. We secretly fear that Christ is not in control of time. We covertly doubt that he is truly the sovereign Lord of history. On the contrary, we believe that we must busily save ourselves.

Behold what such hurry has done to our churches. They should be founded on the solid rock of Christ's patient salvation, on the sure conviction that God's grace alone saves us, and that our busywork can only damn us. Instead, we have done worse than the religious folk of the first century. Jesus accused them of having turned the house of God into a den of thieves. We, by contrast, have made it into a beehive of busyness. A couple recently confessed to me — not altogether in jest

— that, if they ever get a divorce, they will name their church as the co-respondent. Their marriage is being virtually devoured by their church's endless activities.

The devil, says Denis DeRougement, is the one who keeps the clock. He tells us that our time is short and that we had better hurry up. In every aspect of our lives, therefore, we are a people made manic about time. In our cars, we are transformed from otherwise tranquil folk into veritable speed demons filled with road rage. In our sex lives, we are in a frenzy for quick happiness, for instant ecstasy. In our obsession with money, we want to get rich quick. Notice the time-haunted character even of our metaphors. "Fools rush in," said Alexander Pope, "where angels fear to tread." We declare that someone ran into trouble, not that they walked into it. The drug world calls methamphetamines by the name of "speed," and we describe the sensate thrill of drugs as a rush. And fast food has become our preferred culinary sustenance.

No wonder that witchcraft and occult religion are burgeoning in America: they are spiritual drugs that offer shortcuts to hope and happiness and truth. Yet we should be very careful not to regard David Koresh and the Branch Davidians as mere crazies. If we do, we will have failed to recognize that our own more socially acceptable addictions are what the New Testament regards as demonic possessions. The Greek word for witchcraft and sorcery is *pharmakeia*. The devil drugs all of us with a hurried desire for pleasure and power and position. For when we are in a hurry, we start to gild bricks, to shave edges, to tell little lies that gradually become the Big Lie — until we end by believing our own untruth. Total self-deception is the mark of the devil's final triumph.

III

The Good News called the gospel is that the devil has been defeated. He is desperately busy because he knows that his time is short. Like the sands of an hourglass, his days and years are draining away. He may be the ruler of this present evil age, as the New Testament calls him, but he is not the King of Time. And so his reign is coming to a rapid end. "The Prince of Darkness grim, we tremble not for him," we sing with Martin Luther. "His rage we can endure. For lo! his doom is sure. One little word shall fell him." No wonder the demons were the first to recognize Jesus as the Messiah. They knew that this one little Word — this rabbi-God in the flesh — would put them literally out of business, out of "busyness." John's Gospel is emphatic about the matter: "Now is the judgment of this world, now shall the ruler of this world be cast out; and I, when I am lifted up from the earth, will draw all men to myself."

What does such drastic language mean for such workaday folk as you and me? It means that we are all called to lift high the cross, to learn that our time is in the hands of the Savior who died for our sins and who was raised for our salvation, and thus that we are summoned to wait and watch with Christ. Jesus was short-tempered with his disciples when they grew weary and fell asleep during his all-night ordeal in Gethsemane. "Could you not watch with me for one hour?" They had drowsed off because they did not recognize the real battle Jesus was fighting: it was not against flesh and blood, but against principalities and powers and wickedness in high places. To make clear that his battle is with the father of all fraud, Jesus commanded the disciples to "watch and pray that you enter not into temptation." To stay alert and awake with Christ is not to be deceived, as Peter was, concerning the real enemy. Peter thought he could identify and handle evil quickly, and so he took matters into his own hurried hands by slicing off the ear of Malchus.

To watch with Christ is to discern the subtle deceptions of the devil. Chief among his deceits is the notion that a busy life is a good life, that the early bird gets the worm, that to hurry is to arrive first. The slow pace of the Christian life, by contrast, requires a sense of modesty about our own allotment of time and about the things we might accomplish in it. I learned this lesson from a next-door Methodist saint who lived one month short of 101 years. I once asked him to tell me the secret of such longevity. He said quite wittily that he first of all went out and found himself a pair of long-lived parents. Then, less ironically, he told me that he had never, in all of his ten decades, gotten in a hurry. "You, on the other hand, haven't yet learned to walk. You always run. You don't want things done tomorrow. You want them done yesterday."

This chastening admonition to slow down, to stop hurrying, to walk patiently, can also be learned from our wisest writers. Milton's sonnet "On His Blindness," which wrestles angrily with God for exacting day-labor of a man who has been deprived of his sight and thus cannot work even in conditions that are bright, ends ever so patiently: "They also serve who only stand and wait." Pascal once declared that most of the world's mischief is caused by our inability to sit still in our rooms. The opposite of a watchful waiting is a furious fidgeting. Somewhere in *Alice in Wonderland* there is this wondrous injunction: "Don't just do something. Stand there!" Best of all is this injunction from one of Peter De Vries's characters: "Never, ever put off until tomorrow . . . what you can put off indefinitely."

So it is that we are called to wait for the Lord God, to go slowly, to renew our strength in Christ, to mount up with wings like eagles, to run and not be weary, to walk and not faint. The race we run is not the race to get there first and thus to finish among the world's winners. We are running in order to be the least and the last of God's servants — to be found faithful rather than triumphant. The great cloud of witnesses surrounding us is not a crowd of secular spectators but rather of all the faithful dead: all those saints who, having gone before us, have thus made possible our own path. Jesus is the pioneer and perfecter of this new way. He is the one who took no detours or by-ways, who persevered to the end, who did not get in a hurry, even though his lifeblood was drained out at age thirty-three. He set aside all privilege and equality with God in order to endure the dishonor of the cross. He converted that cruel instrument of death from a sign of shame into the mark of true joy for those who take its slow path — the way of suffering and perseverance, the way of resurrection and eternal life.

Many of you will remember that Martin Luther once drove out the devil by hurling an inkbottle at him. A far more revealing story concerns another time when Luther faced yet another demonic temptation. It was so fierce that Luther ran to his slate board and chalked down but two words: *Baptizatus sum.* In that succinct phrase, "I have been baptized," Luther was declaring to the devil the deepest of truths: "I am the property of Another! You cannot lay hands on me. This is my indelible mark. I am stamped with the character of the cross, with the ownership and lordship and forgiveness of Jesus Christ." For in baptism we receive a new character and identity. We are given a name that the world cannot give and Satan cannot take away. It is not the name "rich" or "poor," not the name "Democrat" or "Republican," not the name "black" or "white" or "yellow" or "brown" or "red," but the name Christian. We are here today to give thanks for this incomparable gift: that we are God's property and not our own possession, that he has bought us at the high price of Calvary, that he will take all of his time and even eternity to reclaim us, and thus that nothing can make us hurry our way into hell. Amen.

Baptism in a Coffin

A former student of mine, Jim McCoy, the pastor of a rural Baptist congregation in central North Carolina, recently invited me to lecture at his church. After finishing my duties on a Saturday morning, I was preparing to make a quick exit for my two-hour drive home when my pastor-friend halted me with a hesitant question: Would I accompany him to the local minimum-security prison for a baptism? The prisoner's family and hometown preacher would probably not attend, and so the cloud of witnesses celebrating the new birth of this convert would be small indeed. My presence might in fact double the congregation. Thinking of all the yardwork I could do that Saturday afternoon, I was tempted to decline, but in the end I reluctantly agreed.

Over lunch I learned that the newly professed Christian was no ordinary prisoner. He had been incarcerated not for stealing cars or selling dope, but for the crime that our society is perhaps least prepared to pardon. In a drunken stupor this man had molested his ten-year-old daughter. He had thus committed a triple violation: he had violated the girl's sexual integrity, her filial trust, and her moral innocence. No wonder that child molesters are the most despised of all criminals and that their fellow inmates call them "short eyes." Convicts understand, as many of us do not, that no clearly considered human motive, no matter how sinister, could prompt such an act: it must spring from a blindness made all the more terrible for being self-inflicted.

My suspicions were instant and numerous. Was this a convenient jailhouse conversion that might lead to a quicker parole, a sentimental

---

"Baptism in a Coffin" first appeared in *Christian Century,* October 22, 1992.

turning to God because there was nowhere else to turn, a desperate search for pastoral acceptance when societal rejection was sure to come? The pastor confessed something, however, that caused me to doubt my doubts. He said that this criminal did not make his profession of faith amid abject panic. His conversion was not prompted by the dread that, unless he reformed his life, no one — least of all his family — would ever accept him again. The real turn had come several days earlier, when the man's wife and daughter had visited the prison in order to forgive him. It was only then, when freed from the burden of his sin by God's humanly mediated grace, that the molester got on his knees and begged for the mercy of both God and his family. Surely, I thought, this is the true order of salvation: our repentance is always the consequence and not the condition of divine grace.

The baptism turned out to be an event for which joy, though a good biblical term, is altogether too tame and tepid a word. It was as close to a New Testament experience as perhaps I shall ever have. A guard escorted the prisoner from behind a fence that was topped with razor wire. His family was not able to attend because their broken-down car had failed yet again. There were just the three of us, with the guard looking curiously on. To the strumming of the chaplain's guitar we sang a croaky version of "Amazing Grace." We did not balk at declaring ourselves "wretches." After a pastoral prayer, the barefoot prisoner stepped into a wooden box that had been lined with a plastic sheet and filled with water. It looked like a large coffin, and rightly so. This was no warmed and tiled bath in the baptistery of First Baptist, with its painted River Jordan winding pleasantly into the distance. This was the place of death, the watery chaos from which God graciously made the world and to which, in rightful wrath, he almost returned it.

Pronouncing the Trinitarian formula, the pastor lowered the new Christian down into the liquid grave to be buried with Christ and then raised him up to life eternal. Though the water was cold, the man was not eager to get out. Instead, he stood there weeping for joy. When at last he left the baptismal box, I thought he would hurry away to change into something dry. I was mistaken. "I want to wear these clothes as long as I can," he said. "In fact, I wish I never had to take a shower again." And so we walked to nearby tables and sat quietly in the autumnal Carolina sun, hearing this newly minted Christian explain why his baptismal burial was too good to dry off. "I'm now a free man," he declared. "I'm not impatient to leave prison because this wire can't shackle my soul. I know that I deserved to come here, to pay for what I did. But I also learned here that someone else has paid for all my crimes, my sins against God and my daughter and my wife."

We warned him that his new life in Christ would be rough, that temptations would be fiercer than ever. The pastor recalled Luther's confession that, even in baptism, the old Adam remains a frightfully good swimmer. Our baptism signifies, all three of us confessed gladly together, that we belong not to ourselves, not to our guilty past, not to our fearful future, nor to the demonic powers of alcohol and sex. In our baptism we have been reclaimed as the property of Jesus Christ and his Kingdom. The pastor then fetched his guitar and sang a down-home gospel song about what it means to be free in Jesus.

Before returning to the prison yard, the new Christian made a final affirmation. He said that he had once doubted he could ever go back to his hometown, so great were the shame and scandal of what he had done. But now he was determined to return there, to take up his work as a carpenter, and to become a faithful father and husband. More important by far, he declared his hope to join a local church and to live out his new life in Christ as a public witness to the transforming power of God's grace. "When I get out of this place," he added. "I want to do two things. But without a car, I can't do either one. I want to find a church where I can get on my knees and thank God, and I want to get home to my family." The pastor assured him that he would provide both the church confessional and the ride home.

The wonder that I witnessed on this Saturday could prove a sham. The repentant molester may return to his old abusive habits, destroying both himself and others. It will take careful and prolonged nurture in the faith in order to free him from such bondage. But I believe it wrong to insist — as many voices would insist — that this man's family should never have forgiven him, that to do so was to sanction his violence, indeed to collude in rape. I believe that this mother and daughter brought a dead man back to life. Their act of forgiveness opened him to the one reality by which our common slavery to sin can be broken — the power of salvation in Jesus Christ.

PART V

THE CHRISTIAN YEAR

Waiting, Watching, and Enduring to the End

Mark 13:1-13

AN ADVENT SERMON

First Sunday in Advent, December 2, 1990
Quail Hollow Presbyterian Church
Charlotte, North Carolina

For us Christians, the new year begins not with January 1 and the gradual return of the sun as the days begin to lengthen. For us, the new year starts with Advent, with the coming of the Son of God as the Word made flesh. Yet Advent is not only a time to prepare for Christmas but also a time to ready ourselves for the Second Coming. What began at Bethlehem will be completed only beyond the bounds of time. Advent is thus the season of purple: a time of sober reflection and remembrance and preparation for the Christ who is coming to judge the quick and the dead, to divide the sheep and goats, to separate the left and right — amid weeping and wailing and gnashing of teeth. Yet Advent is also the time of rejoicing. For the Son who is returning to wage war at Armageddon is the same Christ who made peace at Golgotha. The first Coming was so wondrously merciful that we eagerly welcome our Lord's Second Advent, in the confidence that it will be more strangely gracious still. In this firm hope, we wait and watch and endure to the end.

I

In Mark 13, Jesus prophesies the destruction of the Jerusalem temple. Nothing could have seemed more horrible to a Jew. Here was the very dwelling place of God: No. 1 Temple Mount! Here was the ark of the covenant, the holy of holies. For God's temple to be cast down and its sanctuary defiled by gentiles was, for Jews, an unspeakable abomination. Thus did Jesus' prophecy of the coming destruction of the temple seem to signal the death and end of *everything*. The disciples are staggered by this news. They demand that Jesus tell them when the terrible event will happen. But instead of giving them a calendar of expectation, Jesus warns them not to get in a hurry, not to be led astray by false signs of the end, but to wait patiently on God.

We, too, have cause to believe that we are near the end. I sometimes alarm my students by telling them that the West has worn itself out, and that history as we know it may be nearing its conclusion. Our culture seems indeed to be sinking into the sunset of its permanent decline, as Oswald Spengler and Alexandyr Solzhenitsyn have long warned us. In the East, Communism has collapsed of its own bloated weight — not from the triumph of Western liberty and democracy. East Germans fleeing to the West have thus been accused of modifying Caesar's famous motto as follows: We came, we saw, and we shopped.

What is our own desperate Christmas shopping but an attempt to silence our fears of the end? The fear that our present recession will slide into another grueling depression such as our parents knew sixty years ago? The fear that the slumbering ease of the eighties will become the bed-thrashing nightmare of the nineties? The fear that the thousands of hospital beds that the Army has prepared in England and Germany will soon be filled with our dying sons and daughters if we go to war in the Persian Gulf? The fear that the crisis in Kuwait will incinerate us all, amidst a series of bomb bursts that will darken the sun, drench the moon in blood, and cast down the stars?

Yet the nearing end that we fear is not the end that Jesus prophesies. The incineration of our planet is but a lighted candle when compared to our Lord's Second Advent. He enjoins us thus to wait without fear in the face of all the false signs. There will indeed be wars and rumors of wars, says Jesus. Nation will rise up against nation, kingdom against kingdom. Earthquake and famine will strike. Despite the silly song in *The Sound of Music,* our own recent Hurricane Hugo has taught us that hurricanes can indeed horribly happen. "But," says Jesus, "the end is not yet." We are not to be panicked. We are to wait patiently on God, trusting that his Son's coming will bring the world not to its desperate but its proper end.

A rightful waiting is perhaps the most difficult task of faith. Patience is the virtue that I, perhaps like you, am most conspicuously missing. We are all busy and bent on getting things done. How often, alas, is our hurried doing our very undoing. And so we are called at Advent to stand and wait — perhaps even to stand and wait in the Arabian Desert.

To wait patiently for Christ's coming is to wait rightly for everything else. There are wives waiting at the bottom of Fool's Hill for their adulterous husbands to tumble all the way down, there to help them put their lives back together again. There are the chronically ill victims of cancer waiting for their disease to run its awful course, and perhaps to drive them into the ground with it. There are the elderly waiting alone in nursing homes, with little to anticipate but the final word of the Great Filmmaker: "Cut." There are parents waiting for their twenty-five-year-old children to grow up and start behaving like adults. There are thirty-year-old women waiting for men who will take interest in something more than their bodies. There are teachers waiting for the academic fads of our time to fail of their own silliness. There are preachers waiting for their congregations to stop acting like adolescents in wanting the church to meet their petty needs. And there are congregations waiting for their preachers to get real about the reality of the gospel. We are all waiting. Advent is the time when we learn the right kind of waiting: a faithful waiting on the God of Jesus Christ.

II

Advent is also a call to watch and to endure. "Watch," says Jesus, "for you do not know when the time will come." Like the servant who has no idea when his master will return, we are to watch and not be found sleeping. Faith is not a Sominex life, but it is a divine alertness to what is really happening. To the disciples who snored their way through Gethsemane, Jesus spoke some of the sharpest words in all of Scripture: "Could you not watch one hour?" To watch is to be on guard, to sense keenly the dangers of evil, to fathom the world's mystery and, above all, not to miss the tricks of God's grace. In Advent we learn this kind of watching: how to see straight, how to have true vision, how to detect what really counts from what doesn't matter a whit, how to discern the passing and ephemeral from the lasting and eternal.

To watch for Christ's coming is also to know that God watches over us. Not a sparrow falls, not a hair remains unnumbered, without God's watchful concern. We are vigilant about what we think and say and do because we know that God stands vigil over us. But he is not the Great Snoop who's making a list and checking it twice. He is the sovereign Lord who will not let his good creation get flushed down the sinkhole of history. Thus does Christ sit at the right hand of God, watching patiently over all time and space, making intercession in our behalf. In his repeated injunctions to "wait upon the Lord," the psalmist was steeped in such patience. He also knew the meaning of watchfulness: "Unless the Lord build the house, those who build it labor in vain. Unless the Lord watches over the city, the watchman stays awake in vain." In Advent we learn to stay awake, to wait and to watch for the coming of the one who watches over the world with grace and truth.

Advent is above all a call to endurance. You Presbyterians have a fine name for it: the "perseverance of the saints." Jesus warns his disciples that they will be hailed into court and brought to trial because of their witness to the gospel. This prospect seems comically remote from us. Far from being persecuted, we are often congratulated for being Christian. Church-going is as American as pro football and PTA. Yet our Advent text suggests a radically different vision of the church, the church not as a safe haven but as a perilous place indeed. My student Steve Blakemore has suggested that, if we were to worship God aright, we would wear crash helmets and seat belts in church. Why? Because here we enter the dangerous presence of God. Because here we eat Christ's broken body and drink his bloody cup. Because here we receive the Word which pierces like a two-edged sword, dividing joint from marrow, causing brother to betray brother, making children strike their parents dead, leading the world to hate us for Christ's sake. Because here we are called and equipped to persevere to the end.

Surely, we are inclined to protest, Jesus is not talking about us. In fact, he is. There is not a person in this sanctuary whom Christ has not given crosses to bear, sorrow to suffer, persecution to endure for his sake. By his power, we have staying power. Christians are called to stick fast and not to fall away. We are summoned to sweat it out to the end. The Presbyterian theologian George Hendry has wisely said that "the inspiration of the Spirit does not eliminate the perspiration of the saints."

Endurance comes through hardship rightly borne. Such was the witness of the great Christian curmudgeon who died last week, Malcolm Muggeridge. Not a solitary thing, Muggeridge confessed, did he learn from all the success he achieved, nor from all the happiness he so desperately pursued. "Pain and desolation taught me everything that enlightened and enhanced my life," said St. Mugg, "because they drew me to the Cross."

We begin the new Christian year, therefore, with the banquet of the Cross. At this meal we proclaim the Lord's death until he comes again. At this feast we learn to bear our load because Christ has carried our afflictions and borne our sorrows. At this banquet we find the burden that is easy because it brings joy, the yoke that is light because it pulls real weight. At this carnival of the kingdom we receive the Advent power of the Christ who has come and is coming again, the Christ who enables us to wait and watch and endure to the End.

Benediction: Wait on God the Father, and you shall renew your strength. Watch with Christ the Son, and you shall mount up with wings like eagles. Endure to the end by the power of the Holy Spirit, and you shall run and not be weary; you shall walk and not faint. Amen.

Jesus as Both Savior and Lord

A LENTEN MEDITATION

Robert E. Lee Memorial Episcopal Church
Lexington, Virginia
March 15, 1989

The joke about bringing a Baptist to explain to Episcopalians why Jesus is Savior and Lord is altogether appropriate. I never heard about Lent until I was in college, and at first I thought it referred to the stuff that collects on one's socks when washed with cottony clothes. Many Protestants of my kind do indeed find this forty-day season of repentance too Catholic, as if the climactic Christian event were not the Resurrection but the Crucifixion. Yet, however much the ancient church may have misunderstood the nature of repentance, its instinct was quite right to make us see the connection between Easter Sunday and Good Friday. Lent joins them together so as not to be put asunder.

Not by accident is our central symbol the cross and not the empty tomb. Not only would a vacant grave be difficult to make into an emblem; it would also miss the real point of the Christian faith. There have been many empty tombs but only one risen and living Christ. And he is living and risen in confirmation of what he performed upon the tree at Calvary. God raises Jesus from the dead to confirm and not to deny what happened there. Admittedly the Easter event was a great surprise that staggered the apostles' expectations. Yet it served to validate and verify the far more drastic surprise that the Messiah would be killed, that Jesus would suffer and die for the sins of the world rather than triumphing in political and religious power. We worship the God of Easter morning, therefore, only because he is first and last the God of Good Friday, the God of Golgotha, the God of Lent.

I. Justification by Grace Alone

Ephesians 2:8 was the watchword of the Protestant Reformation: "By grace alone are you saved through faith; and this is not your own doing, it is the gift of God — not because of works, lest any man should boast." Justification thus points to Jesus as Savior, who justifies us *sola gratia,* by grace alone. Sanctification points to Jesus as Lord, who sanctifies us *sola fide,* by faith alone. Concerning justification by grace alone, Luther said: "Of this article nothing can be yielded or surrendered, even though heaven and earth and all things should sink to ruin. . . . And upon this article all things depend, which we teach and practice against the Pope, the devil, and the whole world. Therefore, we must not doubt but be sure concerning this doctrine; for otherwise all is lost. . . . This is the position on which the church stands or falls."

We Christians believe with Flannery O'Connor's serial killer called the Misfit — though in wonderfully cornpone grammar he is protesting rather than affirming — that "Jesus thrown everything off balance." Christ is indeed Savior because he throws everything out of balance by dying for our sins. We do not claim that Christ was the perfectly innocent man whose goodness was so great that he earned enough merit in God's sight to outweigh all the sins we have committed. On the contrary, he inherited our own fallen nature, was tested and tempted in every respect as we are, yet maintained total faithfulness to God and total solidarity with his fellows. Jesus Christ is thus the one and only man who has given God his due. God thus let fall upon him the wrath that was reserved for us, because he alone could take it as the One True Man. Unique among the world's religions is this Jewish and Christian reversal of the claim that God is the reconciled and man the reconciler. The essence of pagan religion is that the gods can be placated if we are sufficiently moral and dutiful in our regard for them. Here alone, in the Judaeo-Christian formula, is God the reconciler and man the reconciled. God does what no earthly judge could ever do: through Christ our Savior, he judges us sinners not only as forgiven but as righteous, as justified.

Voltaire, the great eighteenth-century French skeptic, liked to say that God must forgive sin because that's his business: *Dieu pardonnera, c'est son métier.* This would mean that God would renounce his justice, let bygones be bygones, and forgive us in the hope that we will do better next time. This, alas, is the nature of most parental pardon. But God is no such soft sell. He demands his due by creating what he requires. God insists on his honor, claims his own due, and reclaims his lost property by restoring the broken covenant and thus putting us on the hook of his grace. He puts aright what we have set wrong. He reknits the cords that we so sinfully break. He places us alongside him despite our attempt to separate ourselves from him. He does not acquit us but makes us righteous. He justifies us by his grace alone.

Jesus Christ is the saving answer who makes us redefine the nature of sin. The popular notion of sin understands it as individual evil acts, moral mistakes, ethical errors — all of which are said to make us bad persons. Thus was I taught this nifty little ditty: "We don't smoke, and we don't chew, and we don't go with girls who do." This banal rhyme misunderstands the difference between sins (plural) and Sin (singular and capitalized). Not just smoking and drinking and dancing (and going with girls who do), but even thievery and adultery, cheating and lying, swindling and murder, even nuclear war and the Holocaust are sins in the plural. Horrible as these are, they are symptoms of a much worse disease. All human attempts to rid ourselves of such sins are at best a rearguard action in a losing battle.

The Bible thus understands Sin (singular, capitalized) as the permanent state of alienation from God through unbelief and distrust — namely, the rejection of God's grace. Genesis makes clear that sin may be something as small an act as eating forbidden fruit but have the huge effect of distrusting God, wanting to be our own lord and masters, and thus seeking our own autonomy. From the tiniest personal peccadillo, such as tardiness, to the largest corporate evil, such as war, all sin is the refusal to trust God's goodness, to be justified by his grace, to believe in his salvation. Thus is Golgotha the measure of all sin, the act that we in twentieth-century America would have committed no less surely than did first-century Jews and Romans. We totally rejected God's total help. I an opposed to capital punishment, not because there are no sins heinous enough to merit the destruction of a human life, but because every human being who has ever lived, except for this one man, Jesus Christ, deserves the death sentence, because we were all complicit in his death: we crucified the mercy of God.

The final pages of Walker Percy's *Love in the Ruins* reveal the true terror of God's mercy. Dr. Thomas More, lineal descendant of the Renaissance saint but also a physician who cannot heal himself, has come to his end. He has lived a dissolute and despairing life in anger over the cancerous death of his daughter Samantha. Yet suddenly the truth breaks upon Dr. More: he has feasted on his own remorse; he has made his bitterness strangely delectable; he has perversely enjoyed his suffering. Without his daughter's death, he would have had no excuse for his massive self-indulgence. Thus was it in fear of healing rather than in dread of failure that More did not take Samantha to Lourdes: "I was afraid she might be cured. What then? Suppose you ask God for a miracle and God says, yes, very well. How do you live the rest of your life?"

This is the central question raised by Lent. How dare we repent when the request for forgiveness is the one prayer that never goes unanswered? What shall we do with something so fearful as divine mercy? Is not this the real wrath of God — to be condemned by exoneration, to be imprisoned by having the prison door flung wide, to be enslaved in the service that is perfect freedom? When Jesus embodied this divine offense in life and deed no less than in word, he was hanged. Here, I believe, lies the real poignancy of Jesus' plangent lament over Jerusalem. "How often I would have gathered your children together as a hen gathers her brood under her wings, but you would not!" It is not Christ's anger but his mercy that offends. Like his original accusers, we are able to answer condemnation with legitimating excuses. We find pardon intolerable precisely because it permits no such self-justification. To receive the miracle of God's grace is to be robbed of all defenses, to be rendered bereft of all self-protection. We are left with nothing else to do but to rejoice, to give thanks, and to get on with the utterly wondrous, utterly ordinary business of living the rest of our lives.

Our human attempts at self-justification are endless: work, health-and-beauty, power, possessions, thinking too lowly of ourselves because of failure, thinking too highly of ourselves because of success. Precisely because we do not believe in the justifying grace of God is ours such a desperately self-justifying society, a culture obsessed with certification and self-improvement and all the other forms of do-it-yourself salvation provided by the self-help books. And the worst kind of self-justification is the one least likely to recognize itself: the doing of good and thinking well of ourselves for it. John Updike has the Reverend Thomas Marshfield, the hero of his novel *A Month of Sundays,* confess the real source of his marital difficulties: "My wife doesn't believe in God. She believes in doing the right thing."

II. Sanctification Through Faith Alone

During Lent we are called to remember, with special acuity and gratitude, that salvation is utterly and totally unconditional. We do absolutely nothing to earn, deserve, or merit God's grace. On the contrary, the surest way of blocking and insulting God's good gift in Christ Jesus is to set up conditions for receiving and accepting it. The glorious and incomparable thing about this salvation is that it is to be celebrated and feasted on with a joy that is not grudgingly or guiltily worked up.

Through Christ's once-for-all, unrepeatable deed on the cross, we are now justified and set before God as able to live for him. We are not second or little Christs seeking to imitate his life. Justification is God's gracious turning toward sinful man. Everything depends on the prevenient and anterior act of God: his seeking reconciliation with his faithless people from the foundation of the world, calling us before we were even born, seeking partnership with us from all eternity. Sanctification is God's faithful turning of sinful man toward himself, enabling our obedient and free response. But this second turning is no less God's act than the first: he gives, we receive. Justification reveals how Christ is the Savior who adopts us as his children and determines to be our God. Sanctification reveals how Christ is the Lord who makes us his free people. Hence the inseparable connection between the two doctrines: gift and task, creed and deed, theology and ethics, faith and life, receiving and giving. We are Christians insofar as we are both justified and sanctified (I Cor. 1:30).

This Lenten lesson is nicely figured in a story told of my Catholic friend, Larry Cunningham, about making the hospital rounds in a Florida hospital. Dressed in full clerical garb that could not be ignored — backward collar and pectoral cross — Cunningham was confronted by a Baptist preacher wearing a shiny double-knit suit and carrying a Bible large enough to have served as a weapon of war. Yet the latter was no Catholic-despising Baptist; he was a genial and ecumenical pastor who greeted Cunningham gladly: "Good morning, Father. I'm just a sinner saved by grace." In a swift and apt response, Cunningham replied: "Good morning, Preacher. I'm just a Christian working out my salvation with fear and trembling." In this neat exchange lies the heartbeat of our Lenten faith, the systole and diastole of our salvation: justification and sanctification constitute the single divine act that makes us at once righteous and holy because it is accomplished by the one who is both Savior and Lord.

Forgiveness and repentance are equally indivisible (Acts 5:31; 3:26). They are not something that we do autonomously but something that Jesus Christ enables us to do. The word *metanoia* literally means to "change our minds," to reverse our course, rather than doing God some supposed favor. Being enslaved to sin, we can do nothing of ourselves but display our miserable bondage. Repentance, by contrast, is God's great liberating act whereby he frees us to break loose from ourselves and to embark on the venture of faith. The most effective call to repentance is always the summons to foot of the Cross, where in the presence of God's mercy and forgiveness we see and acknowledge our sorry sin. We are not pardoned because we repent; rather, we repent because we are pardoned. And this most basic and radical conversion we repeat every morning afresh.

George MacDonald declared that the first principle of hell is "I am my own." The positive case can be put more cogently by saying that the first rule of heaven is that "we are God's." This is what the call of the cross — the call to follow Jesus as Lord — is all about. It is not a valiant act of imitating Christ as a mere moral exemplar; rather, it is a glad surrender of ourselves to God's use and glory. We live from our salvation no less than toward it. Christ is the only solid rock on which we can take our stand, all other ground being sinking sand. Sanctifying faith is not the summons to be all that we can be, but to become what we already are: the property of God. If we are the sum total of our acts and decisions, we aren't much; indeed, we are less than nothing. But if we are "in Christ," that is, in the body of believers known as the redeemed, then we are nothing other or less than the sons and daughters of God.

Therefore, we have unconditional trust in Jesus as Lord not in order that he might love us, but because he already has demonstrated his love for us (Rom. 3:23-24). The favorite notion of most Pelagian Christianity is that, unless we do something first, God cannot do anything second. This notion of conditional salvation puts the matter exactly backwards. Because Christ is the Lamb slain from the foundation of the world, the one who entered a covenant with us before we were even born, the Lord who called us (as he called Jeremiah) already from our mother's womb — this is why we are able, gladly and gratefully, to acknowledge and trust his great act of justification on the cross. Thus the witty confession of the eminent English Baptist preacher and evangelist Charles Spurgeon, who said that God must have chosen him before he was born, because he surely wouldn't have done so afterward! "We are justified by his grace as a gift, through the redemption which is in Christ Jesus."

Sanctifying faith is not so much like stepping across Colonel William Barrett's line at the Alamo (or even Jim Bowie's being asked to be carried across it on his cot), nor is it something so presumptuous (as Karl Barth tartly complained) as extending God the right hand of fellowship in something akin to a business deal. Rather, it is more like clapping our hands, tapping our feet, lifting our voices, and thus joining the great parade to Paradise. Barth illustrates the point with the story of a man lost in a Swiss snowstorm who crossed frozen Lake Konstanz at full gallop on horseback, a most foolish thing to do — though it saved his life. He would never have done so willingly; in fact, he broke down in panic and fear after he had been told what he'd done. So does repentance follow faith as the result of forgiveness far more than it precedes faith as condition of forgiveness.

Jesus is Lord because he alone gives us untrammeled liberty to live without condemnation (Rom. 8:1). Freedom of the human sort is produced by following a noble example, by importunate pleas to buck up and do our best, or by dire warnings of the consequences to be faced if we fail. To the alcoholic, we urge the virtues of not drinking. To the anxious and insecure, we commend relaxation and self-confidence. We tell the criminal to stop committing crimes, or he will have to pay. We say to the racist, "Love your neighbor of a different color and cease your inhumanity to your fellow man." To the greedy, we plead for the nonexploitation of others. God in Christ is engaged in no such hectoring and guilt-making enterprise. He condemns us by exonerating us, imprisons us by flinging wide the cell door, frees us in service and slavery to him. "There is therefore now no condemnation for those who are in Christ Jesus."

Jesus is Lord because he alone gives us unstinting regard for every other person as one for whom Christ has died and risen: "From now on, therefore, we regard no one from a human point of view" (2 Cor. 5:16). No one can rightly use this gospel as a means of alienation against one's neighbors; it is meant only and always as the true means of reconciliation. This Lord who provides such sanctifying faith is the ultimate gift that we truly have in common with all others: the glad fact that Christ was nailed to a tree for me and for you and for every human being who ever has or who ever shall have lived. Only as a Christian could the poet W. H. Auden make his excellent declaration that "true democracy begins/with free confession of our sins." Thus is there deep truth in the tired old saying that the ground at the foot of the cross is level. There is no elbowing at the Lord's Table where, as Luther said, we are all beggars. During Lent we prepare ourselves for the twin event of the Crucifixion and Resurrection, knowing that, having looked up for bread we shall not receive a stone. For Lent is the time for learning how to live, as Paul says, in him who is the true Savior and Lord, the one who both justifies us by grace and sanctifies us by faith. Amen.

Hosanna to the King Who Rides upon a Donkey

Psalm 118:1-17; 26-29; Mark 11:1-10

A PALM SUNDAY SERMON

St. John's Wood United Reformed Church
London
27 March 1988

Palm Sunday is one of the most ambiguous days in the Christian calendar. It is the day when we celebrate our Lord's triumphal entry into Jerusalem. There he brings his three-year ministry to its culmination. There he announces the kingdom of God no longer to rural Galilee but to the capital city itself, the home of both the Jewish temple and the Roman state. But there he will also be crucified because of the scandal that the gospel presents to both religious people and secular governments. And so this is a triumphal occasion tinged with melancholy and guilt, because the same crowds that joyfully welcome Jesus to Jerusalem will angrily shout for his death only five days later. We ourselves are there on both occasions, waving palm branches and declaring, "Blessed is the King who comes in the name of the Lord," but also chanting with the mob, "Release unto us Barabbas." This day is thus a bittersweet moment, a day for both exaltation and humiliation.

I. The Lord Mighty in Triumph

The Hebrew Bible is full of gloating over slain enemies. "I shall look in triumph on those who hate me," cries the psalmist. "All nations surrounded me; in the name of the Lord I cut them off." "Hark, glad songs of victory in the tents of the righteous: 'The right hand of the Lord does valiantly.'" It is not hard to discern the meaning of such texts. This is the exultation of victors, the swaggering of soldiers who have defeated the enemy. And like most victors, they credit God with their triumph. It is the right hand of the Almighty who has slain the adversary. As long as armies have fought, they have invoked the name of God in their cause, and our Hebrew forebears are no exception to the rule.

What are we to make of such religious reveling, especially when the Palm Sunday text quotes a passage from one of these same triumphal psalms? "Blessed is he who enters in the name of the Lord! Bind the festal procession with branches, up to the horns of the altar." This is clearly a battle hymn sung after an Israelite victory in war. What place does it have in Jesus' joyous entry into Jerusalem? The standard way of dealing with such matters is to refer to what theologians call "progressive revelation." The idea here is that the Old Testament is a primitive and sometimes bloody-minded version of God's full truth, and not until we get to the New Testament do we receive a full disclosure of God's nonmilitary way with the world. There alone do we discover that he is not the God of righteous anger and battle boasting, but the God of mercy and peace.

This solution is totally unsatisfactory. It is indeed the ancient heresy of Marcionism, which relegates the Old Testament to subrevelatory status. We must not forget that bloodthirsty passages can also be found in the New Testament. The book of Revelation contains chilling descriptions of the final victory at the end of time when Christians shall feast on the heads of pagan kings. The point here is that God's self-disclosure in the Jews and Jesus is unitary rather than binary. There are not two covenants but one: the promise first made to Israel, then renewed and fulfilled in Christ. Therefore, the task of Christians is not to read Scripture either literally or progressively but evangelically: to sift the Bible for the Word of God — using Christ and his gospel as the ultimate criterion — so that it might speak the truth through even the most blood-curdling passages.

The most theologically discerning of all our American presidents, Abraham Lincoln, intuitively recognized this fact when he delivered his Second Inaugural Address. There he sought to bind up the nation's terrible wounds as the most destructive conflict in our history neared its end. Lincoln confessed that both American armies prayed to the same God; yet this God could not have been equally identified with both sides. And lest his fellow Unionists assume that God was dead set against the Confederates, giving the victory to the Yankees rather than the Rebels, Lincoln warned that the Almighty has his own purposes and that these purposes are never to be equated with our little hatreds and victories: "Fondly do we hope, fervently do we pray, that this mighty scourge of war may speedily pass away. Yet, if God wills that it continue until all the wealth piled by the bondsman's two hundred and fifty years of unrequited toil shall be sunk, and until every drop of blood drawn with the lash shall be paid by another drawn with the sword, as was said three thousand years ago, so still it must be said, 'The judgments of the Lord are true and righteous altogether.'"

This same strange truth sounds forth from Psalm 118. The author may have intended it to be an exultant song of triumph over enemies slain in battle, but it also speaks another message entirely: "With the Lord on my side I do not fear. What can man do to me? It is better to put confidence in the Lord than to put confidence in man. It is better to take refuge in the Lord than to put confidence in princes." The reader of this text must ask whether the victorious Israelite soldier is just such a man in whom one must not put confidence? And is not the triumphant king of Israel one of those princes in whom one should not find refuge? And what of that darkest saying of all, "The stone which the builders rejected has become the head of the corner"? It refers to Israel as a nothing nation whom history has spurned, but whom God has honored. But might not the Jews themselves be guilty of casting off one of their own prophets as a worthless rock, and then have God could turn him into the foundation stone of his new house? And might not the festal procession be laid down with palm branches for a king who forbids his followers to take up swords and fight for his kingdom?

II. A Gilded Coach vs. a Lowly Donkey

Jesus himself seems to have interpreted the Old Testament in this way. When at last he makes his entry into Jerusalem, despite the warnings of his disciples to stay away, he asks for a foal of a donkey to ride on. This is hardly a grand and triumphal means for a king to make his processional into his kingdom. Worldly rulers enter via something as grandiose as the Lord Mayor's coach displayed in the Museum of London. It should be pulled by a team of magnificent horses, their harnesses and hooves flashing, the coach itself gilded and resplendent, the king riding high and exalted in state. In his recent novel entitled *Jeshua*, the Welsh poet and Anglican priest Moelwyn Merchant has Judas chastise Jesus for not making such a kingly entry into Jerusalem. In that way, says Judas, Jesus could have impressed both the Jews and the Romans with his true royalty. Instead, he complains, Jesus chose to ride on a demeaning donkey. A man of his spiritual dignity and divine class should not lower himself in such ignominious fashion. It is Merchant's brilliant touch to have made Judas something of a snob.

Yet I wonder whether our Christian churches are not guilty of our own subtle snobbery. It is odd that we should call this Palm Sunday rather than Donkey Sunday, just as it is odd that we should have made the Last Supper into a permanent rite, yet failed to sacramentalize Jesus' practice of washing his disciples' feet. Psychologists call this kind of behavior an "avoidance mechanism": our virtually infinite capacity for avoiding harsh truths, for replacing searing reality with saccharine triviality. Our Catholic and Anglican friends acknowledge the irony of Palm Sunday by later burning the palm branches, using the charred remains for the next year's Ash Wednesday services. Here at the beginning of Holy Week we should focus more attention on Jesus' mode of transportation, for therein lies the essential character of the man whom we call "King."

Not just to fulfill an obscure prophecy in Zechariah did Jesus mount this lowly animal. He entered Jerusalem on the foal of an ass in order to demonstrate the nature of his kingdom. Not by the coercive power of bombs and guns, of swords and clubs, is God's reign established. Jesus' power is the power of a humility that is willing to receive injury rather than inflict it. Jesus is the king whose throne is a cross, an instrument of torture that he freely mounted in order to absorb into himself the cruelty of men and thus to give the world real power for ending it. Only by taking upon himself the sins of the world, like a sheep led to the slaughter, could Jesus reverse the awful cycle of hurting and being hurt, of hating and being hated, that characterizes humanity's sorry history.

The events of recent weeks in Northern Ireland bring home the cruciality of Palm Sunday, the day we celebrate not only Christ's triumphal entry but his also suffering humility. As Peter Jenkins has written in his column for the *Independent,* the violence of recent days does not belong to Northern Ireland but to the human race. We are all capable of feeling the hatred and committing the bloodshed that we have witnessed there. The desire to destroy our enemies, whether with our guns or our words, is the deepest human urge. Nothing pleases us more than to hate those who hate us, whether it be the Communists in far-off Russia, or the mean-spirited next-door neighbor, or, alas, our fellow Christian in the adjoining aisle. We are all too eager to strike them with our baleful stares and to kick them with our graceless snubs. There are more means than one to kill. And this is what it means to recrucify Christ: to live without humility and trust in God — and thus in deadly mistrust of others.

It was not only the bad people but also the good people who killed Jesus. So to speak may sound a bit strange. How could we who are followers of Christ also be his betrayers? Wasn't it the evil King Herod and the collusive Pontius Pilate, the scheming Scribes and Pharisees, the screaming Barabbas-releasing mob — aren't these the people who killed Jesus? Yes, of course. But it was not only the bloody-minded who wanted Jesus dead: most righteous and religious people of the day also wanted that. We good church-going, tea-sipping, rate-paying citizens would also have done him to death. It is this sorry and sobering fact that Christians reflect on yet again on Passion Sunday, the day when we address an accusing word not to the world so much as to ourselves.

III. The Church as God's Answer to War

The theologian Stanley Hauerwas was recently asked to specify the Christian answer to nuclear war and racial hatred and religious strife. The questioner thought that this Duke University theologian would answer with a learned discourse on total disarmament or human rights or political tolerance. Instead, Hauerwas answered with two words: "The church." It is God's answer to war and racism, to cruelty and violence of all kinds, both physical and spiritual. This is to make a drastic claim but also a terrible confession. The worst indictment rendered by the events occurring in Northern Ireland is not made against the Irish people but against the Irish churches. These are not just hooligans and barbarians and professional terrorists but Christians who are gunning down their fellow countrymen and stomping the life out of British soldiers.

The cynics thus have good cause for saying that the church is the source and not the cure for such cruelty. Were the Irish not so spitefully divided over their common Christian faith, they would not be letting each other's blood so freely. There is more than a grain of truth in this charge. In moments of faithless despair, we sometimes wish the Irish would stop queuing up to get into their crowded churches, where sectarian rhetoric serves but to fan the resentment that bursts forth in the flames of violence. Yet it does not follow that, if Ireland became less Christian, it would be less violent. What is needed there — just as it is needed here and everywhere else in the world — is not less faith but more. Not, of course, the false faith of sectarian nationalism, but the true faith of total trust in God to forgive our sins and reconcile us to our neighbors.

This explains why United Reformed churches are called upon prayerfully to remember South Africa on this Palm Sunday. There and in Israel and in Ireland we are being made to recognize that traditional appeals to human rights will no longer suffice. The white South Africans also have rights, and they stand to lose a great deal if they give the vote to the black majority. Not just their governmental power, but surely their property and their possessions will eventually be lost as well. Who of us can honestly say that we would voluntarily give up what the Afrikaners are being asked to surrender? Only in following a Lord who entered Jerusalem on a donkey can any people find the humility that would seek reconciliation rather than domination.

This is not a Sunday, therefore, for pointing an accusing finger at the wicked Botha regime, but for confessing the church's failure to be a humble and reconciling community. We give prayerful thanks for Bishop Desmond Tutu and Dr. Alan Boesak, not only for their great courage in resisting the evils of apartheid, but also for their insistence that Christians must never fight evil with evil. We pay them homage not only for their refusal to submit to the Botha government's repressive measures. We also honor them for their clear denunciations of black violence against fellow blacks, especially the damnable practice of "necklacing," igniting petrol-filled tires that have been placed around the necks of those blacks who refuse to join the militant protests. We stand in solidarity with all the Christians of South Africa, both black and white, confessing our common sin.

Whether in South Africa or Israel, whether in Ireland or London, Christians are called to ride the donkey of humility that signifies our total trust in God. This is what the crowds who threw down their garments on the road and who waved palm branches to greet Jesus failed finally to understand. Christ is not an earthly monarch who establishes his Kingdom by force. Nor is he an ethical teacher of nonviolence such as Mahatma Gandhi or Martin Luther King Jr., important peacemakers though these men surely were. Jesus is the Lord, the Savior of human-kind, the very Son of God. We shout "Hosanna in the Highest!" because he alone is the king who rules through suffering self-surrender. We welcome him as triumphant Redeemer because he alone can enable us to live not in fear and hatred but in trust and humility. Amen.

This Cup

Mark 14:32-42

A MAUNDY THURSDAY MEDITATION

Unity Baptist Church
Winston-Salem, North Carolina
March 27, 1997

The Gospel of Mark stands apart from the other accounts of the Gethsemane scene in one small but significant regard. It adds these words to the story of Jesus' agony in the Garden: "Abba, Father, all things are possible to thee." Scholars tell us that *Abba* is an Aramaic word akin to our English word "daddy." It is a term of the utmost intimacy. Jesus had already shocked his fellow Jews by speaking of God as his father. Now he goes much further: he addresses his father as would a child dandled on his papa's knee: "Abba, Daddy."

Yet this moment of great intimacy in the Garden of Gethsemane is prompted not by Jesus' gladness but by his torment. He cries out for his Abba to exercise the divine power that is uniquely his, to show his mighty hand, and thus to take away the calamity that awaits his suffering servant. "Give me back the new wine of thy kingdom," Jesus cries. "Let me drink the sweet milk of thy gospel. Dear God, please act like the father whom I, as thy son, know thee to be. Deliver me from evil. Lead me not into temptation. Remove this cup of suffering from me."

I

What was the content of Jesus' bitter cup? It was not, I believe, the dread of his coming crucifixion. Many men and women have died more horrible deaths than Jesus was to die. There are people who suffer physical pain so intolerable that morphine will not cut it, and so they chew their lips off. There are people who experience mental anguish so great that they embalm themselves with alcohol and other drugs. There are people who are subjected to political and religious torture almost too terrible to contemplate: their fingernails pulled off, their tongues torn out, their testicles stuffed down their throats. Listen to the searing stories still coming out of South Africa. Many people, I repeat, have suffered greater human pain than Jesus underwent.

Such human horrors are not what Jesus wants chiefly to avoid, I believe, when he begs for his Abba to remove this cup of suffering from his lips. He sweats drops of blood because the world's sin is pressing the very life out of him. Here at last Jesus sees human existence in all of its unbelief, its utter distrust, its total alienation from God. He had come to pronounce God's great Yes upon the world, and instead he receives the world's thunderous No in reply. And yet he has no companions in this suffering, as the weight of the world's evil crushes him. His disciples will not wait and watch with him. They fall asleep because their bodies are exhausted even as their souls are sapped. Like us, their spirits both want and will the good, but their flesh is weak. They are exhausted beyond all faithfulness.

Far worse than the disciples' sleepiness is God's own stillness. Jesus hears not a word from his Abba. He receives not a sign of any kind in answer to his clamant plea. Total silence, total absence. The night has come, as Jesus himself had prophesied, in which no man can work, not even God's own Son. Here is Jesus' true moment of horror, declares the theologian Karl Barth. God has now become indistinguishable from Satan. The Father now seems to be the monster. God does the same thing the devil does: he makes his son drink the potion of sin and death and wrath. He will not lift this cup from him.

Yet God could *not* have answered Jesus' prayer by removing this cup. The Father would have thus made the Son the instrument of sin. If Jesus had escaped this hour, he would have failed his entire mission to become suffering flesh and thus to achieve the world's salvation. Here, then, is the stark irony: the Father who can do all things possible cannot possibly take away this cup from the Son. "For this cause came I unto this hour," we hear Jesus saying in the Gospel of John. Now, at last, Jesus knows what it means to take upon himself the sin of the world and thus, as Paul says, to be made sin for the sake of our salvation.

The silence of the Father in Gethsemane now resembles the noisiness of Satan in the wilderness. There the devil had tempted Jesus with three instant means of accomplishing his kingdom: material comfort (turning stones into bread), supernatural astonishment (angels snaring him as he leapt from the temple), and worldly power (rulership over all the surrounding territories). These were precisely the shortcuts to the kingdom that Jesus had come to deny and repudiate. God does not work his will in the world by means of "bread and circuses," as Julius Caesar famously promised. Even less does he perform his drama by political coercion and military might. It was this last temptation that Judas had again offered him. And when Jesus refused, the money-keeper chose his pathetic thirty pieces of silver over a kingdom of suffering and servanthood.

Now, again, Jesus must do the will of God, even when the face of the Father seems identical to the face of the demonic. His dereliction is total because of the total absence of the strengthening answers that came to the earlier temptations in the desert: "Man shall not live by bread alone." "He will give his angels charge over you." "You shall worship the Lord your God and him only shall you serve." Now Jesus is thrown absolutely into the abyss. His kingdom will come in no other way than his descent into that abyss of helplessness. And so he descends. He does not push away the cup of abandonment; he drinks it. He faces straight on the terrible reality that his kingdom depends on this great and final Yes to his Father and Abba: "Yet not what I will, but what thou wilt."

II

What does it mean for us now to partake of this cup? The great positive import of consuming Christ's body is made clear in a poem by the seventeenth-century Anglican priest George Herbert. Here, verily, says Herbert, we eat and drink the love of God himself:

> Love is that liquor sweet and most divine,
> Which my God feels as bloude; but I, as wine.

This cup that meant a bloody death for Jesus has become the cup of inspiriting life for us. This explains why Jesus instructs us to gather on this night and to drink of this cup. His command (the word is *manda-mus* in Latin) is the origin of the English word "maundy": it means mandated, ordered, required. What we do here tonight is not something we do because we have nothing better to do. We are here because we dare not be anywhere else.

This point is made vivid in Walker Percy's novel *Love in the Ruins*. There a character named Thomas More is talking with his fellow physician and friend, Max Gottlieb. Dr. More is a poor excuse for a Christian. He is a boozer and a womanizer who is also consumed with his own scientific ambition. But he is also a ripping worldly success. As an nonobservant Jew, Dr. Gottlieb cannot understand why More is not happy with his many secular achievements, why he should feel so guilty about not going to church. More gets things exactly right when he tries to explain to Gottlieb why he must not miss the Eucharist: "I won't have life in me." He is recalling, of course, the words of Jesus as recorded in the Fourth Gospel: "Unless you eat the flesh of the Son of man and drink his blood, you have no life in you" (John 4:53). Unless Tom More drinks from this cup, all other beverages are poisonous. Unless he eats of this bread, he is but an animal that guzzles and defecates and dies. For this is the cup of his and our salvation.

As the cup that transubstantiates us into the people of God, it enables us to live amidst suffering and heartache without self-pity. This is the cup that enables us not to think of ourselves as victims, even when we have every right to do so. Ours is a world obsessed with victimization. Everyone is now supposed to be a victim of somebody or something else. Even we men have been declared victims of our oppressive mothers! I for one can attest that my mother was no oppressor; surely the word "liberator" would be a better term to describe a woman so faithful and gracious. Unlike those who seek their salvation in declaring their own victimization, we drink this cup precisely in order not to feel sorry for ourselves.

It is this cup that also fortifies our friend Warren Carr in his great humor and gladness of heart. I recall what he said to me, many years ago, when we were talking about people who fall into the slough of despondency and depression. With his customary wit, he declared: "I've never had time for a nervous breakdown." He did not mean that he was incapable of such a dread calamity. He meant exactly the opposite: like many of you, Warren Carr has had plenty of occasions for despair, for giving up, for quitting, for breaking down. In responding to me, Warren was confessing that such an act of resignation would also have been an act of self-indulgence. Abandoning those many souls who depended on his ministry, he would have declared: "Not thy will, but mine be done." Now that Warren in his retirement has plenty of time on his hands, we are all grateful that he still doesn't have time for a breakdown — being too busy feeding the hungry and watering the thirsty.

So it is with all of us. There is not world enough or time enough for us to live in the dread assumption that Christ has not died and been raised for our redemption. On the contrary, we are here to receive the meal that enables us also to say, "Not my will, but thine be done." Let us gather, then, to drink of this cup and to eat of this bread because they are the blood and the body of him who is our salvation: Jesus Christ. Amen.

The Call of the Cross and the Table

A GOOD FRIDAY MEDITATION

First Baptist Church
Winston-Salem, North Carolina
March 21, 1989

I. The Call of the Cross

Not by accident is our central symbol the cross and not the empty tomb. Not only would a vacant grave be difficult to make into an emblem, it would also miss the real point of the Christian faith. There have been many empty tombs but only one risen and living Christ. And he is living and reigning in confirmation of what he performed on the tree at Calvary. God raises Jesus from the dead to confirm and not to deny what happened there. Admittedly, the Easter event was a great surprise that staggered the apostles' expectations. Yet it served to validate and verify the far more drastic surprise: that the Messiah would be killed for having sought to establish his peaceable kingdom, suffering and dying for the sins of the world rather than triumphing in political and religious power. Therefore, we worship the God of Easter morning only because he is first and last the God of Good Friday.

The final horror of the cross is even more spiritual than physical, horrible though Jesus' bodily torment surely was: his agony afflicts his mind and soul even more than his body. His torment is divine no less than human. For there on the cross he was made sin for our sake, and there on the cross do we understand the horrible nature of our own sin and evil: it is the refusal to trust God's goodness; it is the rejection of God's grace; it is the murder of God's own Son. Thus is Golgotha the measure of all sin, the act that we in twentieth-century America would have committed no less surely than did first-century Jews and Romans: God's total help met by our total rejection. We crucified the mercy of God.

The Musician

A memory of Kreisler once:
At some recital in this same city,
The seats all taken, I found myself pushed
On to the stage with a few others,
So near that I could see the toil
Of his face muscles, a pulse like a moth
Fluttering under the fine skin
And the indelible veins of his smooth brow.

I could see, too, the twitching of the fingers.
Caught temporarily in art's neurosis,
As we sat there or warmly applauded
This player who so beautifully suffered
For each of us upon his instrument.

So it must have been on Calvary
In the fiercer light of the thorns' halo:
The men standing by and that one figure,
The hands bleeding, the mind bruised but calm,
Making such music as lives still.
And no one daring to interrupt
Because it was himself that he played
And closer than all of them the God listened.

This work by the Welsh Anglican priest and poet R. S. Thomas likens the Crucifixion to a violin concert by the celebrated German violinist Fritz Kreisler. The scene has an almost timeless and placeless quality about it. The recital could occur in almost any city, by any great musician, and thus be witnessed at close hand by nearly anyone who arrived late and who was thus thrust onto the stage to see the agony that goes into the making of all true beauty. The divine anguish that wrought our redemption on Calvary is beyond human comprehending, but it can at least be glimpsed through this startling human analogy.

Note how the poet describes the initial scene in sharply etched but purely naturalistic images: the jaw clenched tight with the intensity of performance; the pulse fluttering at the throat like a trapped moth; the pressured veins bulging at the forehead as if penned with unfading ink; the fingers twitching frenetically with contorted energy. Thus far the scene is purely secular, as the Freudian allusion to art as neurosis makes clear. Such sublime human music is but the sublimation of pain, a psychic unburdening, a confession of guilt that brings but temporary relief. Yet there is a hint that Kreisler's performance has overtones beyond the secular. This is a suffering that is not physical so much as mental, a suffering not coerced but voluntary, a suffering endured not because of the musician's own sin but for the beauty and benefit of the audience. In giving himself so totally over to his art, Kreisler has suffered for us in two senses of the word: for our exaltation but perhaps also in our stead.

Hence the startling turn to the overt analogy of the final stanza. The dread truth that great beauty is born of great suffering is akin to the deepest Christian paradox: only out of such suffering as Christ bore on the cross can the song of our salvation be sounded. The cross is a stringed instrument on which Christ himself is stretched taut. Instead of the bright stage lights illuminating a virtuoso, there is the fiercer and darker halo of the shameful thorns. In place of the fingers furiously pressing the strings, there are the grasping and bleeding hands of Grünewald's Isenheim altarpiece. And in lieu of the protruding veins and quivering pulse, there is the bruised but calm head of Christ. No longer does he cry out his dereliction. He has made his final bow and uttered his *Finitus est* ("It is finished"). He has been made sin for our sake and has thus justified and reconciled the whole world unto God.

There is a point at which all human analogies collapse, as the last four lines make clear. Whereas Kreisler's music ends with its performance because it is mortal, this music lives forever because it is the work of the Savior, who is God incarnate. Whereas Kreisler played himself in the sense of performing his own compositions, Jesus plays himself in a far deeper sense: he is the Messiah who presented the music of the coming kingdom, and now as the Crucified he has himself become the music he performed: the symphony of salvation. He has performed this recital of our redemption on no other instrument than his very being, his own life's body and blood. Nor was this Christ caught in a temporary neurosis that can be tamed by art; he was bound in the snares of ultimate sin and final death.

Most stunning of all, there is the difference in Jesus' audience. It is not the three Marys and the faithful John, significant though these human listeners and watchers surely were. Not chiefly to his disciples nor even to us latter-day believers did Jesus play the final concert of his atoning death. Closer than all of them, it was "the God" who listened. The poet stresses the stark and solitary article "the" to emphasize that this was no mere death of a good man, though such a death is cause enough for agony. This was God's own Son abandoned by God himself that he might make the redeeming music of our deliverance. Here alone is our assurance that we have not been abandoned to our own sorry, self-justifying devices but that God hears our cry and delivers us from the bondage of sin. Jesus is the Savior whom we crucified.

II. The Call of the Communion Table

Christian faith would be a grim and gloomy business if the cross did not issue in human transformation, in radical newness of life among those who have heard the call of the cross. The punishment that Jesus Christ bore on the tree of Calvary enables us to live without condemnation, in true and everlasting freedom. Yet the cross is not something we ever leave behind. Golgotha is not a mere stopping point on the road to our salvation. It is the one event we keep returning to even after Easter — to the table that links the cross and the Resurrection.

Love (III)

Love bade me welcome: yet my soul drew back,
  Guiltie of dust and sin.
But quick-ey'd Love, observing me grow slack
  From my first entrance in,
Drew nearer to me, sweetly questioning,
  If I lacked any thing.

A guest, I answer'd, worthy to be here:
  Love said, You shall be he.
I the unkinde, ungratefull? Ah my deare,
  I cannot look on thee.

Love took my hand, and smiling did reply,
Who made the eyes but I?

Truth Lord, but I have marr'd them: let my shame
Go where it doth deserve.
And know you not, sayes Love, who bore the blame?
My deare, then I will serve.
You must sit down, sayes Love, and taste my meat:
So I did sit and eat.

This poem by George Herbert (1593-1633) is always placed at the end of all collections of his poetry because it so clearly and powerfully sums up his entire work. It reveals something of what it means to regard Jesus as Lord by means of a startling analogy between Christ and an innkeeper, thus showing the link between the sacred and the secular, the utterly holy and the utterly ordinary. Herbert envisions a tired traveler approaching a wayside inn. The host of the tavern becomes also the Host of the communion table. But we recognize this fact only gradually, through a surprising dialogue between the Christian pilgrim and the Lord of the eucharistic banquet. The gracious Host is called Love three times, and not only because God is called love, but also because this is a divine seduction, the wooing of a lover not into sin but into salvation.

The Host first beckons the weary wayfarer to make his entry. Yet the visitor hesitates, knowing that he is dirty from the road but also defiled by guilt: he is guilty of both dust (mortality) and sin (immorality). But the Lord is the lover who is not offended by the ugliness of the guest's moral and physical condition. He is quick-eyed with a lover's passion and compassion. He thus draws near with divine concern, seeking not his own welfare but the traveler's. He does not grill the guest with merciless interrogations so much as he sweetly inquires of his need, knowing that mercy elicits confession as mere accusation can never do.

Such confession is the precise result, as the traveler admits that he is not a guest worthy of such hospitality, of such generous welcome. But note that the Host does not make the guest instantly whole, declaring him fit and right just as he is. That would be an awful fate — to be left in his sins, to be declared clean when he is still filthy with sin. Instead, he is given a wondrous promise: You shall become such a worthy and honored guest, but not by your own doing. This staggers the pilgrim's moral imagination. Knowing his own ingratitude and unkindness, his own utter unworthiness, how can he be fêted so royally? How can he even behold the face of so great a Lover and Lord? But the comforting Christ takes him by the hand and gently reminds him who is the sovereign maker of heaven and earth. Were we our own makers, we would indeed be helpless. But our very eyes — the sight and the vision through which we behold ourselves, others, and the world itself — are themselves the gift of God. Nothing can we claim as wholly our own; everything is holy gift.

Note the still slight ungraciousness of the guest's response to this most gracious Host. He is determined to claim something for himself, even if it be only the consequences of his sin. He confesses that he has blinded himself to the beauty of salvation, and thus that he deserves nothing other than the ugliness of his damnation. If he could just send himself to hell, this would be one last desperate gesture of autonomy, one final act of pseudo-freedom. But the Jesus who is the lord of this banquet will not allow him even the wretched self-ownership of sin. For he alone is the Lamb of God who has born the blame and who has thus taken away the sins of the world. Yet even here the pilgrim makes one final but futile attempt to make Jesus a guest rather than the Host: "Then I will serve."

Not a bit of it, replies the Host. You must sit and be served rather than stand and serve. You must taste the food that makes one never hunger again, the meat of him whose body was broken for your transgression. At such a feast you can do nothing but gladly partake. Hence the echo of the prayer of humble access: "We do not presume to come to this thy Table, O merciful Lord, trusting in our own righteousness, but in thy manifold and great mercies." And so Herbert concludes the poem with an almost jaunty admission of our total reliance on Jesus Christ. He is the Lord whose feast we do not guiltily attend but gratefully enjoy: "So I did sit and eat."

Thus do we move ineluctably to the Friday we call "Good." Yet here we also anticipate the event of Easter morning, and thus look forward to that final Easter, when we shall sit forever feasting at the King's banquet. Amen.

Unwearied Hearts Ascend

Acts 1:1-11; Revelation 22:12-21

AN ASCENSION DAY SERMON

First Baptist Church
Winston-Salem, North Carolina
May 28, 1995

Many of us Baptists have never heard of Ascension Sunday. Some of us haven't even heard of the Ascension. A Methodist friend likes to remind me — as does Norman Maclean, my University of Chicago professor, in *A River Runs Through It* — that Methodists are Baptists who have learned how to read. He also suggests that folks of our religious stripe are likely to confuse the Ascension with the transmission or some other mechanism under the hood of our automobiles. So let me be clear about our purpose today. We are not merely being high-church Baptists when we celebrate the Ascension of our Lord into Paradise. We are joining with our ancient Christian forebears and with other faithful believers in our own time to declare two great facts: first, that our Lord sits at the right hand of God making intercession for us; second, that he is coming soon from his throne to judge the quick and the dead. Were it not for our Lord's Ascension, we might confuse Jesus with Lazarus, a man who was resuscitated only to die a second time. There have been many resuscitations, but only a single Resurrection: Jesus was raised from the dead to die no more. And because he is risen and reigning and returning, we are called to worship him in the excellence of holiness, living with unwearied hearts.

I

It is important not to be too literal, or unmetaphorical, in our reading of the central Christian doctrines, lest we make them ridiculous. The most important things in life cannot be discerned with the eye: the really Real we cannot see. "Faith is the assurance of things hoped for, the conviction of things not seen" (Heb. 11:1). Yet we have only visual images for dealing with these great invisible realities. I first learned this plain truth on a day in 1947 that I can still vividly recall, nearly five decades later. That day my first-grade teacher, Annie Mae Cameron, asked all of us who could see the wind to please stand up. I leapt to my feet. At the age of five, I was proud to have knowledge that my classmates seemed to lack. Because I was the most eager and the most certain, Mrs. Cameron called on me to describe the wind that I could so confidently see. I pointed to the leaves fluttering on the sweetgum trees outside our window, to the dust blowing on that sandy playground in Kildare, Texas. "You're not describing the wind," my teacher gently replied, "but the swaying trees and the swirling dust. You're showing us what the wind does, not telling us what the wind is."

To be revealed as an ignoramus on the first day of school is not an auspicious way to begin one's education. As both my students and family can attest, and as perhaps you will soon find out, this wasn't the final time I would be proved wrong. I'm still learning. Something I had taken for granted as visible and obvious turned out to be invisible and mysterious. My first-grade teacher was warning me almost fifty years ago — as we should be warned again in our own time, when we are almost wholly oriented to the visible — against the danger of equating the seen with the unseen. There is ever so much more to life, especially ever so much more to eternal life, than meets the eye. Yet in my own childish way, I was stumbling toward the truth that day when I stood so eagerly to describe the wind. We have no way of understanding the great invisible truths except through mental images and verbal analogies and visible effects.

The Ascension, like all the other central Christian events, must be viewed theologically rather than scientifically. I found this rule to be especially true when I visited the Holy Land. My faith was jeopardized when I was shown the rock where the Ascension is supposed to have occurred. There on the Mount of Olives is a large stone containing two indentations roughly resembling human feet. I don't know how those hollow places got there. They may have been caused by eons of water pouring over this boulder, by the long grinding of stone upon stone, or perhaps by some religious huckster who hacked them out with hammer and chisel. Our tour group was told, instead, that Christ ascended into heaven with such rocketing force that his feet left behind these imprints.

I don't know what you think about such a notion, but I know what Mark Twain would have thought. Twain confessed with Voltaire that, after visiting many such holy sites, he had encountered enough fragments of the True Cross to build several battleships. Though I sympathize with Twain's scorn for superstition, I have a different concern than his. My worry is that we make literal and trite what is meant to remain mysterious and holy. All outward and scientific proofs of the Ascension let us forget the true power of its spiritual reality: the Ascension strength by which we are meant to live with unwearied hearts.

II

What does it mean to live our lives before the ascended Lord who reigns at the right hand of God the Father and who is returning to judge the quick and the dead? It means that we worship and serve not a human hero, not even the greatest man who ever lived, but the God who became flesh in Jesus Christ, who made atonement for our sins, who makes intercession for us now, and who will return to finish the kingdom that he is now constructing. Paul gets at the heart of the matter in 2 Corinthians 5:21: "For our sake [God] made him to be sin who knew no sin, so that in him we might become the righteousness of God." The only man who ever deserved to be given his due, to be richly rewarded for his obedience and thus to be set free from the penalty of sin, was instead subjected to the ultimate penalty: he was slain for our sins. He freely and horribly paid the price for our disobedience to God, our rejection of his grace, our attempt to live as if we were our own righteousness. He who knew no sin was made to bear the sin of the entire universe. Yet God raised Christ from the awful death we inflicted on him. And then after the forty days of his earthly resurrection, God lifted him from the earth that he might become our advocate and judge, pleading our case in order that we might become the righteousness of God.

How do such splendid claims impinge on our workaday world? As an elderly neighbor used to ask me, "What do such lofty notions have to do with me, a little old lady who is dying?" A bumper sticker I saw this week gave me a clue to the meaning of the Ascension. It was a secular slogan declaring the creed of this present evil age. "Enjoy Life!" it shouted. "This is not a rehearsal." Such is the pagan plea that confronts us at every turn. In advertising and entertainment, in business and education, in medicine and government, we are everywhere told not to look beyond this world, not to depend on any other savior than ourselves. We are enjoined, instead, to celebrate nothing but our own existence. We are not to think of our life as a rehearsal for any supposed life to come. We are commanded rather to regard this world and this life as being gloriously sufficient unto themselves. So goes the gospel of our unbelief.

As always, our secular friends come close to getting things right. We must thank them for helping us hone our faith on the sharpening stone of their unbelief. God does indeed want us to enjoy life, and exactly because it is not a rehearsal; we are not rehearsing but performing. Our lives are a performance before the ascended and returning Lord. As Kierkegaard said, the preacher is the prompter, we are the actors, and God is the audience for this great cosmic drama. We can, alas, play havoc with the divine stagecraft, turning it into a story of misery and woe. But in Jesus Christ, God has become the central character in the human tragedy, turning it into a divine comedy. The pagan drama ends in final death and defeat; God's drama ends in eternal victory and life everlasting. Every human being — every little old lady and little old man and little old professor — has a crucial role in the play now being performed on God's stage called the world. The ascended Lord demands an excellent performance out of us. He wants us to enact nothing less than his own righteousness by living unwearied lives of worship and service.

III

No such shabbiness is to be found in the great vision of last things that is voiced in Revelation 22. There we hear that outside the gates of Paradise "are the dogs and sorcerers and fornicators and murderers and idolaters, and everyone who loves and practices falsehood." Can you believe that these words were edited out of the lectionary readings for today? Soulless church bureaucrats in New York and Nashville, fearing that our tender sensibilities might be offended, omitted these harsh words. No wonder they excised the following warning as well: "If any one takes away from the words of the book of this prophecy, God will take away his share in the tree of life and in the holy city." The church hacks in their unapproachable officialdom had better beware! How much better to honor rather than to silence such clear indicators of what it means to be judged and redeemed by the ascended and returning Lord. How much more life-enhancing — if also life-terrifying — to know that our existence is not confined to this small little sphere called the earth, but that everything we say and do has ultimate consequence, either for good or ill. How pathetically and damnably sad, by contrast, to love and practice the bumper-sticker falsehood that this world and this life are all there is.

To love and practice truth rather than falsehood is dangerous. This is revealed in the story of the rattlesnake and the bunny rabbit who decided to be honest with each other. Neither had ever seen its own reflection and thus could not know what it looked like. So they decided to tell each other what they looked like. The rattlesnake agreed to go first. He reported to the rabbit that he had a soft cottony tail, long floppy ears, pink glistening eyes, and a twitchy little nose. "Hurray," cried the bunny rabbit, "I'm just who I thought I was — a bunny rabbit." But then the bunny was stricken with fear, wondering whether he dare tell the rattlesnake what he looked like. Yet the rabbit, perhaps having read Revelation 22, decided to risk the truth, no matter the cost. "You are slick and slimy," he said, "and you have beady little eyes set too close together. But at least it can be said in your behalf that you have diamonds sprinkled all over you." "Oh no," the serpent screamed. "Here I've spent my whole life thinking I was a rattlesnake, but now I realize that I'm a TV evangelist."

At the risk of becoming a rabbit who may get bitten by a rattlesnake, I want to declare an unpleasant truth: it is not only our secular and pagan friends who live as if there were no ascended and returning Lord. So do many of us Christians. In our churches no less than our schools and our workplace, there is a terrible dumbing down of worship and preaching and teaching. We might as well call it Church Lite. So thin is our teaching, so banal our preaching, so empty our worship that they seem designed for our own entertainment rather than the praise and glory of God. My own motto concerning the life of the church is this: the less like television, the better. Resurrection Day ought to be the highest and holiest day of the week. Here in our hymns and anthems and prayers, in our Sunday school lessons and our sermons, we ought to be delivered from the littleness of our bumper-sticker lives. Here we should gloriously and humbly be lifted up into the presence of the risen and returning Lord. Here we should encounter the living God, the invisible reality who is more real than anything visible: not Jesus Christ our buddy and chum with whom we desire a chatty visit, but Jesus Christ our mediator and advocate who makes intercession before the Father that we might become the righteousness of God. Because we owe absolutely everything to him, there is nothing left for us to do but to throw off every earthly hindrance and to serve him in gladness and joy.

Only recently I talked with a Christian lady who, though she may not know it, is acting out the righteousness of God. She spends her days and nights taking care of her husband as he declines into senile dementia. He has an ever more difficult time forming sentences, and sometimes he cannot follow an ordinary conversation. The one thing he can still do and still enjoys doing is riding in the car and singing along to hymns and songs played on tape. As they were getting ready to go on their afternoon drive, she laid aside her household chores. "What does it matter," she asked me, "that my floors are not mopped and the house is not dusted?" Here, I suggest, is a Christian woman living out the reality of the Ascension. She is giving away her life gladly and joyfully, knowing that she is answerable not only to her husband and her family and her neighbors but also to the coming Christ. No matter how wearily her body is dragged down, she lives with an ascending and unwearied heart.

The eighth-century British monk and abbot named the Venerable Bede understood what it means to live in worship and service of the ascended and returning Christ. He knew that the cry "Come, Lord Jesus" is not a cowardly desire to escape from the world, but rather a plea for God to complete what he has barely begun. Bede lived in a dark and forbidding world, somewhat like our own. The Roman Empire had collapsed, much as our own civilization is collapsing. The invading Angles and Saxons had brought with them a pagan view of the world that is very much akin to the contemporary notion that this world is all there is. Bede once asked a pagan chieftain what life was like without the hope of resurrection. In a remarkable metaphor, the converted Saxon likened the pagan view of life to a swallow flitting from the night air into one end of a lighted banquet hall and then quickly out the other. From the darkness we come, and to the darkness we return: such was the joyless view of life in Bede's pagan age, just as it is in these latter pagan days. Christian faith in the risen and reigning and returning Lord is the only real alternative to it. Nothing else can enable us to envision the invisible, to worship and serve God in the excellence of holiness, to live gracious and generous lives. Let us thus sing with the ancient and venerable Bede the glorious truth of the Ascension: "O Lord, our homeward pathway bend that our unwearied hearts ascend, Alleluia, Alleluia." Amen.

PART VI

THE VOCATIONS OF MINISTRY AND MARRIAGE

A Fiery Red-Head Called
to the Ministry of Word and Sacrament

A CHARGE TO WESLEY DALE KEYES
AT HIS ORDINATION TO THE GOSPEL MINISTRY

First Baptist Church
Farmers Branch, Texas
June 4, 2006; Pentecost Sunday

I charge you in the presence of God and of Christ Jesus who is to judge the living and the dead, and by his appearing and his kingdom: preach the word, be urgent in season and out of season, convince, rebuke, and exhort, be unfailing in patience and in teaching. For the time is coming when people will not endure sound teaching, but having itching ears they will accumulate teachers for themselves to suit their own likings, and will turn away from listening to the truth and wander into myths. As for you, always be steady, endure suffering, do the work of an evangelist, fulfill your ministry. (2 Tim. 4:1-5)

It's altogether appropriate, I hope, that Wes Keyes has asked a layman to deliver the sermonic charge at his ordination. As one who has never found anybody willing to lay hands on him, I have a perspective on ministers that the clergy themselves often lack. I've known quite a few preachers during my six and a half decades aboard this wobbling world. Some of them have been as sorry as sin. Others have been as dumb as dirt. I have known preachers both fat and skinny, both handsome and ugly, both mediocre and excellent. Yet, in every case, I have refused to look down on these preachers as lesser, much less as inferior, creatures.

On the contrary, I have looked up to them as the chosen ministers of God, as pastors and priests whom the church has set apart for the unique tasks of Christian ministry.

Some of my students are baffled by my admiration for preachers. When they come to my eagle aerie office atop the Tidwell Bible Building, they often envy what seems to be an ideal professorial life. They admire my grand view of the two central quadrangles on the Baylor campus. They ask me if I've read all 6,000 books in my library. (Dodging their hard question, I respond that I've read some of them more than once!) These students are often wrestling hard with their vocation. They want to know what they should do with their lives. Some of them believe that God has called them to be ministers of the gospel. Yet, seeing all the great books of the Western world at arm's reach, and knowing how delightful it is to discuss great texts and debate great ideas, some of them start talking about becoming a teacher instead of a preacher. I remind them that their wish is valid only if they want an easier way of life. For a pastor's work is much tougher than a professor's. I don't have to raise an annual budget, including my own salary. I don't have to keep people smiling when they should be weeping. And I can't be fired unless I am caught fornicating with a coed at high noon on the main campus plaza.

More seriously, I remind these young people that the work as I do as a teacher, important though it is, always remains secondary and ancillary to the direct proclamation and enactment of the kingdom. In grappling with the great books and doctrines of the Christian tradition, I seek to help ministers do the primary labor of the church: to pray with the sick and to bury the dead, to counsel the troubled and to marry the betrothed, to rescue the perishing poor and to care for the dying rich. This evening my emphasis, as we come to ordain Wes Keyes to the gospel ministry, is on the two most important tasks of the minister, the two crucial ones that I as a teacher am not privileged to perform. They were defined by our Reformation forebears, especially John Calvin, as the twofold ministry of Word and sacrament: the proclamation of the Word of God and the administration of baptism and the Lord's Supper.

I

The very first injunction given to Timothy is the one I give also to Wesley: Preach the Word. Do not wander into such myths as the Da Vinci

Code and the Myers-Briggs test and the other modern astrologies that parade as history or psychology. And do not seek the Damned Men (D.Min.) degree, if only because folks would not know how to differentiate you from your physician wife, except to say, "Beth is the kind of doctor who does people some good." The gospel does not consist in old tidings that we can tell ourselves. It is, instead, the radically Good News from beyond the walls of the world, the astounding tidings that God in Christ is reconciling the world unto himself. Yet many ministers turn this startling divine dispatch into banal platitudes about being nice. They transform the gospel into a Hallmark greeting card; they make the revolutionary report of the kingdom into a bland memorandum written by a bureaucrat; they recast the most exciting story ever told into cute clichés; they swab itching ears with the soothing ointment of this or that denominational program. They make a fool of God.

I adjure you, Wesley Keyes, in the presence of God and Christ Jesus, as well as these faithful people gathered to lay hands on you: Preach the Word. The Kentucky Baptist poet, novelist, and essayist Wendell Berry notes the utterly remarkable fact that the church remains virtually the only place in our culture where people actually listen to someone else for twenty minutes once a week. Most of us don't stop to listen to anyone. We are too busy receiving phone calls and taking instant messages, watching television ads and downloading from our iPods. Yet Christians don't come to church to get still more of this stale stuff. They come to hear "what eye has not seen, what ear has not heard, what has not entered into the imagination of man." Therefore, it is ever so important not to waste the precious 1200 seconds that you are given on Sundays. Proclaim a word that is as fresh and original, as surprising and arresting, as the gospel itself. Since God has imaged himself in Jesus Christ, give your people daring images and arresting illustrations of the deep things of the faith.

To proclaim the Word aright will require rigorous study. "Either read," said John Wesley to his fellow preachers, "or get out of the ministry." The Christian tradition is so rich in wisdom and truth, so replete with striking stories and remarkable characters, that you will spend your life just beginning to master it. You must preach the Grand Christian Narrative both in season and out, confident that you will thus make the world relevant to the gospel, not the gospel relevant to the world. For, as a preacher, you are also a stage manager or prompter. Your preaching will enable your people to play their roles, no matter how small, in the great theatrical work that God is performing in our very midst — the divine biblical drama in its four great acts: creation, fall, redemption, consummation.

As a native Mississippian, you are uniquely qualified to understand that, in preaching as in the rest of life, how you say a thing is virtually as important as what you say. Mississippians are experts in saying it colorfully and carefully and right. You know my own motto concerning your native state: "Mississippi: last in literacy, first in literature." You are the legatee of William Faulkner and Eudora Welty and Walker Percy. You are well equipped, therefore, to comprehend the advice given me by my old teacher at the University of Chicago, the Lutheran theologian Joseph Sittler. When asked, near the end of his long and distinguished career, what advice he would give to the church, Sittler replied ever so succinctly and tellingly: "Watch your language." Your people will hear your preaching, in large measure, according to your way of saying it. Search hard for the right word. Remember the wisdom of Mark Twain, who defined the difference between the right word and the nearly right word as the difference between lightning and a lightning bug. Or, I would add, between a dragon and a dragonfly.

Here in the pulpit is your chance to wedge into the world the one Word utterly unlike the myriad other words that bombard us. Such radical proclamation will be the hardest and yet also the most important thing you do. It will be hard because the gospel is hard. It is the most difficult and yet also the most rewarding task in the world to love God with all our hearts and minds and souls, and to love our neighbors as we love ourselves. The love of God is even harder to receive than to give. You will thus be sure to make enemies if you remain faithful in your preaching. Some people do not like to be told that they cannot save themselves, and they will have your hide if you tell them this truth. Eventually, therefore, your youthful cheeks will become creased with care, your forehead lined with woe, your eyes bagged with sorrow. This is as it should and must be. It is the happy price for dwelling in the workaday world with your people. No matter how great your eloquence or how deep your insight, they will not receive your proclamation unless you spend hundreds of coffee-drenched hours listening to and laughing with and suffering alongside them.

During the height of the civil rights violence of the early 1960s, my pastor-friend Warren Carr would rise to the pulpit at the Watts Street Baptist Church in Durham, North Carolina, to proclaim the Word of

God, and on some occasions his preaching bore on the race crisis. In the tradition of the ancient church, he would preach before the offering had been collected, in order that the people might present their gifts in response to the proclaimed Word. But whenever Carr would preach on racial reconciliation, the wealthiest member of the congregation would rip up the check he had planned to place in the offering plate. Vein-bulging angry though he was, it did not take long before this same high-rolling businessman learned what had often happened the night before. Terrified at calling his daddy, the moneyed man's drunken son would instead call Carr to bail him out of jail at 2:00 on Sunday morning. No wonder the rich old ruler would drop his check off at the church office later in the week. The preacher could proclaim the prophetic Word because he was also a priestly pastor.

II

I have dwelt at length, Wesley, on your role as preacher because, as Karl Barth rightly said, preaching has become the singular Protestant sacrament. It is the place where, most often and most starkly, God becomes present to us. Yet there are two other indispensable sacraments. They differ markedly from preaching, for these two actions are not yours but the church's. This explains why this congregation is presenting you with a ministerial gown today: you will wear it to acknowledge that you are no longer Wesley Keyes, the redheaded Mississippian, but an ordained minister of the gospel. And thus, while your preaching will take on the color and flavor of your own personality and style, your baptizing and celebration of the Lord's Supper will not. Here you will recede into the background as an anonymous representative of the church: your robe will cover your perhaps mismatching coat and tie, correctly putting the emphasis on your role rather than your dress.

Concerning baptism, remember to practice it as the church's unique gift — both to those who have been quickly converted and those who have been slowly nurtured into the faith. Their profession of faith is what *they* do; their baptism is what *you* do on behalf of the church. And as a Baptist minister, you will do it right. You will not sprinkle them with the tonic water of social acceptance; you will drown them in the chaos from which God created the cosmos. You will then raise them up to newness of life from a baptistery that is no mere cleansing tub for dirty little sins, but rather a liquid grave for burying the gross condition of Sin itself. Your baptismal act will thus make them what they, in fact, now are: born-again Christians. You will not be initiating them into local church membership, much less into a denomination called Baptists, but into the Christian life itself. And once initiated, always initiated. I urge you not to repeat this unrepeatable act. Remember that Methodists and Lutherans and Episcopalians and Catholics who have been baptized as infants and then later confirmed as adults have thus received believer's baptism. To require their rebaptism is to declare that they have never been Christians! Nor will your people need to be "baptized with the Spirit" later on, via various charismatic renewals, if you have enabled them to take their baptism seriously at its first and only occurrence.

After having baptized the nurtured and converted, you will have transferred all of their important allegiances. No longer will they belong chiefly to their parents or spouses, nor to their country or friends, and least of all to their race and gender. They belong to the body of Christ and thus have they received a new baptismal name: Christian. Their baptism has permanently transferred their loyalties to the body of Christ, with the attendant teachings and practices that the church will inculcate in them. Now they are branded with the cross, tattooed with the indelible mark of their Savior. When some of the baptized fall away from the faith and ask to be removed from the rolls of the church, agree to do so on one condition: that they come forward at the end of the next worship service to make a public repudiation of their baptism. Until then, promise to hound and harass them until they learn happily to honor their baptism.

The same life-and-death business will be transacted as you preside at the Table of the Lord. As with baptism, your personal worth has nothing to do with the validity of your act. For you are not the exalted host at this meal, only the lowly server. Yet you serve no ordinary meal. This supper is no mere symbol or perfunctory memorial. As the eminent British theologian P. T. Forsyth put the matter ever so pungently, memorials are held for dead men. Christ is not dead but risen and reigning and returning, alive and well and active in our midst. Celebrate the Lord's Supper often, therefore, helping your people understand what we Baptists have difficulty comprehending: that this bread and cup feed our souls even if not our stomachs. They have infinite qualitative worth, even if not equal quantitative weight, over the fried chicken and spaghetti casseroles that are our common Baptist fare. For in this sacred act of the Lord's Supper we show forth the Lord's presence until he comes again. It is this mystical act that, as my colleague Barry Harvey points out, is meant to transubstantiate us into the authentic people of God.

III

It is meet and right that we set this man apart for the ordained ministry on this Pentecost Sunday. For it was on this day that fire fell from heaven on the early Christians gathered at Jerusalem. So has the Spirit descended on Wesley Keyes. Your role now is to act as God's lightning rod, the one in whom the divine fire will be brought to earth, ensuring that Christ's people live rather than die by it. Whenever you enter a room, everything will change. It is not that you are morally superior or better educated or even more spiritually mature. Rather are you the catalyst, the precipitating presence that enables everyone else to identify the presence of the invisible God. At times your sacramental role will make people angry, and they will thus strike at you because they can strike at God in no other way. But on most occasions your catalyzing presence will introduce the redemptive reality that everyone is looking to find. Be not ashamed, therefore, to enact this substitutionary role. It's your liberating mask, your true persona, your *sine qua non*.

For, like Abraham, you have been summoned into a far country. Like Jacob, you have been waylaid by an angel of the Lord. Like Moses, you have been shown the bush that flames without being consumed. Like Jeremiah, you were consecrated already in your mother's womb. Like Samuel, you have heard the call of God, and like him you have answered: "Speak, Lord, for thy servant heareth." And so I beseech you, Wesley Dale Keyes, always to be steady, to endure suffering, to do the work of an evangelist, to fulfill your ministry: in the name of the Father, and the Son, and the Holy Spirit. Amen.

A Rock Breaker and a Stone Builder

AN ORDINATION CHARGE TO MATTHEW PATRICK SALAS

Austin Heights Baptist Church
Nacogdoches, Texas
May 4, 2008

Rocks are the most lifeless things on our planet. And yet they serve as a central biblical metaphor, especially for Christian ministry. "Come to Christ," the first epistle of Peter enjoins us, "to that living stone, rejected by men but in God's sight chosen and precious; and like living stones, be yourselves built into a spiritual house, to be a holy priesthood, to offer spiritual sacrifices acceptable to God through Jesus Christ." Yet flint-heartedness is also one of the Bible's chief images of sin. Thus must our hearts be broken before we can be made into useful building stones. Thus, my charge to you, Matt Salas, is that you accomplish two things at once: that you break our hard hearts but also make us into living stones, namely, into altars of sacrifice and praise to God. I enjoin you to fulfill the ancient twofold ministries of the church as both prophet and priest. Christ alone is king, the cornerstone that determines the true alignment of everything else, the capstone that holds the final arch in place. This kingly office is reserved for Christ himself, but you are called to be one of his prophets and priests.

I

Some young preachers can't wait to get their chance to exercise a prophetic ministry. They are eager to burn the ears and sting the consciences of their church members. They are keen to confront them with the tough truths of the gospel concerning war and poverty, racism and hunger and homelessness. Certainly this is part of your calling as God's prophet: you are to cast stones against the glass houses of our complacency. You are to break our stony hearts. For the heart is not chiefly the region of feeling; it is, instead, the symbol of our will and our desire. It is the locus of our most fundamental decisions. We thus turn our hearts to stone when we sin. We become as soulless as rocks, utterly calcified in our disobedience, stone dead in our sins and trespasses.

Having grown up in the stony barrenness West Texas, you probably know what it means to bust rocks. Once again, you are called to be a rock-breaker, but now in a quite different sense. It is exceedingly important to remember who gives you the authority to strike the flint-hearted and teaches you how to do it. Your father is a highway patrolman who may sometimes need to use his billy club to break the heads of criminals. That is his dangerous and noble calling, but it is not yours. You are to take a stick to our hard heads only as Moses does. The prophet is furious at the whining of his people. They have murmured and complained and begged to return to Egypt, preferring the fleshy food they had in slavery to the stringent nourishment of freedom. Hence their constant fault-finding, even though they are being fed with manna and led by pillars of cloud and fire. "Why did you bring us up out of Egypt," they cry, "to kill us and our children and our cattle with thirst?"

If Moses had done what he wanted to, he would have lashed out at his critics, pummeling his people with verbal stones, splitting their rocky heads with his staff. For if God is angry at Israel's hard-heartedness, why shouldn't his prophet also be angry? "Do I not hate them," cries the psalmist, "that hate thee, O Lord?" (Ps. 129:31) Yes, indeed; but you must be angry and hateful only in God's strange fashion. Yahweh orders Moses to strike not his people but rather a rock there in the wilderness wastes of the Sinai. It's an odd — indeed, an outrageous — command. Surely a desert stone is the least likely place to find a hidden spring of water. Yet no sooner has Moses smitten the stone with his staff than water gushes forth, so that complaining Israel is able to quench its thirst at last.

Note ever so well, Matt, that God in his wrath has struck down Israel with his grace. Only now can his people fall to their knees, not in abject humiliation but to drink the newfound water of life. It's always like this. As Karl Barth says, God punishes us by healing us. God imprisons us by flinging wide the cell door. God enables us to see the extent of our sin by forgiving it, making us everlastingly grateful and devoted to him. As God's prophet, you are to do as Moses did. Like a physician, you are to wound in order to heal. You are to strike human stones that they might gush forth with life. You are to shatter only in the assurance that God will build something new and better. Like Francis Marion Tarwater at the end of Flannery O'Connor's novel *The Violent Bear It Away:* "Go warn the children of God that God's mercy hurries terribly near."

II

Here is the point at which your prophetic ministry will always and already be priestly. As prophet you are a breaker of rocks and as a priest you are a builder of stones. Your priestly calling is to help your people rebuild their lives on solid rock, not on sinking sand. Yet it would be dishonest for us to deny, even on this happy occasion, that your people will not always want you to be their priestly builder of transformed lives. Many of us want to spend our time at church congratulating ourselves about what good folks we are and how much we like each other. We do not want a prophet who smashes our houses made of glass nor a priest who builds our houses on solid ground. What we want, instead, is a "hale fellow well met" and thus an all-around "good guy." Will Willimon has described many modern Protestant churches as "conspiracies of congeniality." Some of your church members will thus want you to be "nice" more than anything else. This is a danger far worse than persecution. Søren Kierkegaard, the great Danish thinker and writer, put the problem well. It is not that you will be stoned to death by tormentors, he said, but that you may be trampled to death by geese. Or, as I would put it, you may be pounded into pulp with ping-pong balls.

We are not ordaining you, Matthew Patrick Salas, to become a grinning backslapper or a client-centered therapist, but to be a prophet and a priest of the holy and gracious God. You will be our priest chiefly because you will administer the sacraments. You will immerse new Christians into a baptistery that is the burial vault of Christ's death; and you will raise them up out of that tomb into their new life and their new identity, indeed, into their everlasting vocation. No longer will they belong to their own families or their jobs or even their country. In baptism you will put the church's mark on them: you will brand them with the cross. You will enter their names into the Lamb's book of life with indelible ink. As our priest, you will also feed us with the only bread that does not leave us hungry, with the only drink that does not leave us thirsty — with Christ's own body and blood. Thus will you enable us to eat and to drink either to our damnation or salvation.

In conclusion, listen to what goes into a day's work as a prophet and priest of God. It's a report from St. Augustine, the bishop of Hippo in North Africa. We Baptists don't have bishops, but our pastors are called to do the same kinds of things that St. Augustine did:

> The turbulent have to be corrected, the faint-hearted cheered up, the weak supported; the Gospel's opponents need to be refuted, its insidious enemies guarded against; the unlearned need to be taught, the indolent stirred up, the argumentative checked; the proud must be put in their place, the desperate set on their feet, those engaged in quarrels reconciled; the needy have to be helped, the oppressed to be liberated, the good to be encouraged, the bad to be tolerated; all must be loved.

"The Gospel terrifies me," St. Augustine concluded. So should it terrify you, Matt Salas. And so should it terrify all the rest of us — not chiefly because its duties are impossibly demanding, but because its delights are joyful almost beyond our bearing.

Perhaps this is what the American theologian Reinhold Niebuhr meant when he said that very few ministers are dismissed for preaching too prophetically. Most of them are fired for neglecting the orphans and the widows, or failing to raise the budget, or else (I would add) for confusing their secretaries with their wives. Your people will help you find a wife, just as they will fill the offering plate and grant you the liberty to proclaim prophetic judgments from the pulpit. They will do these things because you will have been their priest, down in the ditch and at the coffee pot with them all week, mending shattered lives with the balm of God's grace. Therefore, I adjure you, Matt Salas, to be a minister of the gospel because you are a prophet and a priest of Jesus Christ the King.

The Redeeming Comedy of Marriage

A HOMILY FOR THE WEDDING
OF APRIL SCHWARZMUELLER AND JEFFREY JOHNSON

The Shrine of the Immaculate Conception
Atlanta, Georgia
July 11, 1992

We are gathered here to do an outrageous thing: to join April Schwarz-mueller and Jeffrey Johnson in making and sustaining their vows of life companionship. We are present as witnesses to a radical act of faith: to the sacramental proposition that two people can live together, in Christian faith and hope and charity, for the rest of their lives.

Surely someone will protest that there is nothing extraordinary about the joining of a husband and a wife in marriage. It happens all the time. Tomorrow morning's paper will be full of pictures and articles about weddings that have occurred in this very city on this same day. We ourselves will be tempted to use the banal and inane adjectives that we so often mouth at weddings. Isn't it all so very pretty? Doesn't April make a beautiful bride? Isn't Jeff a handsome groom? What a lovely occasion! To which I say: well and good — true and right. And may a good time be had by all!

Yes, but this is not the heart of the matter. If it were, then this would be a pagan event indeed. Today, in the marriage of Jeff and April, we are given a surprising glimpse of what life once was like, what life is still meant to be, and what life shall one day become. For Holy Scripture begins and ends with a wedding. History originates with the marriage in the Eden garden, as recorded in Genesis; and it finishes with the marriage feast of the Lamb, as prophesied in the book of Revelation.

Between the time of the first wedding that went bad and the final wedding that will be made good, Jesus brings in his kingdom. Should it surprise us that Jesus likens this kingdom to a marriage where he is himself the groom and we his people are the bride? God himself is thus the maker and giver of marriage because he is the maker and keeper of covenant: the God who has kept faith with us, despite our unfaithfulness, in his people Israel and in his son Jesus. And so today we do a drastic and not a conventional deed: we celebrate with this man and this woman their promise to make and to keep covenant with each other no matter what may come.

I

With consummate human wisdom no less than divine revelation, the Bible's first book declares that it was not good for the man to remain alone. We are not meant to live in solitude but in companionship. April and Jeff are not self-made souls, nor will their nuptial promises make them sufficient unto themselves. Indeed, if they fail to make their union a blessing to their mothers and fathers and brothers and sisters and grandparents — and to the ever-widening circle of their friends and associates — their marriage will have failed in the most miserable way. A true and faithful marriage will bring them closer to us, not take them further away. Loving each other rightly, because they love God first and last, they will love their neighbors more, not less.

Yet the paradox remains: April and Jeff are widening the family circle by breaking it. They are giving themselves first to each other, as husband and wife, the better to give themselves back to God and the world. They are turning inward in love toward each other that they might turn outward in love for others. Again, I say: this is wondrous and not an ordinary thing. Two people who have no natural blood kinship, who should have been strangers and aliens, have been brought splendidly together. And they are promising to do what is more splendid still: to keep faith and hope and love holy until death parts them.

This is what makes marriage such a staggering surprise, such a large and frequent metaphor of God's own goodness: it is a gift and not an acquisition. Jeff could not possibly deserve to have and to hold this woman, nor April this man. None of us is worthy of such a blessing. It is an utter miracle, a work of grace beyond all our fathoming. They are

The Redeeming Comedy of Marriage 223

promising to do the impossible, to give themselves to each other totally. No wonder the Catholic Church regards marriage as a sacrament. Marriage is nothing less than a vital means of God's redeeming and reconciling grace. And so it is that Jesus, far from loosening the sacramental union recorded in Genesis, intensifies it: "What God has joined together," he says, "let no one put asunder" (Mark 10:9).

II

We know, alas, that things did fall apart. The first marriage went sadly sour. The union that should have brought Adam and Eve closer to God separated them from him instead. They sought to be sufficient unto themselves, to be like God. In an act of spurious self-communion, they ate the forbidden fruit and thus divided themselves from God. Their nakedness, once innocent and good, became a curse rather than a blessing. They were ashamed of themselves. Masculine domination and feminine deception were the sorry results of this first disobedience. And so God drove our primal parents out of Eden, lest they make their wretched condition immortal by eating from the Tree of Eternal Life.

Marriage has been shadowed with failure ever since. Many Christian saints have abstained from wedlock lest they be corrupted by it. St. Paul clearly regarded marriage as a lesser condition than his own solitary state. "Better to marry than to burn," he declared, in seeming disparagement of those who cannot restrain their passions for the higher life of the kingdom. Jesus himself, though he blessed marriage, did not enter into it. Therefore, the burden of proof in a fallen world lies not with celibates and singles but with us who marry. How can we justify such a strange act? We will not perform this wedding aright, I say, unless we can answer the objection voiced by an unmarried friend of mine. "It would take a damned good husband," she says, "to beat no husband at all."

This woman has a host of cynics on her side. Wits and wags have been mocking marriage ever since the expulsion of the first couple from the eastern gate of Eden. Hear their complaint. "Love is blind," said Lichtenberg, "but marriage restores its sight." Voltaire was no less caustic: "Marriage is the only adventure open to the cowardly." Samuel Rogers is more sarcastic still: "It doesn't much matter whom one marries, for one is sure to find out the next morning that it was someone else."

Let us confess that the making of a good marriage is a difficult thing. Perhaps at no time in history has it been harder than in the late twentieth century. More than 50 percent of all American marriages now end in divorce; and that rate is rising, not falling. Perhaps we ought to issue separation papers along with the marriage license. With such small odds for marital permanence, all of this ceremony may seem an exercise in splendid futility. Perhaps we ought to follow the advice of Goethe: to celebrate the happy ending of a marriage in old age, and thus to remain silent at its uncertain beginning in youth.

III

But be not dismayed. The good news is that "The things which are impossible with men are possible with God" (Luke 18:27). Today's pomp and ceremony are not attempts to hide the harsh truth; they are the essence of the matter. All the fine flowers and fancy dresses and suave tuxedos, all the candles and rings, all the silk and satin — these are signs that Jeff and April are undertaking no ordinary human adventure. The Eucharist to follow will make the point even more vivid. Here we are the guests, not only of the Schwarzmuellers and the Johnsons, but also and chiefly of Jesus Christ. He is our real host at this wedding feast of the Lamb.

The love of Jesus Christ is the ground and sustenance of all real love. As St. Paul says, this is the love that bears all things — bearing especially each other's burdens. This is the love that believes all things: believing always the best and never the worst about each other. This is the love that hopes all things: hoping to enjoy each other's love in the winter years of age even more than in the springtime of youth. This is the love that endures all things: enduring the failures and defeats that will bind you together even more deeply than your successes.

There is nothing grim or dour about the love of God. Dante, the greatest of all Christian poets, called his work simply *La Comedia,* the comedy. Dante knew that Christian faith is comic at its core because the gospel breaks through the tomb of sin and opens out to new life, indeed to eternal life. Tragedies all end in death, but comedies end in marriage. As we have seen, biblical faith both begins and ends with a wedding. It is about our reconciliation and union with God, as he takes us as his bride.

The American comic novelist Peter De Vries understands the redeeming comedy of marriage more deeply than anyone I know. One of his feuding couples is reconciled when the husband confesses to his wife, "You're the salt of the earth, you louse." A De Vriesian wife admits, in a fit of raging marital truth about her husband, "I wouldn't divorce you if you were the last man on earth." Still another De Vriesian spouse discovers how much he loves his wife only when she starts screaming at him, for it is then that he is brought to confess the truth about her: "As she threw the suitcase on the bed and began flinging things into it with the declaration that she was leaving and never wanted to see me again as long as she lived, I knew, as I had never known before, that she was the woman for me."

And so it is in joy and laughter, no less than sobriety and solemnity, that April and Jeff have come to make their promises. They will pledge their troth before us, yes; yet their real audience is not human but heavenly. God the Father in Christ the Son and the Holy Spirit is here with us. Neither we nor they shall take the name of the Lord in vain. This couple will swear their fidelity to each other by his name. They will do so, not in guilty dread that God will punish them if they break their word. They will do it as an act of worship and not of fear. To call upon God's name is to invoke His presence and power. And so they will make their vows to God and to each other, even as we renew our own promises, in the conviction that he alone has the grace to sustain their love, exactly because it is not their love but his. Amen.

A Latter-Day Rachel and Jacob

A HOMILY FOR THE WEDDING
OF MELODIE WATTS AND SCOTT MARCUS

Rutland Chapel
Ridgecrest, North Carolina
October 28, 2006

Then Jacob went on his journey, and came to the land of the people of the east. As he looked, he saw a well in the field, and lo, three flocks of sheep lying beside it; for out of that well the flocks were watered. The stone on the well's mouth was large, and when all the flocks were gathered there, the shepherds would roll the stone from the mouth of the well, and water the sheep, and put the stone back in its place upon the mouth of the well.

Jacob said to them, "My brothers, where do you come from?" They said, "We have come from Haran." He said to them, "Do you know Laban the son of Nahor?" They said, "We know him." He said to them, "Is it well with him?" They said, "It is well; and see, Rachel his daughter is coming with the sheep!" He said, "Behold, it is still high day, it is not time for the animals to be gathered together; water the sheep, and go, pasture them." But they said, "We cannot until all the flocks are gathered together, and the stone is rolled from the mouth of the well; then we water the sheep."

While he was still speaking with them, Rachel came with her father's sheep; for she kept them. Now when Jacob saw Rachel the daughter of Laban his mother's brother, Jacob went up and rolled the stone from the well's mouth, and watered the flock of Laban his mother's brother. Then Jacob kissed Rachel and wept aloud. And Jacob told Ra-

chel that he was her father's kinsman, and that he was Rebekah's son; and she ran and told her father. (Gen. 29:1-11)

This will surely seem a strange text for a wedding homily. What has the story of the arrogant Jacob being tricked by the clever Laban into marrying the wrong daughter, Leah, and then spending fourteen years in laborious service to this swindler father-in-law before at last getting to marry the woman he should have had in the beginning, his beloved Rachel — what has this bizarre story to do with the wedding of Scott Marcus and Melodie Watts?

I suggest that it has everything to do with it. For this is not a story about love at first sight but about delay and waiting and frustration, but finally about fulfillment under special conditions. Like Joseph, his future son, Jacob has thought himself a clever chap. Yet he turns out, as so often happens in Scripture, to be one of the fraudulent who is blessedly defrauded. The gruff shepherds have no desire to remove the heavy stone from the well nor to draw water for Rachel's sheep. So, in good legalist fashion, they declare that they don't water sheep at noon under the scorching Middle Eastern sun, but only in the cool of the evening, when all of the sheep have been gathered in. Jacob is not allowed, therefore, to have Rachel on his own terms.

He gets her, far better, on God's terms. For Rachel approaches the well as a woman in need. She is not first depicted as a gorgeous lass whom Jacob will lusciously embrace. On the contrary, she is shown to be a woman who requires help. Rachel wants a man who will befriend her, who will help her, who will do what she cannot do for herself. In sum, she wants and needs a husband, just as Jacob wants and needs a wife. And so we learn that Jacob proves his love by first performing an act of courtesy and kindness in lifting the heavy stone and watering her sheep from the well. Such loving deeds will be the basis of their loving marriage. Only after that does Jacob kiss Rachel while weeping aloud for sheer joy. At last he has found the woman he was meant permanently to marry: to help and love and serve Rachel even as she will help and love and serve Jacob.

Melodie Watts and Scott Marcus have not waited quite fourteen years — but at least for ten — after they first showed interest in each other. What they have discovered, upon renewing this long-delayed love, is that it is based on such acts of loving kindness as Jacob and Ra-

chel found at the well, even if those early acts of courteous love have occurred largely by long-distance phone calls between Delaware and
North Carolina! Thereby did they begin to renew an old friendship
that would blossom into marriage. C. S. Lewis teaches in *The Four Loves*
that marriage is indeed the final form of human friendship: it is the
love wherein we share the very deepest commitments and the most lasting virtues. Genesis 2:24 thus describes marriage as the place where we
cease being boys and girls dependent on our fathers and mothers, but
instead become full-fledged men and women. As the King James so
poignantly puts it, we now cleave to our spouses rather than our parents, becoming unashamedly one flesh, in bodily no less than spiritual
friendship.

The blind Cornish poet Jack Clemo understood this matter of marriage as St. Paul did not. Poor bachelor Paul notoriously declared, "It is
better to marry than to burn." How little did he understand, said
Clemo, that it is actually much better to marry than to freeze! Knowing
well the warmth of his wedded life with Katarina von Bora, Luther
called marriage "a school for character." Character has to do with integrity before God and man. It's an integrity that we acquire, always
slowly and often painfully, with the daily practice of Christian virtue.
Our spouses know, above all others, whether we possess such integrity.
They not only know whether we are faithful or fraudulent; they also enable us to have true character. At last Paul gets it right when, in
Colossians 3, he lists the attributes of the faithful life that are also the
virtues of the married life: compassion, kindness, lowliness, meekness,
forbearance, forgiveness. "And above all these put on love," says Paul,
"which binds everything together in perfect harmony. And let the peace
of Christ rule in your hearts, to which indeed you were called in the one
body."

Marriage constitutes a miniature church: Melodie and Scott will
become one flesh only as they are joined in the one body of Christ's
church. Thus will they require us who are their brothers and sisters in
Christ to keep them joined. Here they are making an appointment with
the future: making vows to last not for a day or a year, but all the way to
the grave. They cannot sustain such love by themselves. Marriage is
never a covenant between two people alone; it is always a set of promises made by the entire Christianity community. The Marcus marriage
will build up Christ's church, therefore, only as we also build them up
in a life of utter and endless gratitude. Hence Paul's simple but revolu-

tionary conclusion to his list of spiritual commands: "And be thankful." Those three final words sum up what it means to love each other in the body of Christ called the church and in the holy estate called marriage: "And be thankful."

It's not easy always to be thankful, Luther warned. In one of his wittiest sayings, he declared that it requires great courage to enter both marriage and tournaments. Luther was not referring to basketball tournaments, of course, but to those frightful medieval jousts where lance-bearing knights hurtled full tilt at each other, seeking not only to knock the other off his horse but also to kill him. Well, marriage is a little like that! You will often find it to be a contest of stubborn wills. There will be fierce disagreements, sometimes even outright battles.

The good news is that marriage is the ultimate anti-tournament. It is not about winning but about giving. Scott and Melodie are here pledging not to knock each other off their horses but instead to keep each other firmly in the saddle. They are not about to kill but rather to die for each other in order that they both might live. This bonded marital love that we seal this day in Christ Jesus and his church will enable them to reorder their earthly loves to the love of God. Their wedded life together will thus be blessed and blissful as each lifts the other's burdens, as each draws the water of eternal life for the other, as each kisses the other and weeps not for grief but for joy. Amen.

A Marriage Built on the Solid Rock

A HOMILY FOR THE WEDDING
OF HOLLY HUGHES AND JEFFREY FISH

Memorial Drive Presbyterian Church
Houston, Texas
December 30, 2006

"God is our refuge and strength, a very present help in trouble. Therefore we will not fear." These are the unshakable words of comfort and strength that we will later hear read from Psalm 46. We shall also hear these words spoken by our Lord, as recorded in the seventh chapter of Matthew: "Therefore whoever hears these sayings of Mine, and does them, I will liken him to a wise man who built his house on the rock."

I

This is the Scripture passage that Holly Hughes and Jeffrey Fish have wisely chosen for their wedding ceremony. Together with St. Paul's admonition to the church at Colossae, these biblical words have all of the solidity and straightforwardness of Holly and Jeff's own love for each other. Well do they know that marriage is not based on momentary romantic attraction. Rather, it is based on those qualities enumerated by St. Paul in Colossians: "tender mercies, kindness, humility, meekness, longsuffering." The old wedding ceremony from the Book of Common Prayer stressed the seriousness of the marital covenant by having the couple make the following promise: "I plight thee my troth." These antique words mean, quite simply, "I pledge to you my loyalty, my honor, my truth — my *troth*." So great a promise cannot be kept by human effort alone. It requires the grace of God working through the institution of marriage itself.

The German Christian martyr Dietrich Bonhoeffer was ever so clear about what it means to "plight our troth" in marriage. Writing from his prison cell at Tegel, where he would eventually be executed by a firing squad, Bonhoeffer counseled his niece Renate Schleicher and his former student Eberhard Bethge about their forthcoming marriage. He urged them not to regard it as a prolonged romantic relationship, not as an extended "date." On the contrary, said Bonhoeffer, "It [will not be] your love that sustains your marriage, but from now on [it will be] the marriage that sustains your love." The sanctity and permanence of marriage enables us to love each other even when — especially when! — we are unlovable as, alas, we often are. Hence St. Paul's injunction to bear with one another, to forgive one another, to let the peace of God rule in your hearts. So it is that Holly and Jeff are making radically unromantic but profoundly marital vows: "for better or for worse; for richer or for poorer; in sickness and in health; to love and to cherish, forsaking all others."

That Holly and Jeffrey understand the gravity no less than the glory of their marital vows is evident in their decision not to marry during the season of Advent, as have so many other American couples. Be assured that theirs was no easy decision dictated by the secular calendar of convenience. On the contrary, Jeff and Holly have observed Advent as a season not only of waiting and watching but also of contrition. Thus have they joined the church universal in its four-week period of purple penitence, concluded only five days ago. They and we have spent this time lamenting what the Prayer Book calls our manifold sins and wickedness. We and they have confessed that, in and of ourselves, we are miserable offenders. There is no true health in us, no true hope, no true salvation. Wisely, therefore, have they waited until the birth of Christ has been celebrated in order to consecrate their marriage. Only now, during Christmas proper, do they have cause to celebrate all the rights and privileges and delights appertaining to matrimony. Only through the coming of the Savior do they have a Rock sufficiently solid whereon to build their marital house.

Let us make clear the risk here entailed. The devastating floods of our materialistic culture of ease and entertainment shall surely rise up against Holly and Jeff, threatening to overwhelm the house of their marriage. The winds of worldly mishap shall no less surely beat against the walls of their marital dwelling. They will be buffeted by accident and illness and plain bad luck, even by the deaths of those near and dear. Their matrimonial house will be stricken by the controversies and calamities of our time, not least of all by the petty jealousies of academic infighting. (But they will remember the wisdom of the wag who said that academic battles are so vicious because the stakes are usually so small.) Their holy dwelling place shall stand because it is not built on the sinking sands of time and the tide, nor on the fret and fury of the world. It is built on the immovable foundation of Jesus Christ and his kingdom, against which not even the gates of hell can prevail.

II

Someone has wittily said that Holly Hughes broke the hearts of at least a hundred Baylor coeds when she won the heart of Professor Jeffrey Fish. I count myself among the first to have smoked out their neat little secret. Holly was a student in a course of mine entitled "Christian Literary Classics." We had been reading John Bunyan's *Pilgrim's Progress*. Most of my students find Part II of Bunyan's great allegory to be insufferably dull, for it recounts the rather unadventurous journey of Christiana and her companion Mercie on their way to the Celestial City. With her typical originality of mind and imagination, however, Holly Hughes found Part II to be utterly delightful. So delightful, in fact — Holly informed me last May — that her Latin professor had presented her with a framed portrait of the Bunyan character named Mercie.

Now this struck me as passing strange. Why would a Classics teacher present a former student with so fine a gift? It didn't take me long to detect the reason for the sparkle in Holly's eye whenever she mentioned this unnamed professor. I knew that he and she must be more than mere acquaintants, indeed, that they must be deeply in love. That same semester, I had espied the special relevance of a poem by Gerard Manley Hopkins entitled "Spring." In this fine sonnet, Hopkins celebrates the renewal of the earth after a long and dark English winter. For Hopkins the Roman Catholic, May is not only the month of romantic love but also the month of the Virgin Mary. The two are not unrelated. The natural juices of frolicking lambs and flowering crocuses are distant echoes of the original innocence that our human race once knew in the Garden of Eden. Alas, we lost that primal innocence through the sin of the first Eve and her obsequious husband Adam. And yet God has restored our lost goodness and truthfulness and beauty through the second and true Eve named Mary, the May-maiden who is the mother of the Christ child, the second and true Adam.

Whenever I see Holly Hughes and Jeff Fish walking across the Baylor campus, it never occurs to me to consider their difference in age. What I see, instead, is something akin to the original springtime love of the unfallen Adam and Eve. Hopkins ends his splendid poem with a prayer urging Christ to reclaim the first love of youth as his own possession. Indeed, Hopkins pleads with the Lord not to let such springtime love cloy, not to let it become like a diet consisting entirely of candy. It's a petition worth praying once again on this happy nuptial day:

> What is all this juice and all this joy?
>   A strain of the earth's sweet being in the beginning
> In Eden garden. — Have, get, before it cloy,
>   Before it cloud, Christ, lord, and sour with sinning,
> Innocent mind and Mayday in girl and boy,
>   Most, O maid's child, thy choice and worthy the winning.

What God has brought together in the love of Holly Hughes and Jeffrey Fish through the love of Christ Jesus cannot be sundered by angels or principalities or powers, neither by things present nor things to come, by neither height nor depth, by neither death nor life, by neither things present nor things to come, nor by any other created thing. All praise, therefore, be unto the God who is our refuge and strength, and all glory be unto the Christ who is the solid rock of their marriage and of our salvation. Amen.

PART VII

DEATH AND ETERNAL LIFE

An Unhaloed Mississippian Saint

John 1:1-14

A EULOGY FOR EMILY WHITEHURST STONE (1908-1992)

St. Peter's Episcopal Church
Charlotte, North Carolina
June 27, 1992

Emily Whitehurst Stone gave witness to the light that shines in the darkness. Her life is evidence that the darkness has not overcome the light — indeed, that it shall never overcome the light. For the light that shone in her life derived not from herself alone but from the God who became flesh and dwelt among us. Emily Stone did not always regard herself as a witness to the incarnate Word. She may at times have considered herself a counterwitness. But the God who enlightens every man and woman doesn't pay much heed to our petty distinctions. He doesn't confine his grace and truth to the orthodox and the churchly. Our God loves irony, and so he imbued Emily Stone with his light and made her his ironic witness.

If you or I or anyone else tries to put a halo on Emily Stone, she will rise up out of her ashes to knock it off and to tell us off. She was anything but pious. I do not know the springs of her impiety, but they must have run very deep. Perhaps she had a domineering daddy who convinced her that, if God were such an overbearing parent, then she would refuse to be his daughter. Perhaps there were preachers who gave easy answers to her hard questions, thus prompting her to prefer tough-minded atheism over soft-headed faith. Perhaps her own mental strength and physical beauty persuaded her to reject the props and crutches that conventional religion gives to weak and cowardly souls.

Whatever her reasons, Emily Stone did not approach life with her hands folded in the attitude of a treacly piety.

Let us clearly confess that the evidence for an independent humanism was all on Miss Emily's side. She was a woman of such strong will and hardy character that it must have been difficult for her to believe that she depended utterly on the grace and judgment of God. She was nothing if not an independent woman. She refused to depend even on credit cards. Such fierce independence sometimes got her into trouble. For example, it got her into trouble when, on a trip to visit her husband at the Mississippi State Hospital in Whitfield, she sought to rent a car at the Jackson airport. The man at the counter told her that no one could hire a car without a credit card to back up the rental. Standard procedure, no exceptions: a personal check simply would not do. It was unheard of, he added, that anyone should try to live in the modern world and not carry a credit card.

What this addle-pated attendant failed to understand is that, in a very real sense, Emily Stone did not live in the modern world and had no intention of doing so. She was too prickly and thorny for such a warm-fuzzy world as ours. The bland bureaucrat at the car rental desk was confronting, perhaps for the first time in his life, a woman whose wit and will would not be deterred. And so she asked him: If he would not honor her own personal word, would he honor the word of the Chief Justice of the Supreme Court of the State of Mississippi — who also happened to be her friend? Taken aback at so startling a suggestion, the rental agent relented. And after a flurry of phone calls, the chief justice was summoned from his chambers and put on the line to vouch, ever so willingly, for the good credit of one Emily Whitehurst Stone.

Her credit was good in many other ways. She was an early credit to women unwilling to remain polite society ladies: women who never learned to drive cars, women whose chief role was to keep the silver polished and the china gleaming and the antimacassars straightened, women who belonged to book clubs but rarely read books. Miss Emily was liberated from such an idea of womanhood. She not only drove cars and neglected her doilies; she also read books. To borrow a phrase from the Book of Common Prayer, one can truly say that she read, marked, learned, and inwardly digested the books that meant most to her. Against the will of her husband and the grain of proper Oxford society, she also taught these books in the English Department at Ole

Miss, then later at the All Saints Episcopal School for Girls in Vicksburg, and later still at Huntingdon College in Montgomery.

Though I did not know her as a teacher, I could tell from our conversations that she had conveyed to her students the thrill of learning, the sheer excitement of intellectual work, above all the enduring effect of books and ideas on our lives. For Emily Stone, the great works of Western mythology and literature were not mere texts to be subjected to what the British call Lit Crit. Our novelists and poets and mythmakers were, to her, nothing less than seers into the human condition. Their books enable us to ask, and perhaps even to answer, the essential human question: what it means to be a man or a woman living in the world, and what it means to die.

Emily Stone was troubled over her failure to become a writer herself and to leave a literary legacy of her own. She also feared that her modest degree from the Georgia State College for Women (later to become Flannery O'Connor's alma mater) condemned her to a life of self-education. We are here to testify that she was mistaken in both disappointments. Mrs. Stone was a self-taught woman who possessed the wisdom and understanding that no high-falutin' degree can confer. Moreover, she permanently marked the lives of her students and her family and her friends as books alone cannot do. She has left a legacy of plainspoken honesty and oak-knot integrity that none of us can lay aside as we can put down a book. She understood with Walker Percy that you can make all A's and still flunk life, and that you can create great art and still be a skunk as a person. Let it be said ever so clearly: Emily Stone passed through life with high honors, and as a human being she was not a skunk but a lovely, fragrant rose.

Her high and stoical sense of honor — let it also be confessed — made it hard for her to understand human perversity and evil. She could not fathom why others did not live with her own sense of justice and fairness and decency. The student riots at Ole Miss, when James Meredith was enrolled as the first Negro student there, were a terrible perplexity to her. Whatever view one took of the federal intervention, there was no excuse for brutality. And so, amid the tear gas and flying bricks and overturned garbage cans, Emily Stone took to the streets herself. She braved the mayhem to tell those collegiate thugs that they ought to be ashamed of themselves for behaving like barbarians. They, of course, stupidly ignored this doughty little English professor. In her splendid biography of Miss Emily's husband, Phil Stone, Susan

Snell epitomizes the scene well: "Genteel order could not be imposed on anarchy."

Emily Stone may have believed in humane order, but she was no ordinary humanist. When, in October of 1935, Phil Stone went down from Oxford to New Orleans in order to marry Emily Whitehurst, she insisted on a church wedding. This was an odd demand for a young atheist to make. Despite the smart secularity of her youth, Emily knew intuitively that we make our deepest vows and promises in the presence of another audience than merely ourselves. She sensed, in the deep recesses of her being, that we must reckon with the transcendent. She discerned that at the hinge moments of life — at marriage and birth, in sickness and death — the eternal is made temporal, the hidden is revealed. There a light shines from beyond the confines of the world into the darkness that seems otherwise to engulf us.

Emily's marriage to Phil Stone — "Mr. God," as she called him — was the great light of her life. Her two children, Philip and Araminta, were the luminaries who brightened her days. The family's early friendship with William Faulkner was an enormous gladness to her, if also a cause for consternation. That Faulkner could be rude and ungrateful, beyond all standards of civility, was a fact Emily never denied. But neither did she let their later disaffection ruin the delightful memories of her young years. One of the dangers of growing old is that we forget and thus become ungrateful for the blessings of our youth. The wonder of Emily Stone's old age is that she did not turn bitter and thankless after her early joys were taken from her.

We would be dishonest today if we did not confess that a frightful darkness was, in fact, lowered onto Emily Stone. She was stripped of almost all her earthly loves. She lost her lovely Oxford home to fire, her dear husband to mind-muddling disease, her brilliant son to alienation and untimely death. Emily Stone became more than merely acquainted with sorrow and grief; they were her daily bread. She was made to cry aloud with the Psalmist *de profundis,* out of the depths. Her soul waited and watched desperately for help. She turned to the writings of the Russian mystic Gurdgieff for consolation. There she found access to a spiritual world that made a certain sense of the calamities she had suffered. And with a courage that few of us could muster, she constructed a new life for herself, first in Vicksburg, then in Montgomery, and finally here in Charlotte.

Yet it is not quite right to say that Emily Stone started over again by means of her own gumption. There was something else at work in and through and for her. I call it the grace and truth of the God who became flesh and dwelt among us in Jesus Christ. This is the Lord who declares that he has other sheep that are not of this fold called the church, and that he must also bring them in (John 10:16). I believe that Emily Stone was one of those other sheep. Such confidence enabled me to tease her about being a heretic, even as I also assured her that St. Peter does not guard the gates of heaven with a theological test that we must first pass before entering paradise. And so I joshed with her about the Platonic theology of Charles Williams, her favorite Christian writer. His highly spiritualized religion, I argued, did not fit the rough facts of her own life.

Testing the limits of our friendship, I once accused Emily Stone of being a closet Calvinist. Throwing her head back with that great open-mouth laugh that made her so rare and dear, she affirmed my description. For she knew deep down that God is not a cuddly deity who presides over a no-fault universe. The Christ through whom all things were made, and without whom nothing was made — this Christ, she knew, is not a nice but a fierce Savior. He is the judge who sentences us to a life of free grace, the jailer who imprisons us by flinging wide the cell doors. Such Calvinist paradoxes became clear to Emily Stone only in the last years of her life. She finally understood, I believe, that it is God who creates and redeems and judges us, not we ourselves. She knew in the end that we are not bravely independent souls but creatures totally dependent on God's grace and truth.

This is the Good News of the gospel. Emily Stone was not forced to learn it abstractly or theoretically. God's patience was embodied for her in the kindness of her two granddaughters, Abigail and Jennifer. God's tenderness was granted to her in the care she received from Steve Johnston, the son-in-law in whom she received again the son she had lost so long ago. And God's reconciling love was enfleshed in her dear Araminta, the strong-willed daughter who could have locked horns with her strong-willed mother, but who instead became her friend and companion. These and the many others who nursed her at the end — all of these, I say, were incarnations of God's grace in the life of Emily Stone. Perhaps this explains why, in the last months, all of the bitter memories faded away as she recovered a blissful, almost childlike innocence.

It also explains why we are gladdened rather than saddened on this occasion. We have ever so much more cause for rejoicing than grieving. Indeed, we have cause for laughter. We know that the grammar of paradise has been mightily improved with the advent of Emily Stone into the heavenly precincts. Not even the archangels Michael and Gabriel will be allowed to say, "Just between you and I." No, no, a thousand times no! Mrs. Stone will also correct St. Peter himself if he tries to *sit* her down at the banquet feast of the New Jerusalem; she will remind him that he must *set* her down. And in the unlikely case that heaven contains any medical doctors, they had better be prepared to explain what an *oxymoron* is, since she once used the word in the presence of a physician who had never heard it before.

The word, as she would teach us even from her ashes, is pure Greek: *oxus* ("sharp") and *moros* ("dull"). An oxymoron thus joins contradictory terms in order to give pith and point to a statement or an expression. But for all her etymological wisdom, Emily Stone failed to see that she was herself an oxymoron. She was a saint without a halo. She was a spiky and angular woman whose rough edges smoothed the way for others to follow. She may have thought herself an unbeliever but, to paraphrase Tennyson, there lived more faith in her honest doubt than in half our creeds. Therefore, we have gathered here today not to lament her end, but to say, with T. S. Eliot and all other Christians, that in her end is her beginning.

Let us remember, finally, that Emily Stone could wittily give back the same jibes she so graciously took in. When I would harass her about having a heterodox theology, she would deplore the disability from which I suffer even more regrettably than from deafness, namely, my pitiable condition of being a Baptist. For her, the only thing worse than a Baptist was a Baptist preacher. And so I will prove her right one last time by doing what Baptist preachers are wont to do at the close of their sermons, that is, quote a poem, the politically incorrect original version of a hymn from the eighteenth century, Isaac Watt's rendering of Psalm 90. It sums up the godly grace and truth that buoyed the life of Emily Stone even as it gives ballast to our own:

> Before the hills in order stood,
> Or earth received her frame,
> From everlasting thou art God,
> To endless years the same.
>
> Time, like an ever-rolling stream,
> Bears all its sons away;

They fly, forgotten as a dream
Dies at the opening day.

Under the shadow of thy throne
Thy saints have dwelt secure;
Sufficient is thine arm alone,
And our defense is sure.

A thousand ages in thy sight
Are like an evening gone;
Short as the watch that ends the night
Before the rising sun.

O God, our help in ages past,
Our hope for years to come.
Be thou our guide while life shall last,
And our eternal home.

O God, our help in ages past,
Our hope for years to come.
Our shelter from the stormy blast,
And our eternal home.

All praise and honor and glory be unto to thee, Lord Christ, for the life
and the death and the eternal life of Emily Whitehurst Stone. Amen.

A Man of Godly Fear and Suffering Obedience

PAUL WELLS BARRUS (1902-2000)

A tribute offered at his Vigil Service
St. Elizabeth Ann Seton Catholic Church
Plano, Texas
January 5, 2000

Hebrews 5:7-9: "In the days of his flesh, Jesus offered up prayers and supplications, with loud cries and tears, to him who was able to save him from death, and he was heard for his godly fear. Although he was a Son, he learned obedience through what he suffered; and being made perfect he became the source of eternal salvation for all who obey him."

Paul Barrus was a man of such great and varied gifts that one hardly knows how to pay him tribute. It would be obvious and natural to honor his life as a scholar. He was indeed a diligent student of the great books and ideas of the western world, from the Greeks and the Romans through the English and the Americans. He was also a scholar of languages other than his own, especially Latin. But we remember him mainly a master of his own mother tongue. Knowing that speech is our uniquely human gift, the only thing that distinguishes us from the animals, he sought to use words ever so wisely and well. It would also be meet and right to praise Paul Barrus as a teacher extraordinaire, one whose equal I have never known. I here gladly confess, as could many others, that my own career in the classroom is due almost entirely to his example. Once I had sat at the feet of this teacher, I knew what I was called to do.

It would also be appropriate to laud Paul Barrus for the firmness of his friendships. He knew that friends come as one of life's most remarkable gifts. We find, to our great surprise, that someone else shares our most fundamental interests and loves. Yet Paul Barrus did not cultivate only academic friends who joined him in the life of books well read and words well used. He was also the friend of much less sophisticated folk. He was drawn to common people, and they to him, by their common commitment to the most fundamental virtues: to loyalty and integrity, to honesty and humility, to straightforwardness and the utter absence of pretense. Father Paul was thus the friend of maids and cooks and secretaries, of day laborers and caregivers whose English was halting and imperfect. He was even the friend of eighth graders. Once when this elderly teacher-priest asked his class how many a's there are in the word "cemetery," a sullen boy who was the class renegade and outcast found himself instinctively raising his hand and answering, "None." From that moment onward, this youth whose knowledge had been reluctantly drawn out of him became Father Paul's friend.

Yet I have come not chiefly to praise Paul Barrus for his virtues as scholar and teacher and friend, but rather to salute the Christian faith that was their source. Father Paul's faith was of the kind described in Hebrews 7: it consisted of godly fear and suffering obedience. It was a faith hammered out on the anvil of woe, and thus it had the strength of finely wrought metal. We would dishonor the memory of Father Paul if we did not confess that his Christianity was deeply linked to his sorrow. He was acquainted with grief early in life, when the corpse of his young mother was taken from the bedroom in which little Paul was not soundly sleeping but terribly awake. It was a horror that would haunt him for more than nine decades. Reared by his grandmother in Winterset, Iowa, young Barrus knew intimately the calamities and tragedies that, in rural towns such as Winterset, cannot be covered up and made impersonal as they are in our large cities.

Such griefs and sorrows enabled Paul Barrus to become both a deeper Christian and a better teacher of literature than if he had passed through life unscathed. Unlike certain dilettantes within the academy and certain easy believers within the church, Barrus knew that any faith worthy of our embrace, like any art worthy of our interest, must deal with suffering and fear. He taught us that both our faith and our art must embody, in their own appropriate ways, what the book of Hebrews calls "the loud cries and tears" of our Lord. We who were his students and parishioners were thus drawn to Paul Barrus because he was not scandalized by evil and pain. We learned from him, on the contrary, that pain and evil are the very subject of our literature and the very object of our redemption.

Already as a young man, Paul Barrus felt himself called by God to be a priest of the church. Yet the hardships of his early life had also taught him the biblical virtue of patience, the willingness not to hurry but rather to wait on the Lord. Not until sixty years had passed would Father Paul at last be ordained to the priesthood, in 1978, at the age of 76. The long delay was again prompted by the hard conditions of his life. When he finished his degree in Latin at Drake University in Des Moines, he was not free to follow his religious vocation. Instead, he was required to use his income as a teacher to support his elderly grandmother, a sacrifice that he made not angrily but gratefully. After her death, when at last he was able to finish his doctorate in English at the University of Iowa, it seemed far too late to undertake ordination.

There were other troubles as well. Dr. Barrus's allergies so overwhelmed him during the bitter northern winters that he was forced to seek a more temperate climate. And so he took a job at a school that he had never seen, arriving by train in the eastern Texas town of Commerce on an icy January Sunday in 1949. Surely he must have wondered whether he had exchanged a bad scene for a worse one. For what he faced at East Texas State Teachers College was a strange new life: he was to become the sole Catholic member of a faculty that was otherwise Protestant, in a town that was overwhelmingly Baptist and Methodist, and amid students who — at least some of them — may have suspected that he was a secret agent of the devil!

It would have been ever so easy for Paul Barrus to become a disappointed, even an embittered, man. With considerable justification, he could have pitied himself. He could have bemoaned and lamented the huge gap that stood between the gleaming excellence of his youthful promise and the seeming mediocrity of his middle-aged fate. But he did not. Because he was first and last a believer, Barrus learned obedience through what he suffered. Among many other virtues, he learned self-mocking humor. He knew that he was odd, but then he also knew that we are all a bit strange, and that God himself is the oddest of all. I think that Dr. Barrus enjoyed being eccentric if only because, as a Latinist, he knew that *eccentric* literally means "off-center." Such is the way that Christians are supposed to live: having a different Center from the world's center.

Having endured the difficult years of the Depression, when so many had so little, he had also learned the importance of gratitude. He was thus deeply grateful for his new life in Commerce, and he especially cherished the native courtesy of the young people who came from the blackland prairies and the piney woods of eastern Texas to study with him. Paul Barrus's suffering obedience also taught him humility, and it prevented him from condescending either to his colleagues or his students. He never reminded us that his learning was immensely larger than nearly everyone else's on our campus, nor that his Catholic Christianity had a far older and richer tradition standing behind it than did our own Protestant faith. On the contrary, we were drawn to him because we knew that he stood with us in the things that matter most, in fact, that matter ultimately: in the same faith, the same hope, the same charity. The wondrous result is that he became our brother no less than our professor, our companion no less than our priest.

We also knew that he stood with us in our doubts and difficulties as they are described in the book of Job: "Man is born to trouble as the sparks fly upward." I can still vividly recall the day, nearly forty years ago, when Paul Barrus declared that the deep lines of his face were the battle scars of his life. This plain, matter-of-fact statement came as considerable shock to collegians whose teenaged cheeks were still uncreased by suffering. We didn't know quite what to make of his scorn for the cosmetic disguises that seek to erase the marks of age and pain. Like most other Americans, we were not eager to learn what Dr. Barrus had long ago learned. It is the same lesson that the Hebrew patriarch Jacob learned in his nightlong combat with the angel of the Lord at the River Jabbok. It is the unwelcome but bracing truth that only in grappling with God is our faith made real and lasting rather than trite and ephemeral. A faith that doesn't confront the hard facts of a brutal world — chiefly the hard fact of our own stony hearts — is not true faith. Paul Barrus's faith was true. In obedience to the injunction of the apostle Paul, he worked out his salvation in fear and trembling.

Because his own faith was never smug or falsely secure, Dr. Barrus wasn't panicked by the skepticism and unbelief of his academic colleagues. He wasn't scandalized by the resident agnostics who ridiculed the saccharine piety of sentimental Christians. So long as their scholarship was honorable and their lives had integrity, he counted them as his compatriots. Knowing that the word "catholic" means universal and ecumenical, he was eager to honor excellence wherever it was manifest, no matter how secular the source. It was Paul Barrus, after all, who sponsored the trenchant and thorny writer Flannery O'Connor when she came to our campus on her single visit to Texas in 1962. O'Connor declared, with her typical candor, that sentimentality is to Christianity as pornography is to art. Faith that is sweet and cozy and merely nice is indeed obscene. The Santa Claus deity that Dr. Barrus's skeptical friends refused to believe was also the false god that he refused to believe. The God of Paul Barrus's faith — the one and only true God — is the God who took the form of suffering flesh at Bethlehem, who made his prayers and supplications with tears wherever he went, and who died with a loud cry at Golgotha.

As priest and professor of this same Jesus Christ, Paul Barrus was longsuffering with the moral failings of his students and colleagues, his fellow priests and parishioners. He knew that Christ does not call us to be good so much as to be godly. The good person is beset by the danger of a God-denying self-congratulation. His goodness tempts him to think that he doesn't need God. The godly person, by contrast, confesses his sin and weakness, his doubts and fears, and thus his utter reliance on God. Paul Barrus was indeed a godly man, a man unashamed to confess his own doubts and fears. He underwent a profound crisis of faith in his early sixties when, as he confessed to me and to others, he came to doubt not only whether God is good but also whether God even exists. Again in his seventies, when he was almost blinded by cataracts, he doubted that his life had further meaning or use. And until the very end, he admitted his dread of dying. When I last visited him in September, I found him chair-bound, breathing with the aid of an oxygen tube, and staring at the same four walls all day long. He was clearminded and cheerful, even as he was also candid. "I never thought it would come to this," he said.

The point of my own candor is to stress that the faith of Paul Barrus was the real thing and not a tawdry substitute. It was a deeply biblical and a deeply Catholic faith. Both Scripture and tradition regard the fear and honor of God as the only route to wisdom and holiness of life. Not to fear and honor God, but rather to dwell in cheap comfort and easy contentment, is to live an empty and false life. It is, in fact, to be damned. Paul Barrus's life was full and true. He was saved because he believed in the God of Jesus Christ strongly enough to fear him, to wrestle with him, to doubt him. The world, we must confess, doesn't often look as if God has both created and redeemed it. It often looks like hell. To admit this stark truth is also to admit that the opposite of faith is not doubt but distrust and disobedience. To want an untroubled belief, to want a carefree life, to want a pretty and sin-free world — these are the marks of unbelief. Father Paul was a believer, a man who trusted and obeyed. As the old Baptist hymn insists, there is no other way to be happy. And happy this man truly was. Dread and doubt, pain and death, could not defeat him, for he was faithful to the end, a man of godly fear and suffering obedience. May God rest the soul of Paul Wells Barrus, June 29, 1902 to January 1, 2000. Amen.

Feasting on Manna and Turnip Greens

AN ACCOUNT OF THE FUNERAL SERVICE
FOR JAMES WM. MCCLENDON JR.
MARCH 6, 1924–OCTOBER 30, 2000

Shiloh Baptist Church
Mooringsport, Louisiana
November 11, 2000

Jim McClendon's funeral was a splendid occasion in every regard. Jim's wife, Nancey Murphy, confessed after the service was over that she had doubted whether such a strange collection of people in such a strange place could properly honor Jim. But Nancey was also happy to confess that Jim had been utterly right to think this was the way it all should end.

For northwest Louisiana in early November, it was an uncommonly chilly and gray day. The setting seemed as uninviting as the weather: a remote rural scene out from a village called Mooringsport. Once a bustling town, it had served as the penultimate port for riverboat traffic that plied back and forth between New Orleans and Jefferson, Texas. Not many people know that there was once navigable water linking the Mississippi first with the Red River and then with the Cypress River. It flowed out of Caddo Lake, the largest natural body of water in the region. Named for the local and quite peaceful Indian tribe, Caddo remains a remarkably beautiful place because of its moss-draped cypress trees. Near this once-thriving town and adjacent to the Shiloh Baptist Church, Jim had bought a tract of land where Texaco had clear-cut the timber and destroyed much of the terrain with heavy logging equipment. At this place that had become so dear to him in the last years,

Jim had begun to make his own ecological witness by restoring the land: replanting it in pines, tending it carefully, and thus exercising proper biblical stewardship over it.

During these last years, Jim had also become acquainted with the pastor of the adjacent church and with various church members. He had befriended these black Baptists, and they had in turn bought land from him to enlarge their church grounds. And so Jim had worked out an arrangement with Pastor Leon Robertson to have his funeral conducted at this church. Though Jim had been ordained at the far more prestigious First Baptist Church of Shreveport, he knew that his life and ministry had come to have much more in common with these ordinary rural believers from another race than with the moneyed white Baptists downtown.

How right he was! These black Baptists knew how truly to honor a Christian whom most of them had never even met. There must have been about thirty-five of Jim's family and friends present, and at least as many church members as well. Nancey and Jim's first wife, Marie, sat next to each other in the front row. They were joined by Jim's two sons, James William III and Thomas Vernon, as well their wives. Jim's sister, Marian McClendon, was also there, together with his last physician from Altadena, California, and an assortment of other McClendon cousins and friends. There were also two members from Jim's very first pastorate in Ringgold, Louisiana, plus a handful of us academic friends: Curtis and Debra Freeman and a student from Houston Baptist, Barry Harvey from Baylor, Bob Ratcliff from Abingdon Press, as well as my wife, Suzanne, and me.

She and I immediately noticed that there were no hymnal racks attached to the pews. We soon discovered why. These Baptists have all their favorite hymns memorized! They thus joined us in making that little white-brick church rock with thanksgiving and joy as we belted out the great old gospel songs: "I Love to Tell the Story" and "Leaning on the Everlasting Arms" with the aid of an excellent jazz ensemble, including an organist and a pianist whose sprightly playing seemed to be all by ear. Better still was the singing of the Shiloh Baptist Choir. With both male and female soloists taking the lead, they sang "Amazing Grace" and "What a Friend We Have in Jesus" as few of us had ever heard them sung before. "Have we trials and temptations? Is there trouble anywhere? Are we weak and heavy laden, cumbered with a load of care?" Everyone present knew that the reply must be an honest "yes" and "always." But we also knew that the command to "take it to the Lord in prayer" contains our true cure: "We should never be discouraged" because "Jesus knows our every weakness." Finally, the general Christian assurance became a word of direct personal address: "In his arms he'll take and shield thee, thou wilt find a solace there."

These black Baptists observed rituals that gave the whole service a liturgical quality. A former pastor, now a man of many years, sat next to the present pastor in his place of honor on the podium. Ushers, both male and female, were posted at their appointed places along the aisles. The nurses' guild, women dressed in immaculate white medical uniforms, were seated at the rear of the church, while the deacons sat along one side at the front. Even the choir members, including a lady with a young daughter in arms, occupied their assigned places. Jim's friend Kyle Childress, pastor of the Austin Heights Baptist Church in Nacogdoches, Texas, preached an excellent sermon. Some of us teased Kyle afterward that, with a rousing Amen choir seated immediately behind him, only a deadhead preacher could have failed to proclaim the Word on this happy day. The main burden of Childress' message was to remind us that, as Paul was to Timothy, so was Jim McClendon much more than our friend and teacher: he was also our father in the faith. Kyle thus exhorted us to honor Jim's life and witness by imitating him as Paul enjoined the Corinthians: by serving Christ as fearlessly and faithfully as Jim did.

Childress reminded us that, in order to become disciples of Jesus, we must first learn how to see, how to acquire a new vision. He quoted from Jim's book that is entitled simply Ethics: "The eyes through which we Christians see the world are redeemed eyes; it is exactly through these eyes that we must be trained to look if we would see without double or narrow vision." Kyle gave a wrenching instance of how Jim first acquired such a Christian vision. As a boy growing up in First Baptist of Shreveport, he had overheard his mother talking to their black maid, Rebecca, about a splendid preacher who was holding services at their church. When Rebecca exhibited unusual interest in this man's message, Mrs. McClendon suggested that she go hear him for herself, even though she would have to sit in the balcony. But Rebecca was turned away from the church by a group of white boys who told her that she was not welcome there. On the following morning, when Jim overheard the maid recounting this sorry tale to his mother, he began to see the world with new eyes. Jim recorded his response in *Witness,* his last book, whose published version he was at last able to hold in his hands as he lay dying: "I was profoundly ashamed. Though I could not name it, I was ashamed of the system, the whole entrenched system of division in Christ's church."

Childress made clear the nature of Jim McClendon's witness. He was not outraged simply at social injustice, though surely he hated wrong in all its forms. His conscience was quickened by any violation of the one gospel that has the power to bring peace and reconciliation to the world's warring tribes and nations. As Kyle explained, Jim was not seeking to be a rebel and dissident when he lost his teaching jobs at the Golden Gate Baptist Seminary, for helping send a theological student to march with Martin Luther King in Alabama, and again at the University of San Francisco, a Roman Catholic school, where he helped students protest the war in Vietnam by sponsoring a full-page ad in a leading city newspaper. McClendon got himself into trouble not because he was a troublemaker but because he was a witness to Jesus Christ. "Jim's witness was not perfect," Childress reminded us. "He was better at some parts of the gospel than others." So it is with the rest of us, Childress concluded: "By the grace and mercy of God we are witnesses — broken, fragmented, and partial — pointing to Jesus Christ."

After the service, Childress and the family members went to a remote burial ground on Jim's land to inter his ashes there. There were only four marked graves in this plot that is cordoned off by an ornate scrollwork fence made of cast iron. The name "McDonald" is registered on the gate, and the graves date from the late nineteenth century. They probably belong to the owners of what was once a huge cotton plantation. Yet Jim wanted to be buried in this lonely spot amidst the pine trees, not at a fancy public cemetery. His own gravestone will contain only his name and dates and the following epitaph: "Tree farmer and baptist theologian." Jim insisted on the lower-case spelling of his own denominational affiliation because he insisted that it has links with many others in the believers' church tradition, especially Mennonites and Brethren.

Incidentally, Childress and the Shiloh pastor had been able to locate the gravesite only with the aid of two "good ol' boy" deer hunters who lease the land for hunting and who see to its upkeep. These fellows must have wondered why a white preacher and a black preacher would have been looking for such a place to begin with. As in life, so in death: Jim McClendon brought an odd lot of folks into the common purposes of the kingdom.

While Childress and the family were interring Jim's ashes, the congregation remained in the church to listen as the choir and jazz ensemble continued to sing and play very fine gospel music: "Oh, How I Love Jesus," "When the Saints," and on and on in a similarly joyful vein. In the meantime, Suzanne and I slipped outside to visit the church cemetery. It contains poignant hand-lettered headstones, casket-like blue and pink grave coverings for dead sons and daughters, as well as a handsome marble memorial to Huddie Ledbetter. He is more popularly known by his corrupted slang name, Leadbelly, the famous blues singer, songwriter, and master of the twelve-string guitar. Shiloh Baptist was his home church, and he was buried in its graveyard when he died in 1949.

Christians who celebrate and bury their dead often end their mourning with a faith-affirming and life-restoring feast. So did we. These black Baptists from the Louisiana bayou country really know how to lay out a banquet! They fed us the luscious chicken whose barbecue juices soaked all the way through the white meat. But it was the soul-food trimmings that were really body-and-soul nourishing: turnip greens and black-eyed peas — both of them seasoned with fatback — cornbread and succotash, sweet-potato pie, and an assortment of cakes. It was not a day for dieting. It was a day to learn the real meaning of Austin Miles's great old gospel song from 1911, "Dwelling in Beulah Land":

> I'm living on the mountain, underneath a cloudless sky.
> I'm drinking at the fountain that never shall run dry.
> O yes! I'm feasting on the manna from a bountiful supply,
>   For I am dwelling in Beulah Land.

Ours was indeed a foretaste of glory divine, the banquet of heaven that Jim McClendon helped us all to anticipate by living it out so splendidly here on earth.

A Grotesque Act of Repentance

A MEDITATION ON THE LIFE AND DEATH OF JOHN MILLIS (1953-2000)

John Millis was a man who could not believe. John wanted to believe, but he could not. And in a very strange way, his longing to believe, coupled with his inability to believe, was the mark of John's integrity, in his death no less than in his life. If most of us were as honest as John was, we too would admit our unbelief. The truth, unless it comes by God's grace, is intolerable. If we opened our naked eyes to the world's tragedy and injustice, to its pain and waste and loss, and especially to our own sinfulness, they would blind us. And so we wear corrective lenses of our own making. We invent mechanisms for coping, strategies for surviving. John Millis refused these palliatives. He confronted the awful reality of a graceless world, and it cost him.

I recall John's once describing to me the fright he had received upon meeting Harold Bloom, the distinguished Yale literary critic, during his visit to Wake Forest. "Those huge sad Jewish eyes haunted me," John confessed. "Bloom had stared into depths and beheld horrors that marked him forever." From the time I first met the young John Millis, in 1972, I knew that he too was marked by a similar sight of the abyss. What John could never quite understand, however, is the danger we risk when looking into the abyss. As even Nietzsche, the nihilist, once said, "If you stare long enough at Nothingness, it will stare back at you." The void is not a thing to be toyed with. It can come to have an odd attraction. Our ancient Christian forebears called it "the fascination of abomination." We can become demonically drawn to the very things that we find repulsive, so subtle and deceptive are the allurements that entangle us in their tentacles.

Yet John saw that there is something even more intolerable and outrageous than the mystery of evil. He glimpsed the frightful mystery of God's own goodness: the abysmal depth of the divine love that will not let us go, even if we descend into the depths of hell, perhaps even if we take our own lives, as John Millis has done. He was like the father who brought his epileptic child to Jesus for healing. The boy is foaming at the mouth and gnashing his teeth, falling to the ground and tearing at his own flesh. His condition seems utterly hopeless. Yet Jesus tells the father that all things are possible to the one who believes. The father famously replies, "Lord, I believe; help thou my unbelief." This man found it exceedingly hard to believe that the irreversible could be reversed, that the abyss could be emptied, that a mere rabbi could heal the unhealable. This was also John Millis's problem. He wanted to believe and yet he could not believe. Like the father of the boy afflicted with the falling sickness, John knew that there is but a single alternative to the madness and the horror that the child's epilepsy figured forth. It is the healing power of God's grace, and it is displayed supremely in the madness and the horror of Christ's cross. The one thing worth believing, John knew, is this drastic divine love.

John brought this startling truth home to me on our very last visit. I had given a lecture in Washington on Flannery O'Connor, the crusty Christian writer whom John had studied with me at Wake Forest. After the lecture, John made an astoundingly wise comparison between O'Connor and the much greater Southern writer William Faulkner. "We can squabble about the meaning of Faulkner's work," John noted, "without risking anything ultimate. After all, no one's salvation depends on getting Faulkner right as it does on getting O'Connor right." It was both shocking and bracing to hear John use the scandalous word *salvation.* Few holders of graduate degrees from both the University of Chicago and Banaras Hindu University, fewer readers devoted to the *New York Review of Books,* and still fewer chief liaison officers for the Central Intelligence Agency to the U.S. Congress — John Millis was all of these — want to be caught using such an unfashionable word. Though John was doubtful about his own salvation, his Mississippi upbringing had taught him that no other word will suffice.

John Millis spent his entire life searching for something that he could never find. Yet he knew that the object of his longing was really there. And so he remained a profoundly restless man. St. Augustine's celebrated prayer seems to have been uttered especially for John: "Thou hast made us for Thyself and our souls are restless until they rest in Thee." Standard religion had no attraction for John because it seemed to be a pathetic exercise in cheap delusions. John was rightly disappointed that so many of us accept pitiful substitutes for the Real Thing. Yet I think that John was finally disappointed in himself far more than in the world around him. He knew that it would not do to make the failure of others into an excuse for his own failures. Thus do I read his suicide not as a repudiation of his family or his friends, his colleagues or his superiors. On the contrary, their unfailing support was his immediate evidence for the unfailing love that he had spent his life seeking. Rather, I read his self-destruction as a horrific confession that he had failed those who were dearest to him, that he had failed himself, above all that he had failed God. I believe that his death was nothing other than a grotesque act of repentance.

The central truth of the gospel is that repentance is the sign of faith. We would not repent unless we were already under the pressure of God's salvation. What salvation means, I have come to believe, is that God in Christ holds onto us even when we try to thrust him away. God grasps us even when we can no longer grasp him, latching onto us even in the depths of our own personal hells. Thus are we right to hope and to pray that the deepest of all biblical declarations applies also to John Millis: that neither height nor depth, that neither principalities nor powers, that neither things present nor things to come, that neither life nor death, not even death by our own hand, can separate us from the love of God which is in Christ Jesus our Lord. Amen.

A Woman Whose Name and Life Sparkled

A EULOGY FOR POLLY WOOD SCHIEMANN
(1918-2004)

St. Mary's Episcopal — Christ Lutheran Church
Texarkana, Texas
May 18, 2004

Our names are vital things. They declare who we are and how others are to know us. It's important for us all to know that Polly Schiemann changed her name. Her parents, Donie and Mart Wood, named her Gladys Pauline when she was born in 1918 in the rural east Texas community of Cross Roads. But this name soon seemed far too heavy and serious for a girl who was so happy and spunky. Eventually Pauline became known as Polly. It's a cheerful name. It trips brightly off the tongue. To make sure that no one mistakenly revert to the dreadful "Pauline" listed on her birth certificate, Polly had her name legally altered. And so we are gathered here today to celebrate the life and to honor the death of this woman who, like her name, sparkled. It's altogether appropriate that her stepdaughter Carolyn has prepared altar flowers in Polly's favorite color — the cheerful red of roses.

Yet we are also present to remember that the rose is a symbol of the resurrection, the hope that when we die we do not merely rot and return to the dust, but that we also begin an entirely new life beyond the boundaries of the world. Hence our real purpose today is to declare the Good News that Gladys Pauline had an even more important name than Polly, a name that she did not give herself but that was given to her by the just and gracious God. It's the name that enters Polly Schiemann into the Lamb's Book of Life. It's the name "Christian," the only name granting the real hope that we might all live a faithful life and die a faithful death, as she did.

When I've asked Polly's family and friends what they remember most about her, they have used such words as feisty, bossy, stubborn, opinionated, laughing, jolly and, above all else, fun-loving. Polly came naturally by her delight in the playful and joyful life. She had a fun-loving mother and three fun-loving brothers. Polly's mother once hosted an overnight party for Polly and her friends. Unbeknownst to them, Donie had laced the goodies with Ex-Lax. Remember that, in those days, country houses had no indoor plumbing. It wasn't long before the all-night party turned into an all-night stream of visitors to the outdoor toilet.

Polly's brother Grady taught her how to dance, and she would remain a woman who loved the dance floor well into middle age. Only recently she told me how dancing got her fired from her teaching job at my own high school in Linden. There was almost nothing for a single woman to do with her evenings in this pokey little town. Knowing that Polly was colossally bored, her cousin Bernard Boon invited her to go with him to the dance hall in the nearby town of Jefferson. At the end of the school year, the superintendent called Polly into his office and asked whether she had committed this deadly sin of dancing, thus setting such a bad example that her students might go and do likewise. When Polly refused to lie or to make excuses, the superintendent refused to renew her contract.

Yet Polly was not really cut out to be a teacher. She was not a reader or thinker or grader of papers; she was goer and a doer. She was determined to live the good life because she had seen how cruelly it can be taken away. Unlike many of their neighbors, the Woods were not sharecroppers. They had purchased their own fifty-acre cotton farm. But a terrible flood in the late spring of 1939 completely wiped out their cotton crop, destroying even the terraces in their fields. Mart and Donie Wood were left bankrupt, incapable of making the final $500 payment on their twenty-year loan. The Hughes Springs banker, a wealthy man who did not need the money and who could have easily extended the Woods further credit, coldly foreclosed on their mortgage. Thus did Polly's parents lose not only their family farm but also the nineteen years of hard labor that had gone toward the purchasing of it.

The Woods never really recovered from this devastating financial blow, and the calamity marked Polly for life. She once told me that she could never forget the sight of her father leaving for Linden every Sunday afternoon. He would work there all week at the CCC camp, earning his dollar-a-day wage before returning to Cross Roads late on the following Friday. Franklin D. Roosevelt had created the Civilian Conservation Corps to rescue the little people whom the Depression had ruined, and thus to help impoverished farmers such as the Woods. Because Roosevelt's generous gesture had saved her parents from poverty, Polly became a proverbial "yeller-dog" Democrat. As far as I know, she never voted for a single Republican.

I will spare you Polly's estimate of the current Republican president, though she had a high regard for Laura Bush. Nor will I tell you about the relentless teasing that Polly suffered from her nephews because of her undeviating devotion to Bill Clinton. Whenever one of them slept in Polly's bedroom, for example, he would turn the pictures of Bill and Hilary against the wall. Our anti-Clintonite harassment was merely our means of getting revenge for the embarrassment she caused us as boys. As soon as she would arrive at our grandparents' house in Hughes Springs, she would wrestle us to the floor and plant lipstick marks all over our cheeks and foreheads.

Polly knew, by the time she had become a grown woman, that she did not want to remain in rural Cass County. She liked the bright lights and the high life of the city, and the city was not Dallas or Shreveport but Texarkana. Soon after she quit the schoolroom in Linden, Polly moved there to work at the Red River Arsenal and the Lone Star Ammunition Depot. For several years she rented an apartment from the late Mr. and Mrs. Perot, whom Polly greatly admired, though she did not admire their son Ross. Since he worked later as Polly's paperboy, she became acquainted early with his money-grubbing mentality, though she eventually became grateful for his splendid philanthropic gifts to his native Texarkana.

Polly was the first to confess that she came to Texarkana because she was a party girl. She had good reason for not marrying until she was thirty-nine: she was having too good a time, though she suffered a terrible sadness in the early 1950s, when her fiancé, Dub Blanton, died of cancer. Yet, having promised herself once, Polly remained open to the possibility of marriage. Perhaps it was on the dance floor that Polly met the man who would make her much more than a woman-about-town. Al Schiemann may have been the handsomest man in Texarkana, but he was also a serious man in a way that Polly's other men were not.

Al wanted to marry Polly, and he wanted to live a settled life. Polly admitted that the first year of their marriage, in 1957, almost killed her. Night after night she saw her friends driving off to the dancehalls while she stayed home with Al.

Gradually, however, she discovered that life with Al was much more satisfying than life at the clubs. As I heard her often confess, "Al Schiemann was the best thing that ever happened to me." Together they tramped and camped virtually the whole of this continent, Canada and Alaska included. They witnessed several of the space launches at Cape Canaveral. They played the slots in Las Vegas, and Polly delighted in her trips with her lady friends to the gambling boats in Shreveport and to the country-music shows at Branson. She and Al hunted deer and elk in Colorado, they shot pheasant and quail in Nebraska, and they fished the major lakes of eastern Texas and southern Arkansas.

The Schiemann daughters and grandchildren tell hair-raising stories about Polly's boat behavior on those lakes. She would pull them on inner tubes behind a boat that she drove at full throttle, dodging the perilous stumps of Lake Millwood. Fondly do they remember their many fish fries at the lake. But laughingly do they also complain about Polly's making them sit at the "little table" while they were still in their thirties, never giving them the honor of the "big table" that was reserved for real grownups in the dining room. And what feasts Polly put on for the Schiemann clan at Thanksgiving and Christmas! Perhaps she was making up for her insistence that one of the grandsons come, even on Sundays, to unstop the sewers at the Highway 82 trailer park that Polly operated. What no one doubts is that this woman knew how to have fun, and how to enable her friends to join in the fun. When I asked Polly's niece Juanell why she regarded Polly as her best friend, Juanell offered a tribute that perhaps everyone here assembled can affirm: "I liked everything about her."

There were a few people, however, who didn't like the idea of Polly and Al's owning and operating a liquor store out on Highway 67 here in Texarkana. Polly had never been much of a Baptist to begin with, and the liquor store ended what little Baptist life Polly had left. You've all heard, I trust, that Jews don't recognize Jesus as the Messiah, that Catholics don't recognize Protestants as having a true church, and that Baptists don't recognize each other in a liquor store. Yet even as a bad Baptist, Polly could never stop calling herself a Christian, and so she went in search of a church that wouldn't condemn her for selling whiskey, even to a niece who had never heard of Wild Turkey. It's not surprising that the Episcopalians took her in. As they themselves like to say: where two or more Episcopalians are gathered, there is always a fifth. When Polly was confirmed as an Episcopalian in 1965, she proved the truth of the old claim that perhaps the chief function of Baptist churches is to create future Episcopalians.

Yet Polly's life in the Episcopal church was no country-club or champagne-sipping affair. Let it be said ever so clearly that Polly Schiemann became a serious Christian here at St. Mary's Episcopal — Christ Lutheran Church. She was utterly devoted to its moral and sacramental life, and she served as president of the Altar Guild on several occasions. This fine community of Christ helped make Polly a servant of God in other ways as well. For more than twenty years she volunteered as a "pink lady" for the Christus St. Michael's Hospital Auxiliary. That many of them are present today, dressed in their smart uniforms, is a special delight for us all. As Sister Damian will gladly testify, Polly didn't "run" the hospital Gift Shop: she ramrodded it. Nor can we overestimate how much individual members of this church meant to Polly, not only Father Cal but also such other friends as Voncile and Joan and Louise and Annette — and on the list should go. Lest we forget, let us also note the many hours and the many dollars that she gave to the troubled children at Watersprings Ranch.

It is difficult, in fact, for some of us to comprehend the radical transformation that this former party gal underwent. She once confessed to me, for example, that she avoided retirement and nursing homes because, as she said, they depressed her. Yet in recent years when I would call her on Sunday evenings, I would discover that she had spent the afternoon visiting the sick and the dying, comforting the lonely and the troubled. This woman who had spent her life having fun was now taking care of those for whom fun was no longer possible. Most remarkable all, perhaps, is the story of Polly's care for her dying sister Nora and for her invalid husband during the final months and years of their lives. Polly largely gave up the fun-loving life to care for those who were dearest to her, even though there was no fun in it.

This eulogy would not be complete without mentioning the faithful servants who cared for Polly during her last trials, especially her granddaughter Rebecca. She has earned a reputation at both St. Michael's and Du Buis hospitals that will not be soon be forgotten. If anyone in this sanctuary is planning a stay in a hospital, I recommend that you get Rebecca to serve as your stern and sharp-tongued spokeswoman to make sure that the doctors and nurses behave as they should. And yet as I thanked Pam and Bobby, Rebecca and Reba and Sharon, for their splendid care for Polly during her last days, they said that they were not doing their grim duty. "This was our mother and grandmother," they replied, "and we were doing what we wanted to do — to care for this lady we loved so much."

After Al died last August, Polly hoped to enjoy the travels that she had long denied herself in order to care for the man who was "the best thing that had ever happened to me." She had planned visits to Washington and New York, to Georgetown and Waco, to Holly Lake and Stanley and Del Rio. At last she would have leisure time to spend with her nephews and nieces and grandchildren. Yet in the odd and often perplexing providence of God, it was not to be. The generation of the five children born to Mart and Donie Wood between 1898 and 1918 — a generation lasting 106 years — is now, alas, ended.

And so must I also end, lest Polly shout from heaven for me to shut up. She often groused about my long speeches, complaining that it took her forever to finish them. I replied that it wouldn't take her so long if she would stop moving her lips while reading them. Let it then be ever so gladly proclaimed: Our aunt and mother and grandmother has left us the bright and shining legacy that was ensconced in her cheerful name. Yet Polly has also handed us the flame of her faith. She was a woman not only of good fun but also of gracious service. What Christ says of the man who took his talents and diligently multiplied them must thus be said of Polly Wood Schiemann: "Well done, good and faithful servant; thou hast been faithful over a few things; I will make thee ruler over many things; enter thou into the joy of thy lord" (Matt. 25:23). Amen.

A Teacher Who Demanded Pandemonium

A EULOGY FOR MARGARET WIGGINS LOVELACE (1918-2004)

2 Corinthians 4:16-5:10

First United Methodist Church
Linden, Texas
August 5, 2004

We often regret, when a marvelous woman such as Margaret Wiggins Lovelace dies, that others could not have known her during her prime, rather than in the years of her decline. In most cases, though not always, this desire is right. Most of us end so badly that we want to be remembered, whether in our bodies or our deeds, for what we once were, not for the sorry things that we have become as the years have ravaged us. I, too, wish that everyone gathered here today could recall the brilliance of Mrs. Lovelace's teaching.

My favorite image of her comes from the late 1950s, when she occupied the front classroom on the left side of the old Linden High School building, located where the hospital now stands. She would sit on the side of her desk with one arm akimbo and the other elbow resting on the lectern, often with her chin cupped in her hand and her tongue planted firmly in her cheek after making some sly comment. She was teaching us Cass County yahoos about complex-compound sentences, or about the rootage of our mother tongue in the Anglo-Saxon language, or else about the complex plot and character developments at work in Shakespeare's *Macbeth*. As Rebecca Bowden Narramore and Joe B. Lovelace have both reminded me, she also required us to memorize large chunks of literature, whether it was the Lord's Prayer in Anglo-Saxon, the prologue to Chaucer's *Canterbury Tales* in Middle English, or central sections of Robert Browning's "Rabbi Ben Ezra." Much to your relief, I will not quote the "Our Father" in Old English, though of course I could!

These were assignments hardly designed to grab the interest of hormone-driven teenagers. But we liked her classes because she challenged us, because she did not condescend or talk down to us, because she demanded excellence from us, especially in our writing. She had her detractors, of course, but most of us liked her as well as her teaching. We liked her because she never stood at a scornful distance from us. On the contrary, she identified herself with us. Not that she was our pal or that she went out with us during nonschool hours. Such student-teacher camaraderie was unthinkable in those rather formal and long-gone days. Yet many of us felt that, while Margaret Lovelace was certainly our teacher, she was still one of us rather than one of them. To borrow from the slang of today's young crowd, Mrs. Lovelace was "cool" long before it was cool to be cool.

She taught us to reverence words, especially words that we had never heard before. I especially remember her using the words "insolent" and "impudent" to describe certain members of my class. I thought she was paying us a fine compliment. Eventually, I discovered that the Latin root of the word "insolent" refers to those who refuse to act according to custom, and who are thus rude and disrespectful of proper authority. "Impudent" is even worse. It refers, quite literally, to those who fail to cover their genitals, and who thus remain shameless and uncivil. On at least one occasion, Mrs. Lovelace entered her noisy classroom at the beginning of the hour, slammed her fist on the desk, and firmly declared: "I demand pandemonium!" Thinking that the class was being called to order, everyone fell silent. Gradually they learned, from reading *Paradise Lost,* that Milton had invented this word in 1667 to describe the capital of hell. Mrs. Lovelace was insisting that her class become what she thought it already was: the council chamber of all devils! Thus did she teach us that there are worse things to do with one's life than to learn the meaning of words, if only to distinguish between a condemnation and a compliment, a witty trick and a summons to proper behavior. No wonder that so many of her students did so well in college English courses: so very well had she prepared us.

Nor did Margaret Lovelace's tutelage end with our last days in her classroom. Even during these last sad years, she remained grammatically astute. Before going to visit her, I was often warned that I would find her in mental orbit, so that I would need to reel her in from the airy domain of fantasy. I was told that she might not recognize me or even recall an event five minutes prior, perhaps not even what she had eaten for lunch. But of course I didn't care whether she could remember her lunch menu so long as she could still distinguish between the nominative and the accusative case. And so, after engaging Mrs. Lovelace in idle chat for a few minutes, I would say something like this: "Just between you and I, this afternoon I plan to lay down for a nap." Whereupon she would arch her eyebrows in mock anger and sternly declare: "Hens lay eggs while you and I lie down for a nap, even if — just between you and me — we lay down yesterday for such rest."

So, yes, many of us do want to preserve an earlier pristine image as our essential remembrance of Margaret Lovelace. But as a representative of the church, I am here to declare that Mrs. Lovelace's most important years — though this is a dark and difficult saying — may have been her last years. If so, then the image of Mrs. Lovelace lying paralyzed by a stroke for more than a decade may be the most appropriate way to remember her and to give thanks for her life. This is a radical claim, of course, yet it is nothing other than the hope that St. Paul sets forth in his Second Letter to the church at Corinth: "Though our outer body is wasting away," the crotchety apostle affirms, "our inner nature is being renewed every day." Margaret Lovelace did, in fact, become ever more helpless and immobilized, looking in the end rather like a china doll, as she lay there with the sheets pulled up around her neck. Yet her dying enabled her to learn to look "not to the things that are seen but to the things that are unseen; for the things that are seen are transient, but the things that are unseen are eternal." It's true, of course, that her death was long and torturous, but it's truer still that she became strangely alive during her decade of dying. Hence my conviction — indeed, my proclamation — that today we should salute the way she faithfully died no less than the way she engagingly lived.

Margaret Lovelace learned how to die well, and therefore how to live well, because she had seen her young husband, "Shep," die in a remarkably redemptive way. When he was struck down by cancer at the age of forty-eight, I went to offer her solace. Instead, she comforted me by quoting this splendid line from *Macbeth:* "Nothing in his life became him like the leaving it." Nothing had so elevated and dignified her husband, Mrs. Lovelace was saying to me, as the gracious way that he gave it up. Perhaps this explains why she remained an attractive widow, perhaps knowing that there would not be another "Shep." When Margaret herself was felled by a second stroke in 1993, she began to take her long leave of this earth. She did it as St. Paul enjoins: by focusing not on the things that are seen but that are unseen, not upon things transient but things eternal. Having given up her life long before it was taken away from her, she began to live eternally long before she was dead.

Let it be said ever so clearly that I have no intention of violating the integrity of Margaret Lovelace by making her into a sugary saint. Like many of you, I know that there were moments when she chafed and railed against her fate, just as you and I would, and just as one day we surely will. There were times when she could be a real bother — there is actually a stronger b-word that I could use — both to her caregivers and her kinfolk. When I heard about some of Mrs. Lovelace's less than seemly behavior, I decided to have a little talk with her. Instead of reprimanding her, however, I gave her the same advice I give my students at Baylor: they should save up their swear words so as to use them only when they really need them, lest overuse make them of no effect. She found this advice both instructive and amusing, especially when I added that there are things we really do want God to damn, but that we shouldn't ask him to do it too soon or too often.

Laughter lay at the heart of Margaret Lovelace's faith. When we laugh at ourselves, we transcend ourselves. Laughter liberates us from our clamshell of sinful self-interest, especially when the humor is at our own expense. Mrs. Lovelace laughed at herself all the way to the end. Not long ago she confessed to me her curiosity about what had happened to her leg after it was amputated just below the knee. She instructed her son David to find out what they did with it. Again, with her typically wry wit, she solemnly reported David's story. The owners of a local grocery store had run short of sausage until the hospital gave them Margaret's severed leg to grind into edible fare. Such self-depreciating humor was at work yet again on my last visit with her in early June. I began our conversation by asking my standard teasing question: "Woman, what have you 'mounted to lately?" She paused for a long moment, then with a sly grin and a whispered voice she said, "Nuttin."

But of course she had "'mounted" to a great deal. With immense courage, she had endured the early loss of an infant daughter, the later loss of her beloved husband, then the final and recent loss of her son

David. Throughout it all, she had been a loving grandmother to David's children and grandchildren. His death also drew her closer to her remaining son, Richard, and his family. She was rightfully proud of the accomplishments of both sons. If the raising of these sons, virtually by herself, were all that Margaret Lovelace had amounted to, then her achievement would be a considerable amount indeed.

Yet her accomplishments reach far beyond this county and region and state. Most people here know that Margaret Lovelace taught a young drummer boy named Don Henley. He is responsible for one of her most unintentionally hilarious remarks. Greg Attaway reports that, one day as Don was drumming away with his pencils on his desk, not listening to the lesson, an exasperated Mrs. Lovelace declared: "Don Henley, don't you know that you will never make a living playing drums?" Many years later, when Henley had become a world-famous rock musician both playing the drums and singing, he led the successful effort to preserve Henry David Thoreau's Walden Pond by preventing it from being turned into yet another shopping center or suburban housing tract. For this valiant act of conservation, as well as for his musical talents, President Clinton presented Don Henley with the National Humanities Medal in 1997, one of our nation's highest awards. Upon receiving it, Don reminded the White House audience that he had first learned to admire Thoreau, especially his reverence for the natural order, under the influence of his English teacher in a little place called Linden-Kildare High School, deep in the piney woods of eastern Texas. That Henley has faithfully attended to his former teacher during these last years is surely a tribute to the power of her teaching no less than the boundlessness of his generosity.

We can hardly begin to count how many other former students were shaped permanently for good by the life and teaching of Margaret Lovelace. But permit me but two final examples of her enduring influence. When Faye Jackson Wadsworth, our dear biology teacher, died suddenly in 1963, Mrs. Lovelace became and remained the surrogate mother of the six Wadsworth children, even inviting Anita to live with her. Mrs. Lovelace also inspired me to study at the small college, East Texas State in Commerce, where her own teacher, Paul Wells Barrus, still served as the outstanding member of the English faculty. When I complained that Barrus was a Roman Catholic, Margaret rightly reprimanded me for being such a stupid Baptist bigot! And how right she was, since I owe my whole career to this noble Catholic teacher who burst the cocoon of my suffocating religious narrowness and enabled me to emerge as an ecumenical Christian.

It's as a Christian, therefore, that I close my tribute to our dear teacher and friend, our mother and grandmother and great-grandmother, our cousin and companion. I would have us ponder our own death as we give thanks for Margaret Lovelace's death no less than her life. Ours is a world that fears all limits, especially the ultimate limit of all limits called death. If someone were to ask us, "What is the purpose of life?" most of us would answer, if a moment of unguarded candor allowed, that the "purpose of life is not to die, but to stay alive as long as possible, in order to have a good time." For Christians, by contrast, it's precisely the other way around: the purpose of life is to die well, to die faithfully, to die in Christ — and thus to live faithfully and well in him. The church celebrates its saints not on their birthdays but on the day of their death, for only in death are we made complete.

Our dread of death makes us do dreadful things to ourselves, to each other, and supremely to God himself. In trying to stay alive in order to have an easy time, we fall inevitably on hard times. We refuse to learn what Margaret Lovelace learned: she learned to overcome this deadly desire for unlimited life. When she and I talked about death, we did not speculate about the rewards that await the blessed beyond the walls of the world, the realm that Shakespeare calls in *Hamlet* the "undiscover'd country from whose bourn [boundary] no traveler returns." We spoke not about being reunited with our loved ones, not about streets paved with silver and gold, not about mansions just over the hilltop, not even (to Richard Bowden's disappointment) whether there will be honky-tonks in heaven.

We spoke, instead, as St. Paul speaks. "Whether we are at home [in the body] or away," the apostle declares, "we make it our aim to please the Lord." Mrs. Lovelace and I thus spoke about giving delight to God, about living in ways that please him. Such a life is, of course, the real beginning of heaven on earth. I reminded her that, even in her helpless condition, even as her body wasted away, she was putting on new clothes and thus a new life. By living without fear or rage, by remaining cheerful despite her cruel circumstance, she could still make her faithful witness. She could continue to become what St. Paul calls "a new creation," a woman who was swallowed up by life because she had become the master of death. And so she did. She learned the deeply redeeming gospel truth that those things that, by Christ's mercy, we give away cannot be taken away, and that a life given to the triune God can never be lost, not even in death. Margaret Wiggins Lovelace thus accomplished in her dying body what you and I are called to do in our living bodies: to give ourselves away in the joyful service of the crucified and risen, the reigning and returning Lord. And so I say, "Well done, thou good and faithful servant." Amen.

A Man Alive While Dying

A Tribute to a. j. ("chip") conyers (1944-2004)

Almost exactly a year ago I had lunch with Chip Conyers at a local sandwich shop. He was preparing to begin another semester at Baylor's Truett Theological Seminary, where he had taught theology for the past ten years. Yet he was also working out the complicated schedule that would allow him to receive intensive chemotherapy treatments every week in Houston while at the same time making sure that, with the help of a graduate student, all of his classes would be met. I used the occasion to express sentiments to Chip that I had never voiced before, since it seemed obvious that he was dying of the leukemia that he fought so valiantly for a decade.

I expressed my enormous admiration for the way he had dealt with his illness, neither raging at the injustice of being struck down in the full flower of his career, nor sinking into the self-pity that would have made his disease the defining event of his life. I quoted a Presbyterian friend, a retired pastor who has seen many parishioners face death and who still holds to the difficult Christian doctrine of particular providence: the Pauline confidence that God is at work in all things, not by way of some vague general oversight, but by means of his concrete and particular will. While visiting from North Carolina a few months earlier, a friend of mine had met Chip only briefly, but even this cursory visit had revealed what so many of us had found so remarkable about him. "Never have I seen a dying man face the end with such serenity, with such courage and grace, with such confidence that God's will is being done."

Chip received this tribute with his typical humility, but then he offered a surprising addendum. "Among those splendid words," he said, "there's one that you've left out." I inquired, of course, about the missing word. "It's 'puzzlement,'" he said. How could he not be perplexed at being cut off in his prime? Nearing the end of his fifth decade, Chip knew that his work was blossoming in new and unprecedented ways. He was producing books of remarkably high quality and deep theological insight. His fine little treatise entitled *The Eclipse of Heaven: The Loss of Transcendence and Its Effect on Modern Life* had been reissued by St. Augustine's Press. And his *The Long Truce: How Toleration Made the World Safe for Power and Profit*, published in 2001 by Spence, had enjoyed a positive reception in quarters both political and theological. At the time of our conversation, he was at work on a book dealing with vocation, and he had plans for still others, especially one on baptism. He was also teaching the very best students at our seminary, where he had a large and faithful following. How could a believer in particular providence not be puzzled at so much promise coming to such an unpromising end?

Chip spoke of his puzzlement with a smile, thus assuring me that he was not putting me on the spot, not demanding that I do the impossible by somehow answering Job's unanswerable question. Yet, in a brief moment of inspiration, I recalled what Flannery O'Connor, the salty Georgia satirist, had said upon discovering that her own disease, lupus erythmatosus, would probably kill her earlier than later. "I can take it all as a blessing," O'Connor remarked, "with one eye squinted."

"Yes!" replied Chip. "That's it exactly."

We then talked briefly about Romans 8:28, and about the necessity of authentic faith to include — not to exclude — an eye-squinting perplexity, a pained puzzlement over the seeming godlessness of the world's natural operations.

As a man who spent his last decade dying, Chip Conyers knew that another kind of death suffuses the late-modern world: the moral necrosis of what Pope John Paul II called our "culture of death." From early in his career, Chip courageously made his witness against it, and in behalf of the culture of life. At his very first academic post, while serving on the faculty of Southeast Missouri State University, Chip visited the state prison to teach the dialogues of Plato to inmates, convinced that these convicts possessed a divinely bestowed dignity of mind no less than heart and soul. When his health permitted, Chip also gathered with others here in Waco at 7 a.m. every Wednesday to offer prayers of intercession and counsel of help to pregnant women entering the local abortuary.

Yet Chip Conyers was no reflexive and uncritical pro-lifer. He wanted to plumb the root of things, to uncover the hidden causes that lurk beneath the surface manifestations of evil, and thus to provide an authentic Christian remedy to them. Therefore, when I think of Chip's contribution to Baptist life in particular and to the ecumenical church in general, I think of his steadfast avoidance of cliché. He refused to make the obvious still more obvious, as a wag has put it, in perfectly obvious terms. A single example of Chip Conyers's originality of mind will have to suffice. It concerns the danger that David Solomon warns against when he says that we Southerners and Baptists who came of age in the 1960s cut our teeth on the easiest moral issue of the twentieth century: race. Once we discovered that segregation was a hideous denial of the humanity of our black brothers and sisters, we were then tempted to treat other ethical and theological questions as if they were equally simple.

As a native son of Georgia and a convert to Baptist tradition, Chip Conyers sought, in nonsimplistic terms, to penetrate the evil that has so sorely vexed both his region and his religion. He saw that racism was not a uniquely Southern iniquity but the symptom of a much more pernicious disease afflicting the whole of modern life, namely, the commodification of our entire existence. Chip discerned that the real root of our troubles lies in the sixteenth and seventeenth centuries with the burgeoning of the means for production and conquest. As the rapid triumph of machinery drew the masses into the great industrial cities where the means of manufacture and trade were concentrated, governments also began to operate as impersonal machines backed by large armies, the better to manage their huge territories and to conquer new lands that would enhance their wealth.

With devastating clarity, Chip Conyers came to see that this modern way of life no longer valued human beings as particular persons offering their unique and irreplaceable gifts to a communal enterprise. Rather did the Enlightenment make us into solitary individuals having equal rights because we are regarded as equally interchangeable parts in the gigantic machine of the commercial and martial state. We are little more than instruments of production and profit and warfare. The masters of the market and the military are willing, in turn, to "tolerate" the religion of their drudges and minions only if it is reduced to the private sphere, where it remains essentially harmless. Far from being the regressive invention of benighted medievals, therefore, chattel slavery was what Conyers rightly called "the eldest child of modernity." For in the figure of the Negro slave we moderns created the ultimately autonomous person, one who no longer belongs to family and clan, to region and guild, to community and church and God, but only to oneself in the smallest sense — as the servant of those who possess total political and commercial power. In offering his drastic critique of the slavery that once held black people in bonds, Conyers also revealed that, here in "the land of the free," we also are enslaved to a culture of convenient tolerance and unrestrained consumption.

This gentle radical, this revolutionary conservative, this quietly dissident theologian has fallen, alas, just as his work was beginning to soar. Yet Chip Conyers's final word was not Nay but Yea, not angry admonition but joyful summons. He called us neither to a Luddite smashing of our machines nor to an agrarian rejection of the wondrous technologies that had, as he gratefully confessed, kept him alive for a decade. Instead, he urged that we live in communities of mutual trust and glad obligation, in places that honor an endearing smallness of scale as well as the gritty particularities of history.

Such transcendent unity in community is the theme of Chip Conyers's final book, *The Listening Heart: Vocation and the Crisis of Modern Culture.* The following sentences from it were read at his funeral. Here he seeks to address the clamant late-modern obsession with diversity and difference. Rather than denying their significance in the name of a bland universalism, or else divinizing them by way of a vicious tribalism, Chip defines the way God intends our variety to constitute a splendid symphonic unity:

> It is not only a relief, but positively good news, in the light of a vocational understanding of life, that differences are good also. It is true that in a fallen world they are occasions of distrust, envy, misunderstanding, animosity, and shame. But this comes from the failure to discern that differences are gifts for others, not occasions for animosity. In this they do not isolate us but unite us. Races, genders, language groupings, and the like, are classically [the occasion for] misunderstanding and conflict. But they also represent the way we grasp the world differently, through different cultures and sentiments, through various metaphors and [patterns of] syntax. As such, each of these human differences can be the basis for understanding existence in

a valid, albeit partial, way. Thus with our insights, shaded toward different emphases, enjoying and using the world in our slightly different ways, we are enable to enrich the greater community. While giving expression to what is temporally divided, we begin together to give witness to what is finally united. For the end of all things is the God who calls us, in whom we find rest, by whose one light we find our separate ways toward that city "not made with hands, eternal, in heaven." Those [on pilgrimage] toward that ultimate goal, even while they are separate, and [while] acknowledging that their experiences and ways are distinct, can yet give living witness to the fact that, in the mystery of God's calling, they are one.

After our lunch last September, I never spoke with Chip again about his illness, though we met on several other occasions, including a hospital visit only a few months before the end. Unlike most other Americans, Chip did not seek to avoid an allegedly morbid subject. Exactly to the contrary. He had so fully come to terms with his death that he wanted to get on with his work and thus to talk about the coming semester, the books we were reading, the ideas we were percolating, the students who showed special promise, and the like. He was energized, like none other I've ever known, by the central Christian conviction that the kingdom of God is not an idealistic hope to be realized in some far-off future, but the revolutionary new age that has already dawned in Jesus Christ and his church. Chip Conyers was enlivened by giving himself unreservedly to the God who, as the liturgy of the Eastern Orthodox Church declares, has "undone death by death." He fulfilled in his lengthy dying the splendid saying of Irenaeus of Lyons that "the glory of God is a man alive." Amen.

A Woman Who Waited for the Lord God

A EULOGY FOR EUNICE WALKER WOOD (1908-1993)

Reeder-Schindler Funeral Home
Linden, Texas
April 15, 1993

Out of the depths I cry to thee, O Lord!
   Lord, hear my voice!
Let thy ears be attentive to the voice of my supplications!

If thou, O Lord, shouldst mark iniquities,
   Lord, who could stand?
But there is forgiveness with thee, that thou mayest be feared.

I wait for the Lord, my soul waits, and in his word I hope;
   my soul waits for the Lord, more than watchmen
for the morning, more than watchmen for the morning.

O Israel, hope in the Lord!
   For with the Lord there is stedfast love,
and with him is plenteous redemption. (Ps. 130)

Eunice Walker Wood was a woman who waited for the Lord God, who cried out of the depths to him, who received his plenteous redemption. From childhood to old age, she found her hope in the Christ who does not mark our iniquities but who judges us with a love so steadfast that nothing, not even death, can separate us from it.

Early in her life, Eunice Wood was singled out for a special destiny, even a holy calling. Ten-year-old Eunice was attending the one-room, one-teacher Walker School hidden deep in the worn-out cotton fields of East Texas. Sarah Huggins, the teacher, asked Eunice to stay after books one day. Miss Huggins made a life-turning remark to her pupil: "Eunice," she said, "you are a good girl who earns good marks and who would make a good teacher." From that moment, Eunice confessed, she knew that she was called to make something good of her life, and not to get pregnant, not to quit school, not to repeat the dreary pattern followed by many other farm girls. Eunice knew that she must be willing to wait for the better things that God wanted for her, even when there was little hope for better things.

The Walkers were sharecroppers. They moved from one small Cass County community to another in search of a more prosperous life: from Zion Hill to Lewis to O'Farrell, back to Zion Hill, thence to New Colony and Lanier and Almira. Eunice faithfully attended the rural schools in all of these places. But they stayed in session only six months of the year, and they extended through only the seventh grade. How could she hope to become a teacher when her schooling was so limited?

A perceptive aunt spotted Eunice's talent. She urged her niece to get an education, if only to provide for her parents when they grew old. Otherwise, the aunt said, they will be sent to the county farm — to the poor house — to live with the other indigents. So Emma and Willard Walker, her aunt and uncle, invited Eunice to live with them and their twin daughters, Irene and Alene, in the county seat town of Linden and to attend the Linden High School. There Eunice received three indispensable years of education, which enabled her to enter the sub-college at Commerce, there to earn her high school degree, and thus to be issued a temporary teaching certificate.

As a raw youth of eighteen, Eunice began to realize her dream of becoming a teacher. Yet she never had the money to live in the dormitory as a long-term student at East Texas State Teachers College. Instead, she earned her degrees by attending summer sessions, at least a dozen of them, after teaching all year at rural schools in places such as Almira and Bear Creek. Her grades were always excellent. In fact, someone teased her future husband, who was also teaching at Almira, that he was preparing to marry a woman who had never made a *B*. "So what," Cecil Wood replied, "I haven't either!"

Early in life Eunice had heard the summons to excellence from her own parents. Her father, Jim Walker, wanted to be a preacher or a teacher rather than a farmer. Alas, he had little formal education. As a man who loved books and numbers far more than cotton and money, he raised little of the former and earned little of the latter. Instead, he spent much of his time reading the Bible. Often he would have his four daughters read it responsively with him. And then he would end with prayer. Though he was a rather passive man who let the world roll over him, Jim Walker made one firm act of protest against the hard life of an itinerant farmer: he refused to teach his daughters how to plow.

Virtually blind from a childhood illness, Eunice's mother, Maudie Lummus Walker, was never sent to school. But she would ask her four daughters to read the Bible to her. She committed many Scripture verses to memory, and she could quote and comment wisely upon them even in her old age. Despite her near blindness, Maudie became an accomplished seamstress; and, having learned by her mother's example, Eunice spent most of her last years sewing. Perhaps Eunice was also remembering her own mother when, as an English teacher, she required her students to recite Milton's sonnet "On His Blindness." She was especially moved by Milton's declaration, "They also serve who only stand and wait."

It was not only at home but also at the Zion Hill Baptist Church that Eunice learned what it means to wait expectantly for the Lord God and to serve him in both life and death. Preachers named Hamilton and Chambers and Hollingsworth proclaimed to her the gospel of salvation by grace alone through faith alone. She heard and heeded this Word, and she was baptized in a nearby creek called Jim's Bayou. Eunice lived out her Christian faith in deeds far more than words. She knew that she was not saved by her good works, but she knew most certainly that she was saved for good works.

Eunice was a mere teenager when she volunteered to nurse her Walker grandparents on their deathbeds during two terribly hot Augusts in 1924 and 1925. Three years later, as an unmarried schoolteacher barely twenty years old, she moved her parents into her house at Almira, stretching her slender salary to cover their rent and groceries. Decades later she was to show the same care for her dying mother-in-law, Donie Wood, and for her widowed sister Keron when her life took a downward turn. The countless gospel songs and sermons that Eunice had heard in her youth thus bore rich fruit in her maturity. They taught her that to wait for the Lord God is to live generously: not to save her life but to lose it, not to gain it but to give it gladly away for Christ and his gospel.

Even in her marriage Eunice knew what it meant to wait. She ended an initial engagement in order to spend her life with a fiery fellow teacher named Cecil Wood. His spirit was as wild and willful as hers was gentle and gracious. Thus did they complement each other's gifts, as couples often do. To the surprise of almost everyone, Eunice even took up horseback riding in her fifties to accommodate her husband's love of outdoor life — though photographs reveal that she made a rather unconvincing equestrian. Cecil and Eunice found their true common life, instead, as a splendid team of teachers who shaped their students ever so greatly for the good.

From 1947 until 1959, Eunice Wood was the sole English teacher for grades seven through twelve at the tiny Kildare School, eight miles southeast of Linden. Beyond her teaching duties, she also made annual trips with the senior class, got out the school yearbook, and directed the annual queen's coronation — a pomp-filled pageant that enabled country folk to strut like royalty for an evening. During these dozen years her life was deeply intertwined with students named Holland and Heard, Dooley and Cromer, Wiggins and Whatley, Echols and Rosser and Mott.

These Kildare youths were tough. To the end of her life Eunice vividly recalled the day when the school principal attempted to call down a ruffian who had been misbehaving. This young thug grabbed the man by his shirt collar and twisted it tightly. Getting right in the terrified principal's face, he declared: "Don't you ever again raise your voice to me, cowboy!" The poor man resigned after one year at Kildare, as did many others. Eunice Wood never faced such threats. Even the students who despised her strict discipline respected her sterling integrity. They knew that she stood for excellence and uprightness. One of them conveyed this truth to me only recently. Eunice had reprimanded him for his bad conduct; but when he walked away nonchalantly as if nothing serious had happened, he looked back to discover that his teacher was weeping. Now a sixty-year-old man, he confessed that this event was a major turning point in his life. There he saw that he had injured an innocent soul, that he had breached a moral boundary, and that he would never violate such sacred limits again.

Eunice Wood inspired a similar reverence in her son. His mother was a woman of such steadfast character, such moral and spiritual excellence, that he sought to honor her in his own living. It was sheer respect for his mother and father — not any dubious goodness of his own — that enabled him to avoid many of the troubles that plague young people. His parents taught him the Good News of the gospel that we are not our own maker, that we have been bought at the high cost of the cross, that we are both created and redeemed to live in gratitude to God and in service of others. The son thus gladly confesses that his calling to Christian ministry was enabled to no small extent by his mother's gracious life.

It was a calling to style no less than to substance. Eunice Wood would never let her son say "had took" or "it don't" or "we was." For, while she taught Longfellow and Dickens and Edna St. Vincent Millay, her first love was for English grammar. Eunice knew that to honor the one who is the Word made flesh is to use English words rightly and well.

Her pilgrim journey through the highways and hedges of the world took a stark turn when she lost her dear Cecil to a sudden stroke in 1960. When her mother died the following year, Eunice faced the darkest days of her life. Widowed and alone at age 53, she cried with the psalmist "out of the depths." She pled for God to give her a new life, a real reason to live. The Lord heard her supplication. He gave her a plenteous redemption, not in some surprising new place but in a renewed conviction that she belonged exactly where she was: in the classroom and in the church. Her students were her lifeline.

After forty years of teaching English, Eunice Wood answered yet another call. She went back to school to learn the so-called new math and to prepare for teaching algebra and geometry at the recently consolidated Linden-Kildare High School. The last half-dozen years in the math classroom were among the happiest of her career. Her algebra students won academic prizes, and not only because she was a good teacher, but also because she did not suffer fools gladly. One day she spied a distracted student staring out the window. Eunice announced to the class that one thing only would justify such gazing through the glass: only if there were pink elephants turning backward somersaults on the lawn. She also liked to joke with her geometry students that if πr, then surely cornbread are round.

Eunice's generosity was manifest yet again when W. A. Parker, her school superintendent, called her out of retirement. He asked her to teach a final term in the newly integrated junior high school, located at what was once the Negro high school, Fairview. Mr. Parker knew that

Eunice Wood was no racist, that she would treat her black students fairly, and that she would thus work at a school that other white teachers had declined to enter. It was one of the most difficult years of her life. Yet she refused to believe that true education is "For Whites Only," as the courthouse restrooms and drinking fountains once said.

When she quit the classroom for the last time in 1974, Eunice confessed that there was one thing she never missed: the burdensome task of grading exams. Her dozen years of retirement in Linden were happy days indeed. She was able to spend time with her dear sisters, Jewel and Keron and Oleta, as well as her dear sisters-in-law, Nora Dudley and Polly Schiemann. And how dearly she loved her Linden friends who belonged to her Sunday school class, who shared her taste for fried catfish, and who joined her in playing "42," the deep South domino game whose pleasures the great world has yet to learn.

The winding road of Eunice Wood's life rounded its last bend in 1985. Leaving behind her home of forty-one years, as well as a lifetime accumulation of friends, she moved a thousand miles away to North Carolina. Though she could have pitied herself at so great a loss, she did not. She was willing to walk with patience and cheer this final lap of her life. In Winston-Salem she made many new friends, but no enemies at all. She drew close to her family, especially her grandchildren. And she taught all of us the meaning of prayer. At the end, when her hands were finally stilled from sewing and her eyes too blind to read, she kept alive the most important thing: she held us up hourly to the mercy of God.

Eunice Wood was prepared to meet the Author and Finisher of her faith. Though she did not want to die alone, she had no fear of death. She had put her trust in the Christ who has robbed death of its sting and the grave of its victory. This deep belief made her a teacher to the very end. Her last lesson was perhaps the best of all: she taught us how to grow old generously and how to die graciously. The way she ended her life summed up the whole of it. Its meaning is figured nicely in the last stanza of her favorite poem:

I shall be telling this with a sigh
Somewhere ages and ages hence:
Two roads diverged in a wood, and I —
I took the one less traveled by,
And that has made all the difference.

About the roads that diverge into final destinies, Eunice Wood knew even more than Robert Frost. She lived and died in the hope, not that she would sigh away the ages in a vague "somewhere," but that she would forever sing the wondrous story and shout the victory of God's glory. She began her journey to this paradise of praise and thanksgiving eighty-four years ago in the piney woods of East Texas. There the paths of her life soon diverged. God called her to wait for him, to take the road less traveled, to follow the way that makes all the difference. Her earthly pilgrimage ended at the hour of Christ's own triumph, at the dawning of Easter 1993, when she crossed over death's deep river into Campground. Now her traveling days are over. Now she's home. Amen.

A Fearless and Funny Preacher of the Gospel

Romans 5:1-5; Genesis 6:5-8

A EULOGY FOR WARREN CARR
(1917-2007)

Wake Forest Baptist Church,
Winston-Salem, North Carolina
March 3, 2007

"I can't see; I can't hear; I can't walk . . . and I can't die." Thus in recent months did Warren Carr speak in his typically sardonic and faithful way. Now that he has died, it is our privilege to praise the living no less than the dying of his days. From beginning to end, he was a messenger who, in the eyes of the Lord, found a strange kind of favor. The God who was grieved to his heart that he made such a sorry creature as man, the God who determined to blot out his entire creation because of its evil-doings — this same God saved Warren Carr as he saved Noah, not because Warren deserved saving but because it is God's business to save rather than destroy.

The triune God has made peace with all of his alienated creatures, even a young rebel from Lexington, Kentucky, named Warren Carr. God justified him by faith in our Lord Jesus Christ, pouring out his love on Warren. Christ gave him the grace to do what he could not do on his own: to stand when he could not walk, to see when his eyes were dim, to hear when his ears had failed, to die when he was tired of living but not afraid of dying, and now to live again — eternally. Throughout it all, God equipped Warren to rejoice in the suffering that produces endurance, the endurance that produces character, the character that produces hope, and the hope that does not disappoint because it springs from the inexhaustible divine love pouring into our hearts through the Holy Spirit.

I

From the beginning, Warren Carr understood the meaning of prevenient grace, the grace that goes before us and enables all our doing of the good. The gospel is not the bad news that, if we sufficiently grovel in the dirt repenting our sins, then God will perhaps condescend to redeem us. The logic of the gospel runs exactly the other way: it's the great glad news announced in Romans 5:8. "God shows his love for us in that while we were yet sinners Christ died for us." We are enabled to repent because we have already been forgiven. Warren learned this profoundest of all lessons from his mother as she lay dying of cancer in a Lexington hospital. She summoned him to her bedside for a final leave-taking. Knowing that his mother had wanted him to become a minister, Warren expected to get a stern tongue-lashing. He assumed that she would admonish him against his hellish ways, and, by his own admission, Carr was indeed a hellion who deserved such an upbraiding. Instead, his mother offered him an utterly gracious and freeing word. She assured Warren that he was a splendid son and that he had not disappointed her at all. Warren was astonished at these last words from his dying mother. They were the words of God's astonishing grace. They not only opened him to a drastically altered life; they virtually required him to embark on that life as a minister of such grace. Years later, whenever someone would ask Warren how he came to be a preacher, he would reply by saying: "I didn't have any choice. I had to make an honest woman of my mother."

Warren Carr attended Transylvania College in Lexington on a football scholarship. Weighing but 145 pounds, he was nonetheless a much-feared blocker and tackler. In those days of leather helmets without face guards, Warren lost most of his front teeth. Fierce though he always was, he also remained both handsome and winsome. Photographs of Warren in his twenties reveal a striking resemblance to the movie actor James Dean. No wonder that Warren won the heart of a lovely Transylvania student named Martha Knox. Though both he and she had many other chances, they patiently waited for each other until her graduation. Theirs was to be a partnership of sixty-one years, not only in marriage but also in ministry. Martha never sought to do the spectacular deeds of Mary, but the commonplace, out-of-sight chores befitting her humble namesake.

Nor did Martha demand that Warren find pastoral circumstances suited to her cultured upbringing as the daughter of a violinist in the Louisville Symphony. She did not complain, for example, about the pathetic condition of their first parsonage, even though, when she took a bath for the first time, one leg of the tub pierced through the floor. During Warren's days as a student at the Southern Baptist Seminary in Louisville, she gladly accompanied him to his weekend pastorate at a crossroads village called Red House, Kentucky, and later to his work as an associate pastor at the First Baptist Church in Winchester, Kentucky.

Because the church in Red House abutted the railroad tracks, not even the strongest-voiced preacher could outshout the passing trains. Instead, an elderly man named George Dozier would rise and lead the congregation in lustily singing "Jerden" (the Southern pronunciation of the key word in "On Jordan's Stormy Banks I Stand") until the caboose at last rolled past. Unfortunately, Mr. Dozier was also prone to somnolence. On one particular Sunday, he fell so deeply asleep that he *dreamt* that a train was passing through, and thus leapt to his feet to begin the singing of "Jerden" in a loud voice. Rather than embarrass the old codger, the congregation joined in, as if a train were in fact barreling down the tracks. Many years later, Warren was invited back to Red Bank to preach Brother Dozier's funeral. In typical Carr fashion, he opened his funeral sermon by saying, "Well, old George is doing what he always did — sleeping in church."

The choir minister at the church in Red House was also a dairyman. When he was charged with keeping an unsanitary dairy, Warren offered to serve as a character witness. The prosecuting attorney held up a quart of milk that had been produced at the music minister's dairy; it clearly contained dark sediment in the bottom of the jar. "What is this," asked the attorney, "if not fecal matter?" "That's not fecal matter," replied Carr's choir minister, "that's cow shit." Rarely would Warren have to defend such hopeless cases, but many of his church members would be just as colorful if not quite as clueless.

Warren's fearlessness landed him in a good deal of trouble, not because he was always spoiling for a fight but because he was always defending the little guy and the underdog. On Warren's very first day as a student at Southern Baptist Theological Seminary in Louisville, after morning orientation and registration had left the afternoon free, Warren and his best friend walked to downtown Louisville to see a movie. Later that evening, the two of them were invited by the president of the senior class to come to his room for a nightly prayer session that he held. Thinking this to be a generous gesture by a much-honored upperclassman, Warren and his friend agreed to attend. Their host seemed to be still more gracious when he offered for the guests to pray first. When finally it came time for the senior to pray, he immediately sought the mercies of the Lord God upon such grievous sinners as these two first-year seminarians who had so wickedly wasted their afternoon at the movies. When finally he had finished, the senior turned to Carr and his friend to assure them that they would be welcome to return for these nightly prayers in the future, and that he hoped they had not been offended by his intercessions in their behalf. "Not at all," said Warren, "and we'll be glad to come back — so long as I get to pray last." Vengeance may belong to the Lord, but Warren Carr was its clever carrier.

During his years as a student in Louisville, he was more than once ordered into the office of Dean Harold Tribble, there to be threatened with expulsion for his obstreperous behavior. (In one of the most delicious of divine ironies, Carr would eventually become Tribble's pastor, right here at the Wake Forest Baptist Church). On graduation day, however, it looked as if Warren would be the only member of his class who would be unable to follow the custom of announcing the name of the church to which he had been called. Like Noah once again, he was saved at the last moment by the uncanny favor of the Lord. While standing in the graduation line, Warren was summoned to Dean Tribble's office to be told that he had indeed received a call. It came at the last minute because it was a pastorate no one else wanted, a tiny Baptist church located in a remote coal-mining town deep in the hollows of southwestern Virginia called Coeburn.

II

The reason no major church called Warren Carr is not hard to find. In those days, as in ours, the chief requisite for being a minister is to be "nice," and if there is one word that would never describe Warren Carr, it surely is that word "nice." Lest this seem an awful condemnation of Warren, we would do well to ask ourselves about the applicability of the term "niceness" for describing the prophets and the apostles and the saints of the church, much less Jesus himself. Yet if Warren wasn't "nice," he was something far more important: he was at once courageous and humble.

Though the people in Coeburn loved the Carrs, he could not help but chafe at the smallness and insignificance of his first pastorate. There were many nights when he would roam the silent streets of the town at three or four o'clock in the morning, restless and troubled, pondering his pathetic backwoods ministry, envying his classmates and friends who had found prominent pastorates in central places, feeling the consequence of not having played by the rules of "niceness" during his seminary days. He was deeply vexed that his consignment to Coeburn was the price he was now having to pay. Then he heard a voice — it was his one and only "religious experience," he later confessed — and the voice spoke ever so clearly: "Carr, I didn't call you to be successful; I called you to be faithful." Warren went straight back to the church, tore up the sermon he had been preparing, and composed a new one, entitled "A Proclamation of Emancipation." There he confessed to his congregation that he had sinned not only against God but also against them for wishing he were in a bigger and better place. On the contrary, he said, this is where God had emancipated him to proclaim the gospel, and this is where he would seek to be a faithful preacher.

Coeburn was a rough place. One of Warren's church members was the owner of a local coalmine, and this man generously filled the parsonage basement with coal in order for the Carrs to be warmed during their first harsh winter. Yet it soon became evident that it wouldn't be the winter alone that he and Martha would have to survive. Warren noticed that four young girls in their late teens had arrived in town and were living at a house of questionable repute. When Warren inquired about these girls, he was told that they were sisters who had just moved to Coeburn to stay with their aunt. Penetrating the lie, Warren went straight to the madam and warned that he would report her for the prostitution of these girls if she didn't get them out of town immediately.

It wasn't long before the church member who was also the mine owner appeared at the parsonage door. He had come to warn Pastor Carr that he had better mind his own business. Better still, he should remember where that load of coal in the basement had come from. Warren knew why the coal baron was angry: he didn't want anyone, least of all his preacher, interfering with the pleasures of the miners who worked for him. The pastor was undaunted: "As far as I am concerned, sir, you can come take that coal back today." Warren Carr was a preacher and a prophet who was not for sale. Having himself been "bought with a price" — the incomparable cost of Christ's death on the cross — Warren would never sell out his Savior. Not by chance did he have this hymn as his favorite: "O Jesus, I have promised to serve Thee to the end; O give me grace to follow, my Master and my Friend."

There was so little to do in Coeburn that Warren began to cultivate a practice that would permanently shape his ministry. He went to the drugstore every Monday morning to buy a novel for 25 cents and to read it during the week. It was a way of enriching his imagination, the better to engage the gospel with the world's problems and promises. He learned early that stories are not simply a way of preserving memory but of embodying the Truth as pure ideas cannot. One of the novelists whom Warren picked from the drugstore rack was named Peter De Vries. When I arrived at Wake Forest in 1971, Warren urged me to read De Vries, especially *The Mackerel Plaza* and *The Blood of the Lamb*. I eventually devoted two chapters to De Vries in my book entitled *The Comedy of Redemption*. Through the long and winding trail that began there in Coeburn, De Vries was eventually awarded an honorary doctorate at Wake Forest in 1978, forty years after Warren began reading his work.

The Coeburn congregation came not only to admire but also to expect wonders of Warren. When the town's most notorious criminal came to die, some of the church members urged Warren to visit him. They hoped that the scoundrel might undergo a deathbed conversion and repent of his loutish ways. On the contrary, the impenitent brute taunted Warren: "I have not bothered with God during my life, so why should I bother with him now that I'm dying?" "Sir," replied Warren, "that is not the question. The question is not whether you should bother with God now that you are dying, but whether God should bother with you. And you had better pray that He will." Then Warren turned and walked out. Shaking the dust from his feet, Carr had made a far more powerful witness to the gospel than if he had begged the brazen sinner to "accept Jesus as his personal Savior" in what would have amounted to desperate and selfish act of last minute life-insurance.

Word soon spread that Warren Carr was helping coach the high school football team and thus that he was no milquetoast preacher. Even the town toughs heard the news. One Saturday afternoon, as Warren and Martha sat in their car on the village square, three of the town rowdies approached them and began to make snide remarks. As long as the insults were directed at Warren, he held his wrath. But when the hooligans began to demean Martha, he could not let her honor go undefended. Emerging swiftly from his automobile, Warren didn't wait for these goons to strike first in order to turn the other cheek. Instead, he exercised his own version of Christian charity. Just as Christ drove the moneychangers from the temple with a whip, Warren flattened the chief malefactor with a single blow to the chin. Suddenly one of the three thugs declared that he was switching sides: he had rather fight for this fist-swinging preacher than against him.

The match was now even — two against two — but it was no less bloody. In fact, two Sundays later, when the pulpit committee from the First Baptist Church of Princeton, West Virginia, came to hear Warren preach in view of a ministerial call, the preacher still had a black eye from the dustup on the town square. Warren Carr may be the only preacher in Christendom to have been called to an important pulpit while sporting a shiner from a fistfight.

III

The church in Princeton gave Warren a much larger venue than he had previously known. Soon he was being invited to speak not only at other churches but also at college campuses across the entire South and to occupy pulpits as far north as the Sunday Evening Club in Chicago. In those long-gone days, campus revivals and religious emphasis weeks were held not only at church-sponsored colleges but at secular schools as well. As always, Warren proclaimed the gospel fearlessly but humorously, refusing to dilute the "scandal" for the sake of his audiences. They either loved him or hated him for it.

During the revolutionary sixties, students had begun to grow restive at having to attend compulsory religious services. At one particular college, the undergrads proved especially rude. They had talked loudly and sailed paper planes and exhibited similarly boorish behavior during the previous speaker's presentation. When Warren came to the lectern, he declared that he had carefully prepared his speech, that he had traveled a considerable distance, and that he had sacrificed considerable time to be present for this occasion. "But since you aren't willing to treat us courteously," he added, "then you can go to hell." Whereupon he walked off the stage. He was soon accosted by a student who desperately confessed, "Sir, I'm an atheist, but I've never had a preacher tell me go to hell. I need to talk to you." Later that evening, Warren expected no one to attend the discussion period he was slated to lead. Instead, the room was packed. Even churlish students could recognize oak-knot integrity when they encountered it.

At another of these campus sessions, a young collegian approached Warren to announce that he was an atheist, only to notice that Warren never paused to answer him. The next day, the young fellow again accosted Warren and repeated the datum that he didn't believe in God. Warren continued walking past him. Exasperated, the youth finally said, "I keep reminding you that I am an atheist, and yet you won't try to convince me I'm wrong." "Why should I," said Warren, "when you're having such a good time parading your atheism? I wouldn't want to spoil your fun." Instinctively and profoundly, Warren Carr understood the great wisdom of Søren Kierkegaard, who declared that "to defend God is to make a fool of God." This young man who was rich in intellectual possessions did not go away sorrowful so much as perplexed. Warren's serene confidence in the convicting power of the Spirit had planted the seed of belief far more deeply than if Warren had played intellectual games with him.

Already the pattern was beginning to form that would characterize the whole of Warren Carr's ministry and life. The more prophetically and faithfully he announced the Good News, the more the Baptist bigwigs would ignore him. Three books would eventually bear his authorial name. He also wrote for the *Christian Century* and other important journals, and he had audiences with both Martin Luther King Jr. and Reinhold Niebuhr. Yet Warren Carr was never asked to speak at a state or a national Baptist convention. Even so, I never heard him utter a word of complaint about his neglect at the hands of small-souled denominational bureaucrats.

Instead, he laughed at being passed over and underestimated. He told, for example, about conducting a weeklong revival at a distant church. He had spent all of Sunday afternoon driving hard in order to arrive in time for Sunday evening worship. After an arduous week of both morning and evening services, he arrived back in Princeton to find an envelope in the mail on Monday morning containing a check for $25. Warren returned it with the following one-sentence note: "If I were to accept your honorarium, I would also have to accept your estimate of my worth."

Warren never denied that his courage was deeply entangled with his ego. He liked to talk, and he liked for others to listen, especially to his endless stories. As a result, he dominated most conversations, and some people resented that. Yet Warren knew the wisdom of that distinguished philosopher Satchel Paige, who once said, "It ain't bragging if you've got the goods." Warren Carr had "the goods." He was not only the most discerning man I have ever known; he was the only great man I have ever known. He gave direct and penetrating counsel to all who sought it. He did not simply sit there and offer client-centered Rogerian therapy, which he wickedly described as "the pastoral care grunt" — Unh-huh, Unh-huh. On the contrary, when you sought counsel from Warren, you knew instantly that he understood you, that he had come to grips with your own particular problem, and that he would offer a personal and often surprising remedy.

For example, one of Warren's friends came to the Carr home after he had just been released from the psychiatric ward at the North Carolina Baptist Hospital, where he went regularly to get treatment for his bipolar condition. "Come join your buddies for lunch," Warren beckoned. "Oh, no," replied this friend, "they will all know where I've been, and I will be embarrassed. By the way," the man added, "what are my friends saying about me?" "They're saying you're nutty as a fruitcake," Warren confessed. "Then let's go ahead and join them for lunch," replied the friend. Warren Carr told the truth, because he knew the Lord who is the Truth that makes men free.

Warren also told the truth about himself. Once when he was speaking to a large student group in Florida, perhaps at Stetson University, he was paired with a pretentious professor from Southwestern Baptist Seminary in Fort Worth. After the week's lectures were over, a friend commented: "Warren, your partner was so arrogant that he quoted at least forty authorities during the week's time, as if he had mastered them all. But you were so arrogant that you didn't quote even one." Though Warren had read widely, his wisdom did not derive primarily from books. It came from his long experience in healing broken lives, from his weekly wrestling with the biblical texts that he proclaimed on Sundays, and from the brilliance of his own intellect and imagination.

When Warren did cite others, it was often Reinhold Niebuhr. We pretend, said Niebuhr, that our little bundle of energy and vitality lies

at the center of this vast organization called the universe. "This preten-
sion is ludicrous; and its absurdity increases with our lack of awareness
of it. The less we are able to laugh at ourselves the more it becomes necessary for others to laugh at us." No one needed to laugh at Warren
Carr, for he drowned them out with his own guffaws, joining the Lord
God in laughing his own folly to scorn.

IV

There seems little doubt that Warren Carr reached the zenith of his career at the Watts Street Baptist Church in Durham from 1947 to 1964.
Here the Carr children were raised, and here would his gospel influence
have its furthest reach. Located directly across from the Duke University campus, the church has had a long and important ministry to Baptist students, especially to Baptist graduate students. This was particu-
larly true during Warren Carr's years at Watts Street. Every Sunday
evening, he and Martha invited these divinity students into their home
for vigorous discussion and debate. An entire generation of Baptist
ministers and professors — Charles Wellborn, Dick Smith, and Dan
McGee, Sam Hill and Dan Via and Tom McCulloch come to mind —
was thus formed by this weekly tangle of theological minds. Yet even
there at Watts Street, Warren knew that the openness of the pulpit was
never something to be taken for granted but rather a privilege to be
sustained by weekly proclamation of the uncompromised and uncom-
promising gospel.

A single illustration of his fearlessness in his calling will have to
suffice. Warren had been at Watts Street barely a week when the
church's wealthiest member invited him for lunch at the local Rotary
(or perhaps it was the Kiwanis) club. Upon arriving at lunch, the congregation's only plutocrat proudly introduced Warren to his friends as
his new preacher-boy recently arrived from Princeton, West Virginia.
Warren said nothing during the meal but returned straight to his office and called to ask the wealthy man's secretary for an immediate appointment. When Warren arrived a few minutes later, the gentleman
wanted to know what was on Warren's mind. "Just one thing," replied
Warren. "I've come to tell you, sir, that I'm your preacher but I'm not
your boy." The rich man looked at Warren straight in the eye, smiled,
and said, "I understand." Warren turned and bade him good day. Im-

mediately they became the best of friends, despite their fierce disagreement about the race issue.

The hallmarks of Warren Carr's ministry in Durham were his work with Alcoholics Anonymous, his support of parents with Down syndrome children, his ordination of Addie Davis as the first Southern Baptist female minister, and his courageous leadership concerning the race issue. He was instrumental in forming the first Mayor's Commission on Racial Reconciliation in the entire South. And though it cost him a firebomb thrown against his living room window, he never relented in proclaiming the gospel that Jesus Christ has died and risen for every human being, "red and yellow, black and white."

V

Warren Carr must have been tempted to remain at the Watts Street Baptist Church for the rest of his already distinguished career. The congregation of 1200 was growing, a new educational building had been dedicated, and Warren was preaching with uncommon eloquence and passion. To the surprise of many, however, he left Durham in 1964 for a new challenge here at the Wake Forest Baptist Church, a congregation in steady numerical decline since the heyday of student church involvement during the 1950s. Warren felt a veritable Macedonian call to "come over and help" this church that had gone into a nosedive. He wanted not only a new challenge but also a different kind of ministry. Though he proudly called himself a liberal to the end, Warren mastered the truth that most liberals miss, namely, that it's a dangerous thing to cut your moral teeth on the easiest ethical issue of the twentieth century — that is, race.

To deny black people their rightful place in restaurants and restrooms, in hotels and schools and other public places, and especially to keep them, as our fellow Christians, from joining us in the worship and service of God — these are outrages so obvious as hardly to need marking. Yet precisely because racial justice is so patent, it tempts liberals to a preening kind of righteousness, as though all moral problems were so evident, all spiritual evils so readily remedied. Warren knew that others could take up the cause of racial justice when he left Durham. And so, in a remarkable act of downward mobility, he accepted the call of the Wake Forest Baptist Church. More remarkable still was the purgatorial act that Warren performed before leaving Durham: he burned all of the sermons he had preached during his seventeen years at the Watts Street church. Unlike us professors who so shamelessly return to our yellowed class notes semester after semester, Warren made it impossible to dip again into his homiletical barrel. He was determined to preach the perennially fresh gospel in a fresh way on the Wake Forest campus.

Once he arrived here at Wake Forest, Warren began to see that the great unrecognized problem for our late modern world is not race or gender or class, but rather the church itself. With remarkable prescience, he discerned that the word "Christian" appears only three times in the New Testament, and that it is never used by Paul at all. The apostle always describes his fellow believers as those who are *en Christo*. And to be "in Christ" is not to have a private and subjective relationship to Jesus via religious experience, no matter how intense. Rather, it is to belong to Christ's outward and visible body called the church. "It is decidedly illogical," he wrote in 1972, "for anyone to think that he may be related to Christ without His body." In baptism, we are taken into Christ, he added; and in communion, we take Christ into us. The church, in turn, is the world's unique multicultural and multiracial and multiethnic community. But if this unique community — and the Word that it uniquely announces and embodies, "God was in Christ reconciling the world unto himself" (2 Cor. 5:12) — if this Word is ever silenced and if this community dies, then all of the world's magnificent social and moral and technical advances will fail.

They will not become null and void so much as vain and vicious. For then men and women will begin to turn and tear each other apart in the name of their righteous causes, whether right or left, precisely as so-called "red" and "blue" America is now doing. Everyone will want to do justice, but none will want to love mercy or walk humbly with their God. Gone will be the gospel that in Jesus Christ there is neither Jew nor Greek, neither slave nor free, neither male nor female, because in him and his church alone are we all made one. And so Warren Carr discerned the need for a new and ironic kind of evangelism: not the winning of souls to Christ for the first time, but rather the keeping of Christians in the church when they are tempted to leave it. He wittily called it "rear-door evangelism," for its aim was to snare believers as they were attempting to exit the church. And so he aimed his ministry at the hardest of all heads and the flintiest of all hearts, namely, those hearts and heads ensconced in professors and administrators. I happily attest that many of us were saved at the back door, our lives being utterly transformed by the ministry of Warren Carr.

As always, Warren remained both fearless and funny in his proclamation of the thorny and offensive gospel here at Wake Forest Baptist. His friends often observed that his preaching was saddest at Christmas, gladdest at funerals. Warren was rightly downcast that the world makes such a mangle of the Christ's birth with its yearly debauch of getting and spending, laying waste the power of the gospel. Yet the world has not been able to co-opt Christian funerals. Here we are able to declare the one Truth that the world knows not: that this is not our end but our beginning. Stanley Hauerwas, one of Warren's favorite theologians, has declared: "If you ask us Americans to define the purpose of life, we will reply (if we're honest) that 'The purpose of life is not to die, but to stay alive as long as possible, in order to have a good time.'" Warren knew ever so well that, for Christians, the logic runs exactly the other way: the purpose of life is not to stay alive at all costs but to die rightly and graciously, to die above all in Christ. Here in death we find our final fruition. Here our lives achieve their ultimate point and climax. Here we return our talents multiplied and blessed and taken by God into his final keeping. And so we celebrate our saints on the day of their death rather than their birth. Hence Warren Carr's repeatedly declared motto: "Nothing matters but the Resurrection." February 23 we will ever remember as the day of Warren Carr's resurrection.

Warren celebrated the blessedness of those who die in the Lord by telling the truth at their funerals. At the final rites for one of the church's finest busybodies, Warren began by declaring, now that this lady had arrived in paradise, it must surely be a much better organized place. On a far sadder occasion, the memorial service for a suicide, Warren did not balk the truth. "We must confront the fact," he said, "that this man took his own life." Other ministers would have spent the whole sermon trying to dance around what everyone knew to be true but what no one was willing to admit. After openly confessing it, Warren then proceeded to preach one of the most redemptive and hopeful sermons I have ever heard, emphasizing the ways in which God redeems all our sins, even suicide.

Warren always "preached truth to power," but always comically, never self-righteously. In tribute to his fundamentalist friend and fellow pastor Mark Corts, Warren said that they were like two dogs pursuing a covey of birds, one on the left and the other on the right, but both of them seeking the same quarry called the gospel. Yet Warren could also be caustic. After one especially biting sermon, Warren was approached by President James Ralph Scales at the rear doors of Wait Chapel. Said Scales: "I don't appreciate your trying to run the university from the pulpit." Warren was undaunted by this scolding. He replied: "Dr. Scales, I'm not trying to run the university from the pulpit. I'm preaching from the pulpit so *you* will know how to run the university." Needless to say, Carr and Scales remained the closest of companions to the end.

Surely the funniest moment of Warren Carr's ministry at the Wake Forest Baptist Church came in May 1985 on his final day as pastor. After his brief and poignant sermon, we repaired to the Magnolia Room in Reynolda Hall for a magnificent celebration. There were several fine speeches in his honor, and then it came time for him to respond. But to everyone's hilarious surprise, Warren said: "My heart is full, but so is my bladder. I'm an old man, and it's time for me to *go*."

It's also time for me to go, but not without a final word about Warren Carr's family. In looking again at Warren's important book of 1964, *Baptism: Conscience and Clue for the Church,* I found this simple dedication: "To Martha and Her Gifts: Ellen, Lynn, Martha Gail, and Debbie." Those were not perfunctory words of blessing. They echo Warren's remarkable tribute to Martha on their fiftieth wedding anniversary. "Never once," he declared, "has Martha tugged at my sleeve and urged me to hold back. Though my public exposure has often been painful to her, she has never asked me to back off or to let up." I have come to know the Carr daughters, especially during these latter years, and I can testify that they are exactly like their mother in this regard: they have never wanted their father to soften the scandal or to water down the strong stuff of the gospel. Well do they know — as do their children Marti and Meredith, Rob and Chasie, Heather and Ty, Ellen and Joshua, and eventually also the children of this second generation — how well all of them know that they are immensely privileged to be the offspring of Warren Carr, the inheritors of this fearless and funny preacher of the gospel, the legatees of this undaunted proclaimer of the one and only hope that does not disappoint. It is voiced in his dear wife Martha's favorite hymn: "Great is thy faithfulness, O God my Father. Morning by morning new mercies I see; all I have needed thy hand hath provided, great is thy faithfulness, Lord, unto me." Amen.